Ranching, Mining, and the Human Impact of Natural Resource Development

NEW OBSERVATIONS

Howard S. Becker, series editor

The close and detailed observation of social life provides a kind of knowledge that is indispensable to our understanding of society. In the spirit of Robert E. Park, the books in this series draw on an intimate acquaintance with their subjects to make important contributions to the development of sociological theory. They dig beneath the surface of conventional pieties to get at the real story, and thus produce ideas that take account of the realities of social life.

Ranching, Mining, and the Human Impact of Natural Resource Development

Raymond L. Gold

With a Foreword by
Elizabeth Moen

Transaction Books
New Brunswick (U.S.A.) and Oxford (U.K.)

Copyright © 1985 by Transaction, Inc.
New Brunswick, New Jersey 08903

MLA

Library of Congress Catalog Number: 84-16355
ISBN: 0-88738-025-5 (cloth)
Printed in the United States of America

Library of Congress Cataloging in Publication Data

Gold, Raymond L.
  Ranching, mining, and the human impact of natural resource development.

  (New observations)
  Bibliography: p.
  Includes index.
  1. Cattle trade—Social aspects—West (U.S.) 2. Coal trade—Social aspects—West (U.S.) 3. Economic development projects—Social aspects—West (U.S.) 4. Natural resources—West (U.S.) I. Title. II. Series.
HD9433.U62A1714 1985   307.7'2'0978   84-16355
ISBN 0-88738-025-5

Contents

Acknowledgments   vi
Foreword   vii
    Elizabeth Moen
1. Introduction   1
2. The Community Before Development   15
3. Impacts of Anticipated Development   31
4. Impacts Experienced at the Outset of Development
   and During Construction   53
5. After Construction: The First Year   71
6. Conceptualization and Analysis   93
7. Toward Socially Enlightened Natural Resource Development   133
References   167
Index   173

Acknowledgments

At various stages in the preparation of this work I received valuable advice from anthropologist James Boggs of Helena, Montana, from sociologists I.W. Evans and John Driessen of the University of Montana, Elizabeth Moen of the University of Colorado, Howard S. Becker of Northwestern University, and Irving Louis Horowitz of Rutgers University. Philosopher Albert Borgmann of the University of Montana collaborated with me in writing about some of the ethical problems and positions in natural resource development projects. My longtime research associates at the University of Montana, and, in recent years, at Social Research and Applications in Missoula, Montana, Alice Sterling and Kathy McGlynn, have helped me in countless ways in all aspects of generating and organizing the data and composing, typing, and proofing the essays which evolved into this story of a coal development project at Sagebrush. My greatest debt is to the residents of the many small communities in the rural West who, over the past ten years, have allowed me to enter their lives and pick their brains concerning the deeper, as well as the more evident, aspects of their experiences with coal and other development projects. My thanks and salutations to all these and others who have assisted me in producing this case study of rural industrialization, for which, to be sure, I nevertheless assume overall and final responsibility.

Foreword

Elizabeth Moen

I've always wanted to be one of those authors who could begin a book with ". . . sitting on the veranda of an Italian villa overlooking the Mediterranean Sea." But I'm pleased enough to be able to note that I am sitting on the roof of a Turkish pension overlooking the Agean Sea. This information is not entirely irrelevant, since behind me lies a once small, quiet fishing village that is now a tourist boomtown. The environmental and social problems evident here would be very familiar to readers of *Ranching, Mining, and the Human Impact of Natural Resource Development*. This book is about boom and bust, especially the social consequences of rapid demographic and economic change in rural North American communities caused by energy and other natural resource development. This book is also about sociology: how the social dynamics of a community can be revealed, how concepts and theory are developed and used, and how sociology can be put to very practical and valuable service in social impact assessment (SIA) and planning.

Although SIA is not a new concept, it is only recently, with the enactment of the National Environmental Policy Act in the United States and similar regulations in other countries, as well as massive efforts by many nations to develop domestic energy supplies, that the field has become a rapid-growth profession. Along with a proliferation of documents has come some criticism, often quite severe. However, the practitioners of SIA are not entirely to blame for these shortcomings; after all, academic sociology had little to offer them in the way of theory or method. Areas of major concern about the professional standards of SIA include:

- failure to define what is "social";
- failure to utilize or generate theory, resulting in ad hoc and non-cumulative research;

- such a great emphasis on quantitative data over qualitative and phenomenological data that social impacts are often made to appear to be largely a matter of roads and sewers;
- heavy reliance on readily available data even to the extent that the impact assessor has little or no first-hand knowledge of the study site;
- results which often appear to reflect the source of funding;
- pretense of value-free research which enables the impact assessor to evade questions as to whether a given project is really necessary, whether there should be private profits when the public is incurring avoidable negative externalities, and whether the same could be achieved through means which would generate fewer unavoidable externalities.

It is a pleasure to write a foreword to the Sagebrush story because it provides answers to such criticisms of SIA, thereby making substantial contributions to rural/urban/community sociology.

Since the early 1970s, Raymond Gold has been studying a wide variety of rural and urban communities undergoing boom and bust. He has observed and listened carefully, allowing the residents to describe, define, and interpret their own experiences. Through patient, long work he has been able to uncover and understand basic values and objectives, to learn how a community organizes itself to achieve its goals and how it reorganizes to protect itself during times of rapid change. Gold circumscribes the domain of social impacts and employs time-honored sociological concepts. Equally important, he proposes the extension of modification of his theoretical perspective. Moreover, since the Sagebrush story is based on Gold's studies of several communities in all stages of boom and bust as well as the long-term study of one rural Western boomtown, the analysis of Sagebrush is probing and comprehensive. In addition, the results are integrated with other studies to further develop and refine theory and policy recommendations. Gold is well known as an outspoken critic of the energy industry, and yet much of the financial support for his research has come from that industry—a testimony to the quality and integrity of his work.

Gold recognizes that value-free research really means the implicit acceptance of status quo values. Since in the United States these values emphasize consumption and maximum profit, they run counter to Gold's stated belief that the well-being of communities and people affected by a development project should be the primary concern of social impact assessment and related decision-making processes. The resulting policy recommendations are very different from those that would have been made under the pretense of a value-free posture.

The Sagebrush story not only makes many important contributions to SIA but also to sociological theory and method, social epidemiology, public administration, and private management. For example:

- Gold unifies the classical concepts of *Gemeinschaft* and *Gesellschaft* and thoroughly refutes the belief that they are mutually exclusive states which characterize the beginning and end of an evolutionary process of urbanization.

• The dynamic and interdependent nature of *Gemeinschaft* and *Gesellschaft* is established through Gold's demonstration of their "waxing and waning" cycles. (The dynamics of *Gemeinschaft* and *Gesellschaft* will be of particular interest to social epidemiologists who have linked stress-related illness to the absence of social bonds and networks.)

• He shows that the maintenance of *Gemeinschaft* through its modification is essential if rural longtimers are to overcome "agonizingly painful and difficult . . . imposed modernization and urbanization," and safeguard cherished community values. Similarly, *Gemeinschaft* is present in urban communities, and its expression is modified as a protective device against rapid change.

• His explication of two important concepts, inner and outer structure, helps solve the problem of measuring *Gemeinschaft* and *Gesellschaft* and enhances the understanding of why the consequences of boom and bust vary from one community to another.

• The strong rationale Gold provides for why and how ethnography should be done fits in well with his excellent examples of the substance and process of sociological thinking. (Gold's candid account of his own mistakes and his demonstration of the development and use of sociological concepts and principles should make this book very helpful to students.)

• Gold demonstrates the folly and injustice of planning based primarily on profit-motivated values and monetary cost-benefit analysis. He also shows that in the long run the accommodative industry, which puts the well-being of people above profits, will generate fewer externalities and more profit than the contentious industry that seeks only short-term monetary gain.

If I were wealthy, I would send a copy of the Sagebrush story to every official of the U.S. energy industry and the federal departments of interior and energy. Both have been much too careless with the lives of people and communities. Booms, busts, and the high externalities borne by community residents, company employees, and the environment are the logical and inevitable result of a profit-first economic system and a federal energy policy that primarily aims to satisfy any and all demand through profit-motivated production. In recent years, numerous books and articles have demonstrated the costliness and inefficiency of this policy which has clearly failed to deliver on promises of energy security and energy "too cheap to meter." Quite the contrary. The authors of these works (see for example Lovins, *Soft Energy Paths*; Stobaugh and Yergen, *Energy Future*; Krenz, *Energy: From Oppulence to Sufficiency*) call for the development of decentralized, renewable energy resources and for conservation of energy through more efficient production and use along with the appropriate matching of energy resource and end-use. In *Ranching, Mining, and the Human Impact of Natural Resource Development*, Raymond Gold has provided additional evidence that the costs of a business-as-usual approach to energy and other natural resource development are just too high.

1

Introduction

Background

This book is about the waxing and waning of the *Gemeinschaft* style and quality of life, particularly in communities which are in the throes of being industrialized. For the most part, it examines the experiences with coal development projects of rural America's Western people, illustrated by those residing in and around the tiny, isolated, ranching community of "Sagebrush." It shows what has been happening to the values of Sagebrush residents and to other aspects of their way of life when confronted by the forces of rapid growth and change associated with an industrial project. Having utilized ethnographic methods to gain the intimate knowledge of this community needed to perceive and understand its values, this study provides a fresh perspective on what *Gemeinschaft* is, how it works, and how it interrelates with *Gesellschaft*.

In the past twenty years or so, but especially in the past few years, students of community have marshalled data in attempts to show that communal life in cities is not dead after all, that various supportive social networks abound there, and even that the quality of life in the metropolis is about the same as that in the small town (Fischer 1982; Hunter 1974; Suttles 1968). However, their analyses have relied heavily on questionnaire data (which, by its very nature, does not enable the investigator to gain intimate knowledge of the subject matter), and, for the most part, they have restricted themselves to studying urban, suburban, and semirural places. By focusing on a very rural community, the present book takes a firm step toward completing sociology's coverage of the entire range of contemporary American communities in its analysis of what *Gemeinschaft* and *Gesellschaft* are, how they work, and how they handle forces of change. As indicated, however, the focus is on *Gemeinschaft*, its persistence and its ebb and flow.

First discussed at length by Ferdinand Tönnies in his renowned book

1

published in 1887, the concepts of *Gemeinschaft* and *Gesellschaft* have greatly influenced subsequent sociological thought regarding community change and development. *Gemeinschaft*, a form of social organization historically typified by informal lifestyles, is characterized by strong interpersonal bonds based on shared values, traditions, and activities. While life in such a society is not devoid of formal aspects, it is dominated by the members' deep-seated personal ties to the community and by their unswerving commitment to kinship, friendship, and neighborhood relationships, all of which are based on common sentiments and values and, above all, on mutual trust. As a result, *Gemeinschaften* are widely considered to be vulnerable to the relationship-disrupting and trust-straining forces of externally induced and controlled change. *Gesellschaft*, on the other hand, is historically typified by the relative formality of urban lifestyles. These lifestyles are enmeshed in multifarious complex organizations and are marked by rationalistic and calculative (nonsentimental) behavior. *Gesellschaft* is characterized by bureaucratic ties and relationships based on organizational rules and other formalized norms of social interaction. Elements of *Gemeinschaft* are evident, but the dominant way of life is impersonal and legalistic (based much more on formal contractual arrangements than on informal mutual trust), enabling it to weather diversifications, alterations, or other modifications quite readily. This book departs from the traditional thinking regarding both concepts by presenting evidence that, everywhere and always, *Gemeinschaft* and *Gesellschaft* are interdependent as well as interrelated: each exists only in and through the other. This departure from the traditional evolved as I sought to make sociological sense of empirical research findings which documented usual and unusual instances of the ebb and flow of *Gemeinschaft* as found in American rural Western communities undergoing rapid and massive industrialization of natural resources in or near their vicinities.

According to the evolutional thought in sociological theory, modernization and urbanization, usually accompanied by industrialization,[1] have been steadily transforming the nation's (and the world's) rural areas into urban ones. The standard sociological expectation fostered by some of the discipline's most respected theorists for the past century has been that, whenever and wherever the light of *Gesellschaft* is turned on a *Gemeinschaft* community, the latter's traditional way of life is quickly superseded by the culturally more brilliant lifestyle of the former. According to this viewpoint, the two forms of community organization do not long coexist: a community has one way of life or the other, not both. Its attitudes, values, relationships, and modes of interaction are, at most, only a temporary mixture of the two as the unilinear forces of evolution unceasingly energize the process of changing *Gemeinschaften* into

Gesellschaften. When the evolutional forces have done their work and this transition is completed, naught but *Gesellschaft* will remain. Robert Nisbet (1966, p.77) leaves no doubt about this point of view: "With the advance of *Gesellschaft* and its cultural brilliance, must go the disintegration of *Gemeinschaft.* On this point Tönnies is clear and emphatic."

Ten years (1972-83) of research by my colleagues and me, along with some other recent community studies (Gold 1974-82; Fischer 1982; Hunter 1974; Suttles 1968; Liebow 1967; Gans 1962)—and with that marvelous pre–World War II adumbrator of many of our recent "discoveries," Hughes's (1943) study *French Canada in Transition*—has forced us to realize that this either/or assumption about the relationship between *Gemeinschaft* and *Gesellschaft* is incorrect. Although my research associates and I did not set out to study *Gemeinschaft* and *Gesellschaft*, we gradually realized that our findings were not in accord with this and some of the other standard sociological assumptions—to which we subscribed—about these two forms of human organization. It took us several years to face up to the need to revise our concepts of these organizational forms in light of our recurring findings about what was happening to industrially impacted *Gemeinschaft* communities in sparsely populated areas of Montana, Idaho, Wyoming, Colorado, and North Dakota. What was happening, and continues to happen, was that, instead of being taken over and transformed by the forces of *Gesellschaft* unleashed by natural resource development projects, the essential *Gemeinschaft* quality of the affected rural Western communities has been changed only superficially. (Lest anyone jump to the conclusion that this kind of change is easily managed, I hasten to point out that much of this story of Sagebrush is about how agonizingly painful and difficult even apparently superficially imposed modernization and urbanization are for members of a rural community.) Such findings led us to conclude that *Gemeinschaft* has much greater staying power than sociology has long assumed it has. Furthermore, comparisons with metropolitan areas which we (in an established section of Detroit) and others have studied have shown that *Gemeinschaft* also persists in what traditionally have been considered to be *Gesellschaft* areas (Gold 1974-82; Fischer 1976; Palen 1979; Suttles 1968).

These findings indicated to me that the evolutionists' widely accepted assertion that *Gesellschaft* tends to engulf and supersede *Gemeinschaft* had to be modified. This assertion and the assumptions associated with it[2] have led many sociologists into a self-fulfilling, albeit erroneous, prophecy regarding the impact of industrialization on traditionally rural areas. For example, rather than being taken over by the forces of *Gesellschaft*, rural Western residents have managed to tighten and revitalize their established social circles and turn their backs on and take out of account some of the more disruptive impacts of modernization and urbanization as a way of preserving their community and way of life, much like the French Canadians of Cantonville did as their community underwent substantial growth and change (Hughes 1943). This interpretation of Tönnies has also kept many sociologists from the unexpected finding that the difference between actual and ideal *Gemeinschaft* in rural Western towns is smaller, not larger, after they are impacted by the forces of *Gesellschaft*. These residents have found ways to preserve what they consider the key elements of their social organization and culture by shifting from relatively fanciful to relatively actual realizations of ideal *Gemeinschaft* relationships and lifestyles.[3]

Examination of such behavior revealed a serious error in the usual sociological prediction that *Gesellschaft* will replace *Gemeinschaft*, for it failed to take into account that the latter is so fundamental to the existence of a human community that it cannot be displaced if community life is to be maintained. It followed that even an ideal-typical conception of *Gesellschaft* must allow for the significant presence of *Gemeinschaft* in its midst. This conclusion seems certain enough now, but it took the findings of several years of boomtown research in the rural West to begin jarring me loose from my tendency to cling to the evolutionary interpretation and thus to engage in either/or thinking about these two basic forms of community.[4]

About a year after I had completed fieldwork on Sagebrush, Rudolph Heberle's (1966) insights into Tönnies's conceptualizations came to my attention. Although Heberle's understanding of Tönnies has not had the influence on sociological thought that the evolutionists' position has had, his understanding of *Gemeinschaft* and *Gesellschaft* enabled him to anticipate, quite precisely, the essential "discoveries" I made many years later when doing fieldwork at Sagebrush. Here is an especially illuminating excerpt of what Heberle (1966, pp. 150-51) said about Tönnies's intended distinction between ideal-typical and empirical meanings of these two forms of community:

> The two categories of *Gemeinschaft* and *Gesellschaft* stand in a complicated relationship to each other which is not always understood by critics. The objection has been raised that these concepts represent, on the one hand, antithetical conceptional categories and, on the other hand, stages of historical development and that they also are mere classificatory concepts. The last of these is certainly not Tönnies' meaning. Though he sometimes designates the family or the village as a *Gemeinschaft* and the city or the state as a *Gesellschaft*, this is only as a paradigm. To him *Gemeinschaft* and *Gesellschaft* are pure concepts of ideal types which do not exist as such in the empirical world. They cannot, therefore, be applied as classificatory concepts. Rather, they are to be regarded as traits, which, in empirical social entities, are found in varying proportions. If one should, for example, define the family as a *Gemeinschaft*, the road to sociological understanding would

thereby be barred; it is the peculiar task of the sociologist to find out to what extent a family in a concrete situation (e.g., a wage-earner's family in a great city) corresponds more to the type of *Gesellschaft* than does a family in another situation (e.g., on a farm). If one takes the concepts in this sense, it will be possible to apply them to historical phenomena without doing violence to the logic of the system.

A peculiar difficulty lies in the fact that the two categories are not strictly antithetical, inasmuch as a purely *gesellschaftliche* empirical condition of social life is, for Tönnies, inconceivable; for, since man in his behavior is never motivated alone by intellect and reason but, whatever the stage of social development, by inclinations and emotions, that is to say, fundamentally by *Wesenwillen* [affective-traditional] and only partially by Kürwillen [*zweckrationale*], all empirical "associations" must have a *Gemeinschafts* [sic], or "community," basis.

After the research at Sagebrush had forced me to modify my assumptions about the "clear and emphatic" meaning of Tönnies's conceptualizations, Heberle's insights helped me to understand why. Further confirmation of the Sagebrush findings on *Gemeinschaft* and *Gesellschaft* came from an unexpected source.

My associates and I obtained strikingly similar findings from "Poletown," a segment of Detroit made up of several adjoining communities.[5] Having incorrectly assumed that this urban scene—indeed, *any* big-city urban scene—would be more or less representative of the ideal-typical *Gesellschaft*, this similarity came as a great surprise. We found that a thin veneer of *Gesellschaft* was covering the local *Gemeinschaft* and, as we had interrupted our studies of industrially impacted rural Western towns to do social impact research on a similarly threatened section of Detroit, we were understandably much more keenly aware of the powerful presence of *Gemeinschaft* in this area of the metropolis than were those who resided there. The residents took for granted their thinly veneered coupling of *Gesellschaft* with *Gemeinschaft*, but our sociological findings on their Detroit community complex so dramatically revealed a totally unexpected case of the persistence of *Gemeinschaft* that we felt compelled to risk the generalization that this persistence is inherent in all established human communities, regardless of the setting. While the evidence supporting this generalization emerged from the quantitative as well as the qualitative impact data we gathered over the last decade, the most revealing and significant findings on *Gemeinschaft* came from our use of comparative and longitudinal ethnography.

Ethnography is a method by which the sociological fieldworker systematically establishes relationships of mutual trust and respect with people he selects as representative community informants. In and through these relationships, the fieldworker is able to become intimately acquainted with the structure and way of life of their community—both the larger community and the smaller social circles where the members have their principal communal experiences and form their views on what life in their community is and should be about.[6]

The present portrayal of the community of Sagebrush evolved from over 1,000 interviews which focused on the views and reactions of both the townspeople and the landowners (cattle ranchers principally, but also a few farmers) in the vicinity. Using a sociological sampling approach, which enlists the help of informants in identifying and locating persons locally thought to be good representatives of various groups and points of view of interest to the research, the informants contacted represented a variety of occupations and professions, including government officials, merchants, ranchers, ranchhands, store employees, land brokers, financiers, health professionals, welfare workers, students, educators, laborers, engineers, housewives, clergymen, tribal representatives, law enforcement personnel, industrial managers, construction workers, senior citizens, newsmen, and lawyers. One of the major themes which surfaced in interviews with these informants concerns the importance of membership.

Membership and Gemeinschaft

In established rural Western towns and agricultural neighborhoods and in the metropolitan area studied, *Gemeinschaft* continually affirms and reaffirms a person's sense of who he is and where he fits into the community as he goes through his daily routine. One of the greatest fears of impact concerns losing this social and psychological sense of belonging and becoming instead a "nobody."[7] There is also a great desire to pass all this good membership on to the next generation—a strong reason for not wanting young people to move too far away. In rural communities most grown children cannot stay on unless the residents are willing to risk the impact of industrialization in order to provide additional job opportunities. Taking this risk means exposing the community to the forces of rapid economic growth.

Vulnerability

Because people in the rural West are so committed to doing things informally and personally, they resist using legal or formal channels to protect their *Gemeinschaft*.[8] They find such procedures, even when ostensibly in their own interest, to be anathema. This stance turns their greatest strengths as isolated rural communities into their greatest vulnerabilities when impacted by industrialization. For example, they are helpless in trying to deal with the formal, bureaucratic, legalistic, impersonal world that is suddenly thrust upon them, although certain individuals may be able to get some protective action going, such as city zoning ordinances, on the strength of their respected membership in the community.[9] Such vulnerability may well be a universal theme in rural communities which have no political clout for dealing with interventions of *Gesellschaft*. Even so, the residents generally find ways of protecting the structural integrity—and thus the *Gemeinschaft* form—of the community.

Inner and Outer Structure

Regardless of its type, the structure of a community is essentially twofold. The most obvious aspect is outer structure, which consists of readily observed organizations and behavior. It is evidenced behaviorally in the way people present themselves, their community, their organizations, and their way of life to outsiders—that is, in ideal, formal, categoric, guarded, normative, impersonalized, and similar terms. It is observable in the fronts people display when functioning as bureaucrats; as organizational, community, or lifestyle representatives; as questionnaire respondents; and as public relations persons for, or defenders or advocates of, their way of life. It is also seen when people are putting their best foot forward; are deliberately and perhaps self-consciously being polite or diplomatic; are directing their words and deeds to posterity or to other unseen categories of those whose judgment of their behavior they might wish to be favorable, positive, or approving; and are willing to negotiate definitions, meanings, functions, and uses of the organizations and activities of which they are a part.

This kind of guarded, calculative action serves to protect one's position in outer structure, to keep self shielded, and to insulate inner structure from the essentially nonsentimental, untrustworthy, and impersonal character of outer-structural behavior. Acting guardedly lends itself to trying out versions of reality under conditions of perceived risk to role, self, and position. It also lends itself to making a practice of using versions of reality which are calculated to meet the perceived expectations of one's associates (e.g. telling them what they want to hear): to project to them certain desired images of role, self, and position, and thus to reach the essentially rational, instrumental, and other nonsentimental objectives of outer-structural interaction. As a consequence, relatively little has to be inferred about outer structure even in the early phases of community study, when the fieldworker is just starting to develop relationships with informants and to achieve the deeper understandings of the social life of the community which are needed for gaining relatively direct access to inner structure.

In the same sense that outer structure includes, but is more than, rational and calculative behavior, impersonality, emphasis on "associative" relationships, formality, bureaucratic organizations and roles, and the like, inner structure includes, but is more than, sentimental and traditional behavior, strong bonds of kinship and friendship, emphasis on primary and communal relationships, informality, encouragement of behavior which gives rise to and affirms the basic human (and humanizing) sentiments (loving, caring, belonging, being morally accountable, etc.), and so on. Inner structure is the foundation of community life and, in contrast to outer structure, is relatively hard to see and change. It is also intrinsically vulnerable to forces of disruption because its great, inherent strengths are the human bonds of sentiment, trust, and reliably familiar surroundings. In relatively slow-changing times, these bonds suffice for coping with the usual recurrent vicissitudes of life, but they are much more subject to rupture and dissolution when continually bombarded by adverse forces of rapid change, such as rationality, impersonality, calculativeness, and strangeness. These bonds are regarded by those concerned as so natural and intrinsic to their existence that they are exceedingly difficult to put into words, however they may be perceived, defined, and socially accounted for. Accordingly, it takes considerable time, effort, and fieldwork skill to reach the point where relatively little inferring has to be done about the social circles which comprise a community's inner structure.

When making inferences about a community, it should be kept in mind that the concepts *Gemeinschaft* and *Gesellschaft* indicate the essential features and qualities of two contrasting modes of communal organization and attendant ways of life. The concepts of inner and outer structure help to explain how residents of the two kinds of communities characteristically fashion behavior so as to make their communities work. The concepts of inner and outer structure are more process-oriented than those of *Gemeinschaft* and *Gesellschaft*. The latter are relatively static and do not adequately account for how and why people engage in social interaction. The former are more process-oriented in the sense that they direct attention to the process by which people define their situations and, in light of these definitions, fit their behavior together so as to make society in the ways which characteristically take on the patterning of inner or outer structure. Accordingly, the concepts of inner and outer structure help to show how, in given situations, people size each other up and why they decide to act toward each other in given combinations of sentimental/personal and rational/impersonal ways.

The experiences of newcomers in the small Western towns I have been studying illustrate these points. Ordinarily new persons in such a community first come into contact with its outer structure when they arrive and look for a place to live. Personalized attention, usually a part of the local mixture of formal and informal interactions which make up the outer structure, is naturally withheld from newcomers when they contact court-house employees, grocery clerks, and other outer-structural representatives. Those who happen to be present when local inner-structural behavior ordinarily would occur find they are either taken out of account (e.g. established residents act as if there were no newcomers present) or the inner-structural behavior is displayed to them via an outer-structural veneer (e.g. the locals engage in polite, guarded behavior of the kind reserved for company or other nonmembers). Only those who can be "placed" as members qualify for personalized interaction in outer-structural contacts.[10]

It ordinarily takes two to three years for newcomers who genuinely want to make a place for themselves in the community to become accepted as residents in the process of fitting into the community and becoming members. Until they have put down roots and adopted the local values and lifestyle, their ability to remain in the community is almost exclusively dependent on the particular job they have and is otherwise related to outer structure. In contrast, longtimers are likely to find a way to stay whether or not they are able to continue their present line of work; they have a place within the community's inner structure no matter what happens to their jobs or other outer-structural positions (see Hughes 1943, pp. 46-47).

Members of small communities like Sagebrush tend to avoid and suppress conflict, because they view such disharmony as intolerably incompatible with the folksy, consensus-making processes which they depend upon to live together in the *Gemeinschaft* manner. Because inner and outer structure in such a community are so intertwined in so many respects, conflicts which directly affect cultural values and social relationships in the one structure readily spill over into those of the other. Accordingly, when faced with conflict or other threatening impingement upon any aspect of community life, members naturally feel compelled to find ways to fend off or otherwise dispense with such disruptions so as to protect their values and relationships and thus the integrity of community structure.

Inner and outer structure always occur together no matter how definitely and explicitly one predominates or fronts for the other. Thus, informal interactions and relationships always arise in even the most formalized organizations; and, at the other extreme, there is always a certain amount of rationality and calculation in even the most sentimental and enduring relationship. In the former case, people find ways of using their potential for being human (sentimental) beings and whole persons (not just role players) even in the most bureaucratic, ritualistic, or otherwise controlled interactions. Likewise, in the inner-structural case, even the deepest sentiments of the most loving and caring relationships are ordinarily talked about, accounted for, and protected in rational terms—in the language, expectations, and social practices of outer structure.[11]

The same social and cultural mechanisms which are needed to portray and shelter inner structure can also be used as disruptive agents of *Gesellschaft*; for example, the bureaucratization and formalization fostered by a mining project may change the size and character of a small Western town's outer structure so much and so fast as to severely damage its established relationship with the community's inner structure. Impacts on local outer structure may lead to confusion of ends and means in a family business,[12] damage a community's way of fitting in newcomers, make for uncertainty about sense of community and of place in it, and otherwise disturb the existing *Gemeinschaft*. If the latter is to survive, inner structure has to make substantial adjustments to rapid and far-reaching changes of this sort in its outer-structural façade and shelter. Such references to these key aspects of *Gemeinschaft* and *Gesellschaft* occur throughout this book,[13] which is organized around the experiences which a typical rural Western community had when impacted by a large-scale development.

Focus on Sagebrush

Extensive interviewing of rural residents in five Western states revealed that small communities here have much in common even though their individual histories and population makeups may vary markedly. This fact prompted me to utilize the various sociological features these communities have in common to construct a composite community, then place a typical energy development project there in order to indicate what life in the rural West is usually like before, during, and after such industrial intervention. I have given this composite community the rural Western name of Sagebrush, and I use the natural history of Sagebrush's experience with a traditional (i.e. relatively socially unenlightened) coal development project to bring the sociological phenomena of concern in this book into much sharper focus than would be possible were descriptions of several of the studied communities and their predevelopment lifestyles presented separately. Other named places in the region are also composites and are similarly representative of the many such places in the rural West.

Once the typical predevelopment situation is understood, the reader can readily appreciate the impact of sudden, massive industrialization on the lives of local residents. The discussion follows Sagebrush through the typical impacts of construction of a coal strip mine and an associated power plant as experienced by rural Westerners whose lives and communities are being changed by such overwhelming industrialization in their midst. As development proceeds, locals must cope with various and unavoidable impacts on their values and lifestyles. Their demonstration of ability to ward off or accommodate to the forces of modernization and urbanization and to maintain at least the essentials of their predevelopment social organization and culture is surprising. Even more surprising is their ability to revitalize their *Gemeinschaft* way of life while in the throes of experiencing massive industrial intervention. This book attempts to account for the ebb and flow of *Gemeinschaft* as residents of Sagebrush do. Dovetailed with, but clearly distinguishable from, their accounts are my own efforts to make relatively formal sociological sense out of this remarkable phenomenon.

Notes

1. Lauer (1982): "Modernization is a more inclusive term [than industrialization], for modernization can occur apart from industrialization. . . . In the West modernization proceeded by commercialization and industrialization, while in some non-Western areas modernization has proceeded by commercialization and bureaucracy. . . . Both modernization and industrialization involve the crucial element of economic growth, but that growth can occur apart from industrialization, while it is always integral to modernization [p. 280]. Urbanization is generally occurring along with modernization. There are ways in which urbanism facilitates that modernization—the provision of centralized political control, the stimulus offered to literacy and education, the enhanced ease of coordination, the breaking down of localism, for example. Urbanization can occur too rapidly and become an impediment . . . [and] a debilitating experience to large numbers of people . . . [for example, in] slums created by the influx of more people than the economy can absorb. . . . Any nation committed to modernization, therefore, must deal with the serious problems presented by—and take advantage of the opportunities offered by—the process of urbanization" (pp. 318-19).
2. Nisbet (1966) is the best-known subscriber to this interpretation of Tönnies.
3. As Sagebrush's experience has shown, this strengthening of *Gemeinschaft* is not merely an ephemeral "flash." To the contrary, some aspects of *Gemeinschaft* waxed at Sagebrush through the construction period and for some time beyond it before entering a waning phase. Overall community *Gemeinschaft* waxed particularly at the outset of construction and after the project became operational.
4. I was not unaware of the urban ethnographic research that had shown the presence of *Gemeinschaft* in the big-city slums, in occupational groups, among factory workers, and the like, but I tended to view the urban and rural lifestyles as much more fundamentally different than my research findings of the past several years have shown them to be.
5. These communities were predominantly composed of Polish and Albanian Catholics, Black Protestants, and Yemini Moslems (City of Detroit 1980).
6. This research method is an invaluable tool for understanding why such views are held and what they mean to those concerned; it facilitates reporting on the issues as all categories of community residents see them and, in these ways, portraying the changing research scene accurately, comprehensively, and meaningfully. The present sociological portrayal of the community of Sagebrush is a synthesis of the findings of ethnographic research on rural industrialization done by my fieldwork colleagues and me over the past several years.

7. This is a folk way of expressing fear that *Gemeinschaft* can easily be absorbed by *Gesellschaft*.
8. Law can be used to control *Gesellschaft* (and thus protect *Gemeinschaft*), e.g. through controlling the forces of modernization and urbanization. Law can also be used to foster *Gesellschaft*, e.g. through giving it license to engulf *Gemeinschaft*.
9. However, others there are likely to view these people as "bell mares" for the incoming company.
10. However, even in a metropolis, outer-structural veneers are stripped away readily during emergencies, crises, disasters, and other occasions when physically close but socially distant people drop their guards and interact as if they had inner-structural ties. They do so within the framework of the ad hoc, and perhaps quite ephemeral, inner structure they more or less unwittingly and uncalculatingly create to deal with and get through such occasions. Such behavior serves to indicate an important difference between inner structure and *Gemeinschaft*; it indicates that inner structure is a function of emergent definitions of situations, enabling it to take shape and respond to life's contingencies and vicissitudes much more rapidly than *Gemeinschaft* can. With the possible exception of specially trained and equipped groups that fight fires, attend to accident victims, or the like, inner structure is able to take shape and respond to life's contingencies and vicissitudes much more rapidly than outer structure can.
11. When people succeed in talking about, accounting for, and displaying sentiments in frankly sentimental ways, they may be assumed to have achieved some special rapport, such as that between old friends, young lovers, or other pairs whose commitment to the relationship is deep and "forever" and signifies that both the sociological form and the empirical content of their interactions are intimate (Simmel 1950).
12. Most family businesses in rural towns are a means to a preferred lifestyle rather than simply a way to make money.
13. There is an undercurrent of *Gemeinschaft* even in the metropolis, where *Gesellschaft* is manifestly the predominant sociological form. This is so because, as already noted, inner- and outer-structural behavior are so interdependent and interrelated in so many ways that a combination of these behaviors is a necessary condition for the survival of any human organization. This necessity must be taken into account in ideal-typical as well as in empirical portrayals of the human scene if these portrayals are to be faithful to their subject matter. Thus, ideal-typical representations of *Gemeinschaft* and *Gesellschaft* need to be less than "pure" logical opposites in which each totally excludes what epitomizes the other. Mindful of this lack of conceptual as well as empirical purity in distinctions between *Gemeinschaft* and *Gesellschaft*, chapter 7 will make some recommendations for conceptualizing the time-honored sociological distinction between these two forms of human organization.

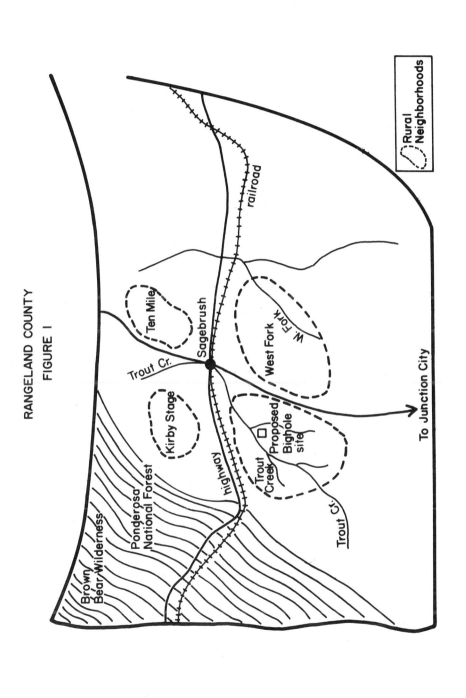

RANGELAND COUNTY

FIGURE I

Rural Neighborhoods

Brown Bear Wilderness

Ponderosa National Forest

Kirby Stage

Ten Mile

Trout Cr.

Sagebrush

West Fork

W. Fork

railroad

highway

Trout Creek

Proposed Bighole site

Trout Cr.

To Junction City

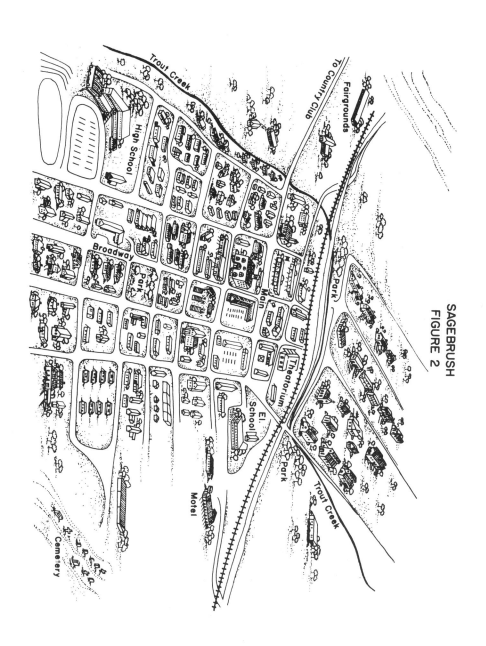

SAGEBRUSH
FIGURE 2

2

The Community Before Development

Physical Description and History

In 1970, two years before large-scale mining and related power plant construction entered the vicinity, the community of Sagebrush had about 1,300 people.[1] The county seat and the only incorporated town in Rangeland County, which then had a population of nearly 2,000, Sagebrush lay in the center of a large agricultural area (see Figure 1). This part of the Old West had some moderately rugged hills about twenty miles to the north and west, beyond which lay the mountainous areas of Ponderosa National Forest and the Brown Bear Wilderness Area. Trout Creek wound its way from the nearby hills in a southeasterly direction. Otherwise, the area was characterized by thousands of square miles of relatively flat and grassy terrain, weathered by a semiarid and often windy climate. The community itself was fairly isolated, given that the nearest town of any size was Junction City (population over 70,000), 150 miles to the south. As a consequence, life in Sagebrush had become quite self-contained over the decades.

Sagebrush has had a varied history. It formed gradually in the latter half of the nineteenth century, functioning first as a trade center for the area's early cattlemen and newer settlers, many of whom were from a number of Western European countries as well as the East Coast. These pioneers had come West at this time to establish themselves, having been displaced, repelled, or uprooted by events in these parts of the world. Gradually the town grew and was influenced by the development and utilization of the railroad which served this part of the state and ran through Sagebrush. By the turn of the century, thick seams of subbituminous coal had been discovered to underlie much of the land close to the nearby hills, and several underground mines were soon established; the town subsequently attracted a large number of miners, most being relatives of Europeans already here. Sagebrush then flourished until mining activity eventually declined, ultimately ceasing in the late 1940s as increasing use of natural gas, heating oil, and diesel fuel eliminated much of the demand for coal. With the exception of a brief period of oil exploration between 1951 and 1954, the population gradually declined as well; and the town's economy more or less stabilized by devoting itself to functioning as a service center for the area's now larger, well-established—but not always profitable—agricultural enterprises.[2]

Although there were some wheat farmers in the county, most of the area's agriculturalists were cattle ranchers. Both had experienced rough times due to fluctuating prices and the region's frequently hard winters. Even the mining days, although fondly remembered by oldtimers as good and prosperous times, did not provide economic stability because production and profit were totally dependent on an unstable mineral market. The Depression of the 1930s also left its mark on this traditionally solvent area, whose ethnic heritage taught the people to work hard, play hard, and pay their bills.[3] Given the experience of many decades, the residents believed that, while mines might come and go, they would always depend on the surrounding farms and ranches as the basis of their livelihoods, reflecting their long-held belief that an agricultural relationship to the land was the only permanent one in this part of the country. Of his rural neighborhood, a rancher said: "[The] Trout Creek [area] has taken care of generations of us, and we must take care of it."[4]

The town itself (see Figure 2) reflected its economic history. The mining lifestyle was built on an ethic of "living for today," and that ethic was still evident in much of the physical makeup of west Sagebrush, where little money was spent on constructing buildings, maintaining them, or making other material improvements. Houses, many in need of paint, were pushed up against one another and crowded into 30-foot lots. Tiny garden plots occupied back corners of yards, where vegetables were planted in clumps rather than in rows and no bit of earth went unused, reflecting the European heritage of many of the residents of this part of town.

Houses in the main residential section to the north and east were largely wood frame, many being of 1930 and 1950 vintage. Retirees who had moved in from ranches and other rural areas over the past two decades had built new homes on spacious lots. Also there was evidence of some remodeling and expansion of older homes situated along the community's dusty tree-lined streets. Three parks, one centrally located and two smaller ones to the north and east, offered nearby space for rest and recreation. Overall, the main residential area was fairly attractive, although many houses as well as trailer homes (set on residential lots or in designated courts), which were arranged in hodge-podge fashion, gave the town a somewhat haphazard appearance.

The downtown area, which altogether occupied about eight square blocks, looked more organized. It had more bars than eating establishments, a bowling alley, a post office, a bank, a weekly newspaper building, a movie theater, a 1-doctor clinic and tiny (20-bed) hospital built in 1958, 1 dental office, 6 churches, a small but expertly run city-county library, 2 motels, and a fair variety of shopping and service opportunities available at several well-established stores. With the exception of a small department store, all local businesses were family-owned and -operated. Two older hotels—occupied almost entirely by single, elderly, or retired railroaders— were located along the railroad tracks on the edge of downtown. One mile beyond was the aging Ranger Country Club, named after one of Sagebrush's founding fathers. The club was established in 1923, adjoining the county fair grounds.

Some of the old buildings in Sagebrush exhibited a European flavor; for example, the country club and the Theatorium on West Front Street were both semi-Gothic in design. The latter was quite elaborate, its interior having been once richly decorated with marble ramps and red velvet seats. Memories of eighth-grade graduation ceremonies, grade-school operettas, and performances of the Eddie Foy Brothers surrounded this old place which was transformed into a distillery, then into a repair shop, and finally into a storage building. The Western motif of the City Hall across the street presented a striking and immediate contrast to the ornateness of the Theatorium.

The city government occupied relatively inconspicuous quarters compared to the grand old county courthouse situated one block south on the corner of Broadway and Main. Built to last for many years, the latter occupied a conspicuous and proud place at Sagebrush's only traffic-lighted intersection. The courthouse was the center for much informal contact among people in the county and was a place in which all concerned felt quite at home. Sagebrush also had a few subregional offices of federal agencies which performed various agriculture-related functions; they were housed in a relatively modern building adjacent to the post office.

Not in the downtown but of central importance to Sagebrush were its two schools, which served the entire area.[5] Jefferson Elementary and Rangeland County High School, located at opposite ends of town, were both built in the early 1920s. The residents were proud of the local school district and of its staff, which had little turnover, and there had never been any particular drug or other delinquency problems. A new gymnasium and large playing field were added to the high school in 1960. Ranchers and townspeople placed great importance on school athletics for both girls and boys and were very proud of the teams. Their games attracted large turnouts and were easily the most popular spectator events in town. During the academic year much of the communitywide social life of both students and their elders traditionally revolved around the schools.

Social contacts were also provided through the local churches, which were scattered about town. The oldest, Saint Andrew's, had about 100 parishioners; and the five remaining Protestant congregations totaled nearly 800. Locals prided themselves on being good churchgoers and supporters, even though they did not consider Sagebrush a religious community. Sunday attendance was high, and between Sunday meetings these buildings were often used as gathering places for various denomination-related voluntary associations. The clergy, on the average, had been in Sagebrush for several years. They were widely respected and were superficially indistinguishable from the other residents; but they served well in their basic role of providing moral leadership, spiritual guidance, and general stability for the community.

The Area's Residents

As a stable and slowly-changing community for many years, it was not surprising that many people in Sagebrush were from second-, third-, and even fourth-generation families. Traditionally most residents were politically conservative; they considered themselves patriotic, prototypical, productive Americans. Almost 80 percent of the residents had lived here much or all of their lives; they stood in contrast to the noticeable number who were employees of the railroad and thus more mobile than most people in town in that they were periodically transferred in and out at their employer's discretion.[6] Many townspeople were related to each other and to the landowners in the vicinity, and everybody knew everybody. Together ranchers and townspeople comprised a readily identifiable social system which people had learned to take for granted and enjoy. Much of what change there was occurred when grown children for whom there was no place in the family ranch or store had to look elsewhere for jobs and careers, as alternative employment opportunities in the Sagebrush area were few and far between. As a consequence, most of these young people had no way to establish themselves economically in this desirable setting.[7]

Almost all older citizens in Sagebrush (nearly 30 percent of the local population) remained in their homes. Some used the help of social service aides and some were assisted by a federal program which subsidized home improvements. Ordinarily locals did not like people who went on welfare, and most were too proud to even consider it, but assistance to the area's elderly was viewed differently because these people had been productive all their lives. Many retirees needed and qualified for such income stretchers as food stamps but would not accept them because they thought of the program as welfare. On the whole, most older residents managed nicely because friends and relatives enjoyed helping out with shopping, trips to the doctor, home repairs, or whatever else needed to be done.

Residents of the vicinity surrounding the town of Sagebrush shared its values and traditions. Whether they had grown up in town or on a ranch, those who did not consider their rural lifestyle more important to them than career or financial opportunities had already left the community. The town's residents were largely relatives or lifelong acquaintances of the ranch families, and both were educated in the same schools and churches, served on the community's various boards, and belonged to the same organizations.

Landowners lived in four discernible rural neighborhoods (see Figure 1) composed altogether of approximately sixty ranches and half a dozen farms. The four functioned well to organize economic interdependencies among neighbors, such as being able to borrow equipment and machinery when needed and to count on help at branding and other roundup times. The rural neighborhoods' interdependencies also occasioned continuing social contacts which enabled ranchers to feel that culturally they were in the same boat and that they had ongoing options to associate with other people who valued a rural lifestyle which was peculiar to ranching in the West. Closer together culturally than socially, residents of these neighborhoods were primarily oriented to a very small number of friends and to their immediate families and other nearby relatives. Like others in Sagebrush, they were proud of their community and had a deep sense of belonging.

Being among the relatively few survivors of a long struggle by many agriculturalists to make a go of things in this part of the rural West, the area's ranchers had developed their sense of membership through learning, with the assistance of neighbors, how to cope not only with the facts of raising and marketing cattle but also with the land, weather, predators, and other factors making for economic ups and downs. For example, ranchers had to steadily increase the size of their herds to deal with continuing inflation.[8] Since land and water[9] in the area were such that it took about thirty acres to support one cow per year, it obviously required a great many acres to have an economically viable ranching operation; and, indeed, the average ranch size in the area was several thousand acres, of which more than half was grazing land leased from the Bureau of Land Management or U.S. Forest Service.

Aside from having to increase the size of his holdings from time to time, the rancher had to become an ever more capable manager of the land and its cattle. It took a very committed, hard-working, skillful, and resourceful person to do all this.[10] The natural selection process of the past few generations had produced at least the recognizable outlines of such a paragon in the person of the modern rancher. He and members of his family constituted an economic as well as a social unit. They worked together on the land and usually managed it either by themselves or with the assistance of one or two hired hands. Only occasionally did they need help from fellow cattlemen.

Although their spreads were large, ranchers still lived close enough to each other to engage in neighboring. Ranch houses and their outbuildings, usually sturdy old frame structures in sparsely treed areas, were generally clustered within a few miles of each other, adjoining county access roads. Few of these roads were paved. Ranchers preferred them that way, believing that unpaved accesses discouraged nosy tourists and cattle thieves. Because vehicles driven on them kicked up a lot of dust, strangers could be quickly spotted—even at great distances. This fact gave ranchers a feeling that, although isolated, they were able to keep a close check on the flow of people through their area without any substantial assistance from law enforcement officials; thus it contributed to their keen sense of independence and self-reliance. Smoke, too, was easily visible and would quickly trigger a communication network for checking out its sources and mobilizing neighbors for miles around to protect threatened grasslands, timber, or buildings. One oldtimer was angry when local ranchers first organized a volunteer fire department because, he said, it was a sign of distrust of their unspoken, but clearly understood, responsibility to each other to handle such matters informally as a community.

Lifestyle and Values

Ranchers and townspeople shared a rural Western lifestyle which represented some very deep-seated convictions concerning what life was and should be about. They valued family-centered life, informality in business as well as in other relationships, and especially the land itself. Since the town of Sagebrush was so much a part of the basic social system and way of life of people in the vicinity, it is not surprising that area landowners considered Sagebrush to be a good, satisfying, and natural retirement place, particularly if their grown children could take over the nearby ranch or already lived in town. Ranchers in particular were keenly aware of the land's fragility and beauty. They unceasingly took this fragility into account as they grew grass for their cattle and turned cattle loose to graze.[11] Locals also valued having easy access to the land's uncrowded and variously splendid outdoor recreation opportunities. Most were conservationists but not preservationists (nor environmentalists). They had trespassing problems under control and were able to take for granted that the people they ordinarily encountered were honest, trustworthy, and fair. They liked being able to recognize practically anybody in the region, living in a stable and familiar environment, and being part of informal life-support systems that really worked; and they were able to manage the vicissitudes of life very well. All this added up to being in meaningful control of their lives. "We really value our ability to control when we will work and when we will do the other things we enjoy doing," said a storekeeper who hung this sign on his door one Thursday morning: "Gone Fishing." The sign was there until the following day when the storekeeper returned.

Believing it was a good land and a good way of life, people did not want change. Sagebrush's mining history was partly responsible for this attitude. As one longtime resident put it: "The people who hung on after the mines closed had to scrape so hard they've become suspicious of changes. This causes considerable complaint about the things that should be done, and the difficulty is in getting people to take the steps to do them."

On the other hand, people here were proud of their independent community accomplishments. In the past, people had gotten together to pave the streets, put in a sewer system and lights, and build a swimming pool. Based on their tradition of neighborliness, residents were more concerned with working together to realize local social and cultural values than with personally acquiring numerous material possessions. A rancher questioned his wife after her first shopping trip to Junction City since they had signed a relatively lucrative oil lease: "Well, now that we're going to be rich, what did you buy?" She replied: "Just towel racks. After all these years of hanging towels on a nail, now I'm going to have real towel racks." One's livelihood was regarded as a means to an end rather than an end in itself. One store owner stated: "My theory of doing business may not be very good but it's sure safe. I want me or my family to wait on the customers, and I want to close up when it's time to go fishing or hunting."[12]

The quality of life in Sagebrush was described as that which comes only from living in a small community where, as one resident put it, "you don't have to worry about keeping your car or your house locked. We have feelings of security and safety at home and in the community, easy access to outdoor recreation, lower taxes than found in places like Junction City, and a slower pace of life that lets us get to know one another as more than casual acquaintances." It was also a function of the local environment's physical amenities. A longtime community member observed: "People live here because of those intangible benefits they get from the environment—the quality of the air, the water from the mountains, and the magnificent open country."

Family life was generally regarded as stable and secure, particularly in the outlying rural neighborhoods, and relatively few family problems were evident. Rules for behavior were informally but strictly enforced within the community's tight social network. Because strangers were highly visible and locals were subject to tight social controls, there were few reports of lifestyle deviations or even minor crimes. Most legal infractions were handled informally even if they were brought to the attention of the sheriff. While visiting health professionals from Junction City had almost no clients in Sagebrush, one of the community's lawyers and the physician (both longtime residents) were expected to deal with a smattering of chronic child abusers, wife beaters, and depressed spouses. The school counselor advised students on class schedules and passed out college brochures, but troubled teenagers turned to an understanding home economics teacher or a particularly sensitive music director. When a slightly retarded uncle was discovered molesting the children he cared for, he was not deprived of their companionship but simply supervised more closely. Generally, the informal helping network served very well for crises and for those with physical disabilities; but members with chronic emotional problems were usually expected to "tough it out." Divorce rates were very low, and few had ever sought marriage counseling, although two of the clergymen in town had had special training in this area of human service. One of the main attractions of the community, its people proudly declared, was that it was a good place to rear children. For example, almost everyone kept an eye on youngsters playing around town and readily provided help if needed.

Such neighborly help was not restricted to children and elderly members of the community. Sagebrush had a tradition of residents helping each other without reservations or hesitation. Rendering assistance in cases of fire and other disasters, loaning each other equipment, pitching in on house construction and repair work, and similar activities were all done naturally, without much self-consciousness and calculation, because this was the way people had learned to get along together. Participation in such neighborly action was based on mutual trust and an absolute willingness to reciprocate; it permitted area residents to establish social relationships and circles which for them made life acceptably predictable and manageable, safe and secure, and—in very fundamental respects—good. In short, people not only looked out for one another but depended upon one another, economically as well as socially. The local druggist noted: "The summer tourist season is good to us [through its economic boost], but we have to live off each other for the other six and a half months."

As webs of interdependency with each other evolved, residents found they could pursue valued individuality and personal independence. Knowing they could count on their fellows to continue caring about them and their place in the community gave them license to explore avenues of self-development and self-expression without fear of losing their place. For example, one middle-aged lady who had spent much of her adult life developing her artistic abilities while raising a family was now a landscape painter of note and spent so much of her time painting that she was just barely able tó maintain contacts with her social circles. Friends and relatives not only accepted her individuality but were proud of her regional reputation and of her ability to attract U.S. senators and other distinguished visitors to her gallery. Individuality of established residents was also expressed in ideational matters. For instance, a dominant community belief was that members were entitled to their own opinions and would not be condemned for speaking them.[13] "You're accepted for yourself rather than for any particular role you're playing," a longtime teacher said. Membership in the community was predictable and secure; always and everywhere the established residents knew who they were and where they belonged.

People in Sagebrush worried about strangers until they found out what they were up to. If the indications coincided with locals' way of doing things and did not pose a threat, the strangers would be accepted as newcomers. While the latter would be evaluated in terms of their deeds and locals would let them know whether they were "fitting in" acceptably, area residents strongly respected the individual's right to control that which was his. However, the newcomer was expected to make substantial progress in earning membership in the community before displaying his individuality. As one lifelong resident put it: "You can be different only after everybody is convinced you are essentially the same as the rest of us—deeply rooted in our traditions." While sociability was expected—even demanded, the area provided residents with never-ending opportunities to be alone. As one local put it: "The only socially acceptable way of keeping to yourself is to go out to the hills or fishing streams." Residents liked the feeling of not being "boxed in," and they had easy access to solitude in the outdoor splendor and recreation areas which abounded in this part of the state.

There was a strong feeling among some older natives that the nearby federally owned and managed recreation lands should have belonged to the locals—or at least those portions which had traditionally been used by Sagebrush area residents as favorite hunting and fishing spots—and that outside recreationists who came here more or less regularly were violating locals' privacy. On the whole, however, most locals did not feel bothered or inconvenienced by the modest number of these recreationists; in fact, some Sagebrush merchants, outfitters, and the like depended on nonresident outdoorsmen for much of their livelihood. For area residents, activities in the great outdoors consisted mainly of camping, hunting, fishing, and snowmobiling.[14] People of both genders and of all but the youngest age groups went fishing in Trout Creek and other nearby streams frequently throughout the season, and the town's adolescent boys and men were all dedicated hunters of deer and other legally allowable big game in the region.

The casual observer would conclude that the locals would rather hunt, fish, and wander over the area's hills and mountains than do just about anything else that life had to offer; but closer examination revealed that much of this activity was not solely for recreation. Most of the older working natives were strong advocates of multiple use of forest lands. This value could be traced back to a heritage which was totally dependent on natural resources found in the mountains and plains; a widespread belief was that any natural resources available should be used. Local townspeople did just that as part of their enjoyment of the outdoors. A retired teacher stated: "Almost everyone uses the area's natural resources to supplement their incomes. The primary activities . . . are gardening, firewood collection, and hunting and fishing—all these are family and social events."

Social and recreational sites in town included primarily the taverns. As one restaurant proprietor noted: "Only one bar in town allows local 'outlaws' to raise hell and pee in the street. The others use various ways to police their place, such as creating a sort of boarding house [or private club] atmosphere to threaten ridicule and ostracism to those who start to get out of line." Consequently most local bars were appropriate places for families to socialize and for adolescent girls to play pool without feeling self-conscious. Since these establishments tended to be the most widely used (and most formally constituted) of the social and recreational centers available, it was not surprising to find some drinking problems there. In spite of a high incidence of drunk driving fatalities, alcohol use was socially acceptable, but "drugs" (e.g. marijuana) were feared. A high-school sophomore reported that he would never use drugs because of the high moral standards he learned in church—"and besides, Lars [a 17-year-old brother] said if I did he'd kick the crap out of me."

Sagebrush's small theater and bowling alley were used extensively, but there was not much else in the way of commercial recreation in town. All this added up to making the best of what little was available. In nicer weather it was not uncommon for youngsters to play touch football on Main Street or for drivers to stop their pickups in the middle of the street to converse with friends who were on foot. To an outsider an atmosphere of lethargy seemed to prevail with one major exception: county fair week activities.

Rangeland County was widely known for its traditionally elaborate late-summer fair and associated rodeo festival, in which almost everyone had some part. Highly ceremonial in many ways, "F-F week" managed to commemorate the seasonal ebb and flow of work and recreation in this part of the region. Exhibits by 4-H and other groups, games and contests, racing events, carnival rides, and nightly fireworks were enjoyed by residents from miles around. Most of the proceeds were used for prize money or trophies, with the rest earmarked for maintenance and improvement of fair-festival facilities. Much visiting took place as part of preparing for, participating in, or simply observing F-F week activities.

The same kind of socializing occurred when doing errands in this very comfortable and unhurried setting. One housewife stated: "Going to the store is a largely social occasion—for drinking coffee and visiting with the storekeeper and other customers. It takes me at least an hour to get out with just a small sack. I suppose I would be disappointed if it took any less." There were no parking problems, and businessmen were interested in pleasing their customers. Merchants often went out of their way to be helpful—especially when the customers were ranchers or farmers who needed machinery or equipment fixed in a hurry, since everyone recognized that such needs were special and deserved high priority. Besides, they were both aware and appreciative of the agriculturalists' great contributions to the town's rather sluggish—but certain—economy.

While deliberately loyal to local merchants in order to keep them solvent and their merchandise consistently available, nearly all families went to Junction City about once a month for various combinations of reasons: to see a health specialist; buy clothing and other merchandise unavailable locally; window shop; attend movies, concerts, or lectures; dine; dance; meet friends whose lives were like theirs but who lived elsewhere in the region; and otherwise enjoy a change of scenery, pace, and social role. Junction City served well as a meeting and social center for residents in this part of the state.

The community's characteristically informal style of interaction even pervaded the staid old county courthouse and all the local government offices, boards, and commissions. For example, following any formal rules of order was anathema, embarrassing, or just simply not in accord with the local style of interaction, even at a meeting of the board of county commissioners, where less formal, obtrusive, and possibly divisive processes of interaction were used to make judgments as to feelings of agreement or disagreement, and formal votes were taken only when legally necessary. Here, as elsewhere in the community's outer structure, the personal, sentimental, folksy flavor of interaction served as a continual reminder of its web of connections with inner structure.

The Future

It was from Junction City's newspaper that locals first learned of Bighole Energy Corporation's plans to build a large strip mine and power plant approximately fifteen miles southwest of Sagebrush and very close to Trout Creek. Junction City's *Daily Times* had begun reporting the proposed coal venture early in the summer, indicating that equipment and an undisclosed number of construction workers and their families would be arriving the following spring. The reaction of area ranchers at this time was generally positive, as they anticipated that this coal project would be essentially what others had been in the past—an unobtrusive and acceptable industrial presence in an otherwise predominantly rural area. The landowners were quite capable of weathering the variables in the cattle business and believed the new activity would pose no particular or insurmountable problems. A few individuals began to fear that their traditional dependence on the land might be weakened by land-use changes, but others, including the veteran feed store operator, disagreed: "People feel they will prevail. We went through this before with the old Clark mine, and we outlasted it. If they go ahead and people come, we will still be here when they're gone. Life won't change; things will still be the same. We'll still depend on the ranches and farms as the base of our livelihoods."

Most locals, anticipating any kind of change, were reactive rather than aggressive. Survivors of two or three generations of killing winters, summer droughts, economic extremes, and the physical demands of ranch life, they believed they could cope with whatever lay ahead. At first, the uncertainties of the future elicited one of these responses: "We will roll with the punches" or "We'll take her as she comes." But as the weeks passed, increased local speculation about the proposed development began to make more and more landowners apprehensive about what the future held in store for them. For example, would the inexpensive federal leases they depended on for profitable cattle operations be threatened by newcomers' demands for recreation developments or home sites on that public land? Most ranchers had deep historical roots as well as site-specific lifestyles, and their inklings that the strip mine and power plant were probably only the first in a series of coal-related industrial ventures destined to move into the Sagebrush area and possibly take it—and them—over made them increasingly guarded about continuing their initial optimism. In contrast, businessmen in Sagebrush generally welcomed the idea of the proposed project because it would give such a boost to the local economy. Although uncertain about how it would affect their own operations, they looked forward to the stimulation and profits new customers would bring.

Some residents who treasured childhood memories of the town's mining past thought it might be pleasant to return to the "campfire and polka" atmosphere of those good old days. But an oldtimer who had recently visited a boomtown in a neighboring state disagreed: "It won't be like 'Snow White and the Seven Dwarfs' here. This time Snow White will come from Las Vegas in a pink trailer." As the development grew closer and more and more unknowns began to surface, such as the impact the newcomers would have on the schools and local housing supply, some of the more discerning residents began to wonder whether the community would be paying a large number of social costs for whatever economic benefits there would be. In anticipating these costs, the effects of "people pollution" on community organization and way of life would gradually emerge as the locals' central concerns.

Summary

The community of Sagebrush was composed of the town itself and four distinct rural neighborhoods located in the center of a large agricultural region approximately 150 miles from the nearest urban center. A number of area residents were descendants of a handful of pioneering families, and most had lived here for many years if not all their lives. Many locals were related to each other, and everyone knew everybody. They were committed to a lifestyle based on shared traditional values rooted in deep-seated personal ties to the land and the ranching way of life.

Over the years, local residents had evolved various interdependency networks which enabled them to cope with the exigencies of living in this sparsely populated area. Participation in these informal networks enabled the individual to be independent and at the same time gave him a highly valued sense of place in the community. For example, neighboring ranchers helped each other at branding and other roundup times without reservations or hesitation; such reciprocal behavior was expected—even demanded. The symbiotic outer-structural relationships necessary for their mutual survival fronted for the continuing predominance of inner structure in this isolated community, making it appear to strangers that Sagebrushians were "standoffish." Given the value locals attached to membership and "fitting in," the latter impression was entirely understandable: the treatment they accorded strangers was genuinely polite, while serving to remind the latter that they *were* outsiders. In contrast, locals' contacts with each other were based on informality, trust, and other *Gemeinschaft* qualities, whether meeting for business or other predominantly *Gesellschaft* purposes or strictly for companionship. Their background and lifestyle made it difficult for residents to imagine and prepare for the social impact of the proposed large-scale industrialization.

Notes

1. The community includes the town itself (population nearly 1,000) and the surrounding area. The four rural neighborhoods more or less directly affected

by the coal development project described in this book are from ten to forty miles away from the town and had a combined population of approximately 300.

2. A slow but continuing decline in agricultural employment and in the number of locally owned farms and ranches occurred in the last few decades. Various financial pressures contributed to the formation of larger, company-owned operations from smaller, less successful ones. However, the great majority of ranches and farms in the area were still owned and operated by individual families, often with the assistance of a hired hand or two.

3. Not much was purchased with credit cards, nor did people buy things they could not afford. A bank officer once mentioned that there were few applications for loans other than annual ones against fall cattle sales, but there was considerable refinancing of mortgaged land.

4. All the quotes attributed to members of the community of Sagebrush and to persons associated with Bighole's project are from the fieldwork files kept by my associates and me on community change studies we did in 1974 to 1983.

5. There were no rural schools left in the county, the last having closed in 1962.

6. While relative newcomers compared to the great majority of local residents, the railroaders were still regarded as members of the community in the fullest sociological sense; and relations between railroaders' families and other people in Sagebrush were quite congenial. In the old days, miners and their families also had been accepted as full-fledged community members. Although most left as mining activity phased out, ending in 1948, a few chose to remain in Sagebrush; all had since retired.

7. Some young people stayed and did seasonal and other part-time work to remain near their families and maintain a rural way of life rather than move to even relatively small urban areas.

8. Usually, ranchers who were unable to acquire enough land to make a living as cattlemen worked occasionally at other jobs to help support themselves. In all basic respects, they subscribed to the same values and lifestyle as their more affluent neighbors.

9. There is not much irrigated land in the area. Most ranchers took for granted their historic claims on local water supplies.

10. Even then there was an ongoing need for "outside" money. In the past, this money had come from marriages that brought "Eastern" dollars with them and from oil leases which provided extra income with almost no disturbance to the ranch, since no oil wells had ever been drilled.

11. The native grasses were very nutritious, and much of what grew naturally could be used for feed throughout the year. Prudent ranchers also grew some alfalfa to help feed cattle throughout the winter; but for the most part, native grasses could be relied upon to continue to reproduce themselves with minimal assistance from modern technology so long as sound grazing practices were used.

12. Suttles (1968, p.24) found the same kind of store in an ethnic neighborhood of Chicago: "[Most businesses in this area are not just a way of making a living but are a way of] enjoying an enduring set of social relations."

13. An important assumption underlying this belief was that people earned this entitlement through subscribing to the local way of life and establishing a place for themselves as members of the community. The few Indians residing in the area were in their own way "old family" in the community, even if not sociologically of it. In plain truth, newcomers of racial categories other than

White would not be welcomed by most Sagebrushians, as they were inclined to be suspicious and wary of people who looked, acted, and sounded that much different from "regular people" like themselves.
14. These persons were not interested in having more local sites designated wilderness areas, as some recreational activities of the above type would then be limited.

3

Impacts of Anticipated Development

Long before development began, local residents experienced a number of unpleasant impacts related to their anticipation of pending industrialization. Ranchers in the area felt these impacts more keenly than did those living in town, because they were uncertain just how much damage the proposed strip mine and power plant would do to the land and therefore what effect the coal project would have on their ability to continue raising cattle. In addition, they feared that large numbers of construction workers would seriously disrupt the local social system. This system and its common behavioral practices and rules were based on longstanding traditions which depended on certain actions, such as neighboring,[1] and precluded others, especially trespassing. The proposed externally induced and controlled development loomed as a form of "industrial trespassing," even though no disturbance of the land had yet taken place.

"No Trespassing"

One must be familiar with how the tradition of no trespassing originated here to understand both ranchers' and townspeople's increasing reservations about the proposed project. Taboos pertaining to asking indiscreet questions, such as the number of cattle (i.e. dollars) a man owns, imposing rationalistic and impersonal land-use values on ranchers, using their land without permission, and related matters originated on the open range around the 1880s when the area's first ranchers, joined by cattlemen from adjoining regions, began running large herds on the area's public domain. They did not own this land. The profit was very great since the ranchers filed on nothing, except perhaps a little (160-acre) homestead where the water was. As the range became more and more crowded, they grew extremely careful in their relationships with one another because there was no other law—so they made their own. Their law involved, among other things, an absolute taboo on trespassing.

31

They agreed to get together twice a year at roundups but otherwise to stay away from what they understood to be each other's part of the public domain. There was rampant rustling by both Indians and Whites, and so it was extremely dangerous to cross or otherwise use another man's turf except under the strict and rigid formulations of the fall and spring round-ups. When the homesteaders came along in the early part of this century, they absorbed this tradition of no trespassing from their ranching neighbors. While the original reasons for the taboo gradually vanished, the tradition of no trespassing continued unchanged.

Such taboos were not violated because the area's residents perceived that to do so would dangerously weaken the foundation of mutual trust, reciprocal aid, and personal safety upon which their entire social system was built. In other words, ranchers were accountable to each other to maintain this trust and assistance in the practical terms of their symbiotic interdependency, having learned from personal experience that they could not otherwise survive in this semiarid, sparsely populated area. As these symbiotic matters evolved into part of the social act of neighboring and of being members of a community, they became something which the people felt not only needed to be done, but ought to be done in socially acceptable, consistent, predictable ways. Thus, they became morally toned, as is true of all perceptions and behaviors whose evolution makes them socially accountable and thus subject to continual communal judgment regarding whether and in what circumstances they are appropriate, right, and good. In short, practical necessities had gradually become moral accountabilities. The attendant practices and rules persisted through decades and greatly influenced present-day locals' reactions to the proposed coal development. Understandably, then, strip-mining without the surface owner's blessings would constitute "the ultimate trespass."[2]

Any Sagebrush rancher who considered leasing or selling coal-rich land to the strip-mine company was on the way to becoming a trespasser so far as his neighbors were concerned, because he could be unilaterally responsible for permitting coal development to come into the area. In such an event, his neighbors would not know what to do about it because his act would be both an exercise of his traditional right to do with his land what he thought best and an outrageous interference with the ability of his neighbors to use their land as they thought best. As coal seams were the principal aquifers, strip-mining would unavoidably affect the quality of the region's ground water (e.g. its ordinary drinking water); moreover, massive burning of coal would pour pollutants into the air, via which they would come in contact with and be harmful to the grasses and other vegetation in the area, and therefore could negatively affect the health of cattle on neighboring ranches. As time passed, this value dilemma became glaringly apparent to all concerned as they asked what right a rancher had to unilaterally and gratuitously endanger his neighbors' ability to raise cattle. As one cattleman stated: "Nobody has the right to use the land as if they were the last ones."

Local values and social rules extended into business relationships. Ranchers bought and sold cattle by the hundreds; sealing these deals with a handshake was not necessarily an indication that they were more ethical than those who used formal contracts (after all, this informal business practice had evolved in the period when, in effect, they had been stealing the public domain). Mutual trust in local business transactions was no less a pragmatic issue than a moral one: the social system depended on it. In contrast, the outsiders who represented the strip-mine company were fine-print, legalistic types. They told ranchers that others had signed leases to mine coal, whether they had or not. This approach put the individual rancher in the sticky position of having to accept the "lease hound's"[3] word or to check it out, which meant asking neighbors questions which he knew should not be asked.[4] While this kind of deviousness was not necessarily illegal, ranchers viewed it as a form of trespassing. Such unacceptable behavior violated the ranchers' basic tenets concerning doing business; moreover, it was threatening to the entire social system because it suddenly brought into question some of the system's key assumptions, such as taking a person—even an outsider—at his word, trusting each other, respecting a person's right to "do his own thing," being able to count on each other when needed, etc. In short, agents of *Gesellschaft* were trespassing on the local *Gemeinschaft*, which was very vulnerable to external intervention of this type.

Vulnerability of Sagebrush Ranchers

Ranchers' interwoven symbiotic and social ties were rooted in neighboring practices. For some years, however, the amount and quality of neighboring had been drifting away from the ideal to the point where the local social system was held together by much flimsier ties than the ranchers were willing to admit; they shared a culture more certainly and demonstrably than they constituted a society.[5] Although their traditional *Gemeinschaft* community seemed to be on the wane, oldtimers sensed that this had happened before and would happen again as part of the social system's natural cycle of waxing and waning. Being in a period of considerable difference between the ideal and the actual state of their community, it was very difficult for cattlemen to mobilize themselves for collective action related to crises other than fire, critical illness, weather, and the like. Local society simply was not geared to other kinds of group efforts, as networks of relationships had been allowed to languish, and familial social circles had turned inward on themselves as though they were probing for the extremes in exercising their valued rugged individualism and self-reliance.

Being disposed to keep their worries to themselves, or at least confined to the inner circles of their immediate families, ranchers found it difficult to talk with friends and neighbors about the coal development issue and its ramifications. They wondered, and sometimes made erroneous assumptions about, where these fellow pastoralists stood on the question of industrialization. The process of defining the development situation largely in isolation from friends, neighbors, and relatives produced considerable strain in relationships among these ranchers. In some cases this strain was exacerbated as individual landowners took positions and acted on the development issue, but in most instances those concerned later found resolutions which were consistent with maintaining valued community relationships.

In the process, families which felt strongly about maintaining the ranch for the next generation were given a new sense of common purpose, shared with a network of relatives and neighbors similarly committed; and the few who saw development primarily as an opportunity to make money alienated themselves from others in the community by choosing courses of action that were inimical to the local lifestyle.

Ranchers were also experiencing strains in their attempts to deal with the industrial trespassers. Unlike some rural counterparts, Sagebrush area ranchers sought at first to accommodate to development because (1) they identified with big businessmen and therefore assumed that their fellow capitalists and conservatives were kindred souls, and (2) in many respects they genuinely wanted to take this opportunity to contribute to helping the nation meet its industrial needs. They soon found, however, that the company was not interested in being accommodative; rather it seemed to be inflexibly committed to a conflict model of development. Bighole representatives had shown themselves to be untrustworthy, unbelievable, and even deceitful at times; furthermore, they had been caught trying to bluff, pressure, and even intimidate local residents. For example, informants related what a terrifying experience it was to receive a land condemnation threat out of the blue. Upon receipt of such a notice, one has to hire lawyers and spend a lot of time and money trying to defend what has legally and rightfully been one's own land all one's life. One "lease hound" stated: "We sell ourselves on the assumption that we can capitalize on their uncertainties—especially legal uncertainties [regarding surface rights, eminent domain, the future of grazing leases—without which almost no ranch could survive, etc.]—and this turns out to be a good assumption."[6]

Another scare measure used by the land developers was to point out to a rancher what would happen to him if a neighbor decided to lease; he was then encouraged to go along with what his neighbor was presumably about to do: "It helps if they're afraid that their neighbor might lease or might sell out to an outsider like the railroad." Another tactic which land developers routinely used was continually talking in terms of *when* various developments would occur rather than *whether*. Locals noted that this usage made them feel powerless and at the mercy of uncontrollable external forces.

While not always operating in such ways, Bighole's mistakes in being insensitive, paternalistic, and ignorant of local values appalled Sagebrush residents, who believed they should have an equitable voice in determining whether, when, and how development should take place in the part of the world for which they felt responsible. Ranchers soon realized that their own values for doing business (being open, fair, candid, honest, and trusting) increased their already great vulnerability to the calculating, manipulative, and in many respects amoral industrial values being used to obtain leases from them and to secure the various state and federal permits the company needed in order to proceed.[7] Curiously, this recognition was a mass phenomenon. Individual residents were uncertain that their neighbors had come to the same realization as they had because of their reluctance to talk about where they stood on the proposed development. Avoiding discussion of the issue was a way of avoiding the risk of damaging valued social relationships—not just with the individuals at hand but with the many other community members who were intimately bound up with them in the web of relationships called Sagebrush.[8] "Maintaining relationships is very important to us. We sometimes put up with an awful lot because of our traditional inclination to keep in touch with friends or businessmen no matter what" (a rancher's daughter who managed a small clothing store). These relationships were safeguarded temporarily—or so it seemed—but at a price which increased locals' vulnerability to the company's divide-and-conquer tactics and other manipulations.

Concerns and Fears

The proposed mine and power plant—and the suspicion of more to follow—gave ranchers occasion to reflect on how much and at what rate of what kind of development-induced change they could manage without losing control of their community, businesses, and lives. Overwhelming for nearly all of them was the problem of trying to obtain reliable information which might facilitate this imagining. For example, the anticipated impact on water resources was a special concern. Since very few landowners had occasion to irrigate their land and nearly all of them merely took for granted that water would be available as needed, ranchers feared that there would be great and growing problems in competing with industry for scarce water resources and in keeping water from becoming contaminated. They also worried about air pollution and difficulties with reclamation of strip-mined land. Being in a situation in which they believed that important and fateful things were in process of being done to them and their community, they understandably hungered for information about what Bighole's proposed project was causing to happen there. However, they found that accurate and reliable information on project activities was not available. As they struggled to conceive of a future vastly different from their experiences in the past generation or so and tried to imagine what the community structure and way of life would be like if and when the proposed project occurred, rumors regarding their concerns, fears, and fancies naturally emerged. The local rumor mill doubtless did much to help the ranchers and other members of the Sagebrush community to vent their fears and anxieties but, for the most part, it kept the community off balance by continually stirring up feelings of helplessness, cynicism, and despair at the prospect of being turned into some kind of "national sacrifice area." One leasing spokesman offered ranchers this kind of assurance: "If Uncle Sam wants to mine his coal, he's going to do it. We have the expertise to deal with him to protect your economic interest." But ranchers were far from persuaded that the company had any such commitment.

Of all their fears, the kind, amount, and rate of "people pollution" headed the list because most ranchers believed that it would be insufferable to have so many people and cows in the same place, i.e., a large influx of people would destroy their ability to continue being physically isolated and socially distant from others and to remain unchallenged in their attachment to the land.[9] A typical view was expressed by the rancher who said: "I won't die. I'll survive. But the people will be fatal to our way of life." Loss of space, overcrowding of their recreation areas, dilution of their standards of conformity, and "divide-and-conquer" attacks by land developers on their networks of neighboring were all part of this fear. In the final analysis, some ranchers even foresaw having to move.

Those most concerned about the prospect of being uprooted were descendants of the true pioneers of the West. Their family pride had originated out here when their forebears had established themselves in what was then the wilderness and had created successful operations which had become even more successful in succeeding generations. The social and cultural roots of the Sagebrush ranchers in this sense were very deep. These cattlemen felt that here and only here were they socially somebody; they were people who really counted, and if they were to live elsewhere they likely would not be able to take this pride and social position with them. Hence they did not feel potentially mobile nor did they wish to be so.

Commenting on a neighbor whose land the company wanted to buy outright, a rancher wondered: "I mean, what can my neighbor do with $13 million when all he's liked to do all his life is stay on his ranch?" On the whole, these ranchers believed that they had a site-specific status because they could not imagine being able to survive, let alone maintain self- and social esteem, in any other community.

In contrast, a few of the key families in the vicinity of Sagebrush were able to trace their family histories back to the Mayflower and to the old days of the Deep South. In this regard they were very different from the other established ranchers. The former felt that, although they were well established socially and culturally in this area, their roots in this particular segment of the West were not critical to their notion of family pride nor of personal accomplishment. Hence, while far from overjoyed at the prospect, they (along with a few of the more marginal operators) felt potentially more uprootable than did others.

In addition to their deep-seated roots here, both groups shared a common sense of purpose which exceeded any inclination to help the nation meet its energy needs. The majority of the area's landowners felt that their basic responsibility to their fellow countrymen was to maintain the land as a good food-producing area, particularly when good coal was plentiful and available in the East. One rancher stated: "It is especially upsetting to contemplate development here because it is so unnecessary. The coal companies want to develop this just to make a lot of profits in the name of the national energy crisis. They could produce all the coal our country needs by continuing to deep-mine it in the East. To take the good grazing land out of production for probably many years and maybe forever is inexcusable." Given the impression that external energy markets were all that mattered to developers, ranchers realized that they needed to speak up forcefully and convincingly if they were to protect their interests.

Although landowners generally wanted a voice in decisions on coal development on their own and their neighbors' land, they simply did not know of any appropriate and acceptable mechanisms for expressing it. Accordingly, they felt frustrated and ambivalent, given their unfulfilled great desire to make themselves heard in such decisions, their reluctance to impose controls on others, and their fears of what would happen to them. For example, many ranchers in the study area were highly dependent on permits to graze their cattle on U.S. Forest Service land. This important summer grazing land might be mined or reclassified for recreational use only, and the prospect of its loss was real and worrisome. There was also widespread anxiety about what would happen to the character of the area, to patterns of neighboring, to the quality of life, and the like as more and more acreage fell into the hands of big corporations. As one resident said:

"It really bothers me that some of my neighbors would leave and others would be caretakers of corporation-owned land. What kind of community would this be?" In general, ranchers were cynical about the real impact their desires and feelings would have on any aspect of the prospective industrial development. They were growing painfully aware that the development was impinging upon them earlier and harder than on Sagebrush townspeople because of the ranchers' early contacts with land developers, their relatively great attachment to their land, their highly site-specific family pride and social status, and their other particular vulnerabilities to the forces of industrialization.

Mobilization Efforts

Given these varied and mutual concerns, it gradually became easier for ranchers to make corrections in the recent exaggeration of their historic commitment to self-reliance and individualism and to discuss the coal issue with their fellows, particularly after they began to realize that avoiding such discussion left everyone feeling emotionally isolated and politically powerless. Faced with the prospect of externally induced, radical, and basically unacceptable loss of self-identity and social status, they began to explore ways of creating a larger society which would cut across rural neighborhoods, enable them to pool their resources, and permit them to rally together to safeguard their cultural and social interests. These collectively perceived needs paved the way for the formation of the Rangeland Protective Association. The association immediately affiliated with the Mountain State Resource Council, which had formed a year earlier and was designed to serve the interests of the state's landowners and other groups concerned about development. One of its important functions was gathering accurate, timely, and trustworthy information on developmental plans and procedures to help bring the rumor mill under more acceptable control, to help clear up confusions, and to provide for mobilizing group resources. An association member said: "Ranchers have never kept each other informed before. Now we've got to tell each other everything except how much money we got for our calves."

Cattlemen's associations in the West had been around for many years. They performed the same kinds of functions as did other professional, trade, and businessmen's associations. County-level protective associations, affiliating with each other through state-level resource councils, were new ways of getting ranchers (and farmers) together to protect not only their economic investments but their entire way of life. Never before had the exceedingly independent and self-reliant ranchers been able to join forces effectively to protect their common interests and their general welfare. In the space of just a few months after joining together, many previously unorganized, politically inactive, industrially unaware, and legally and bureaucratically naive landowners in the greater Sagebrush area had begun to become knowledgeable about these matters and skillful in dealing with them. Having realized that the company was not interested in their efforts to be accommodative, ranchers sought and began using available administrative and legal leverage to slow or stop development long enough to figure out what was really going on and, in these ways, to become influential in mitigating impacts of the company's colonialistic forays. All this required them to learn about and engage in personal, organizational, and even large-scale planning of the sort they had long disdained—indeed actively opposed—and whose principles still made them feel uneasy. However, they had learned to consider their uneasiness a small price to pay for making progress in achieving a locally acceptable level of control over industrial development in their vicinity.

By this time, the beginnings of a shift of power from ranchers to the new mining industrialists had become evident to all concerned and alarming to most longtime rural residents. How far this kind of shifting might go and what its consequences on the established social structure might be no one at this time could foretell, but appearance of the term *Indianized* was significant. Ranchers had started to use this term to express their feeling that they were beginning to be treated in the generally subservient way in which Native Americans had been treated. Use of the term expressed growing anxiety about safeguarding their culture, their economic independence, and their place in the community as they became conscious and indeed self-conscious of their values and of their community's sociocultural strengths and weaknesses for dealing with representatives of industry. It also revealed that the ranchers were beginning to perceive that they and the few Indians in the vicinity of Sagebrush had much more in common regarding their attachment to the land than they had previously been willing to acknowledge. Native American membership in the newly formed protective association was evidence of this growing alignment.

Positions Emerge

At this time there was no single for/against dichotomy among Sagebrush ranchers and none would favor or oppose the proposed project under all conceivable conditions. Ranchers' participation in protective associations at state and local levels and in related activities revealed that most landowners in the area were very uneasy about the idea of this industrial project and strongly opposed to some aspects of Bighole's approach to carrying it out. One stated his reservations: "I want to start by saying that the mine and power plant are going to raise hell! But the company is big enough that they don't have to let any information out about what they're doing, nor do they have to let us have any say in how they will do it."

The few who tended to favor the project constituted a divergent category, and only one of them lived anywhere near the development site. These individuals were willing to take the great risk of becoming morally detached from the natural community of which they had been a member, i.e., they were willing to risk putting themselves and their community in the position of having to pay big social costs for the big money they were getting for leasing land to Bighole and other coal developers. The pro-development ranchers justified their position largely in terms of helping the nation meet its energy needs. Both sides acknowledged that the proposed mine and power plant would offer marginal ranchers the prospect of earning extra income so they could more certainly continue their preferred lifestyle, and both expected that the development would provide employment possibilities for locals' growing children and others in the area; the proposed development also offered the prospect of injecting new life into the town's stagnant economy.

Members in each category stood to make a lot of money from mining. Several who opposed it nevertheless leased to the company as a hedge against an uncertain future. In the past, money from oil leases had provided extra income with almost no disturbance to the land and local way of life. Some of the first ranchers to sign coal leases did so expecting to have the same nondisruptive experience. An unintended and unwanted consequence of this action was to help bring about the very industrialization they were trying to hedge against, and the irony of this was not lost on these ranchers. Not many people of any persuasion believed that coal development and ranching could long go on side by side if industrialization became large-scale and widespread.

As sides were taken on the development issue and as a neighbor here and there leased or sold out to the company, the vulnerability of the ranchers' social system became evident to all.[10] The imminent industrial invasion had begun bringing to the surface an awareness of some current weaknesses and deficiencies in community relationships—a factor in turning inward, becoming introspective and reflective, and thus becoming self-conscious about basic values which had previously been unspoken and taken for granted. This awareness also sparked informal attempts to revitalize the local version of *Gemeinschaft* to make more real the ranchers' idealization of their community. This attempted revitalization stimulated them to begin redefining their long-held assumption that what a person did on and with his land was his business alone, i.e., they began to realize that their individual land-use decisions could significantly affect neighbors' livelihoods and lifestyles. Perhaps most important of all was the growing awareness of how interdependent they were and how much they needed to work together if they were to safeguard the integrity of their valued community.

Townspeople's Vulnerability

Ranchers felt the earliest impact because the first industry representatives to come to Sagebrush were land developers who were trying to package enough coal leases and surface agreements[11] to be able to offer economically attractive deals to their industrial clients. The same clashes of values, objectives, and purposes which appeared then later emerged in town as these and other industrial outsiders began to present land-use questions and proposals to the appropriate local offices. At this point, activity at the county courthouse accelerated rapidly. Local officials, especially the county commissioners, began to feel unusual pressure, not just from the sudden change of pace but also from the enormous changes in sophistication and expertise their jobs now required. (The county had no planning staff and no administrative or technical assistants.) One landowner whose neighbor was a county commissioner—and a marginal rancher—expressed his neighborhood's concern: "We elected John so we'd be sure to get our roads graded in the spring. How in hell is someone like him going to be able to hold up our end of things when negotiating million-dollar deals with some coal company's big-city lawyer?" The three commissioners (two ranchers and a feed store operator), whose approval was required for various land-use changes, access roads, and other services, were suddenly being wined and dined by visiting industrialists who were seeking special land-use concessions for proposed coal projects, and flown about the country in the executive jets of companies that wanted to educate them quickly about the particular needs of their potential constituents.

While the county commissioners were already beginning to make decisions and commitments about the proposed development—some of which would be irreversible—other local officials (e.g. the school superintendent, sheriff, and public health nurse) were still trying to imagine what problems lay ahead for their agencies. Planning was impossible in the absence of population projections and other data. Similar problems variously affected others in town. For example, although the influx of developers, industrialists, and representatives of natural resource-related state agencies brought a dramatic increase in business for the town's motels and restaurants, most merchants and contractors found the first impacts to be all anticipatory as they agonized over how to make appropriate and timely decisions on expanding facilities, crews, and inventories without sacrificing lifestyle goals in the process. Complicating matters was the concern that if they chose to cater to the new clientele, they would alienate longtime customers on whom they had always been dependent for survival and whom they might again need after the boom was over.

Like the ranchers who viewed leasing land as a hedge against an uncertain future, many merchants saw the prospect of new customers as a potential economic buffer worthy of favorable consideration. On the other hand, however, and unlike the landowners, Sagebrush merchants would have to make certain investments before they could take full advantage of newcomer business. Knowledge of this fact was tied to the realization that a "bust" would very likely follow the construction-period boom, and no one knew how to assess the net effects of these phases of the business cycle and come out with a suitable plan of action. A choice of not expanding would certainly leave them vulnerable to competition from the kinds of chain stores and other shops which typically spring up in rapid-growth communities.

Planning assistance from governmental or private consultant sources had never been available locally. Residents of Sagebrush had a tradition of "making do," and very few demands were placed on their city officials or service providers. With the exception of the schools, for which ranchers and townspeople provided generous support, most local services were marginal at best. The town's water and sewer systems were barely adequate, law enforcement was poorly funded and few felt it needed to be more professional, the phone system was overloaded and worked erratically, and residents agreed that "even the cemetery is overcrowded." Businessmen were described as being in a "comfortable rut" and, like other locals, were more concerned with "just making a living and enjoying ourselves" than with thinking competitively about inventory expansion or land development. No city or county land-use plans had been formalized, and no member of the legally required (city-county) planning board was more than vaguely familiar with the state laws under which it was ostensibly operating.

As rumors about the proposed industrial development gave way to public statements from the company that promised prosperity for the community of Sagebrush, locals were unable to imagine, much less prepare for, the critical housing, health, and other social problems ahead. Residents joked nervously about becoming a boomtown when they met for coffee or at the post office, but they could hardly express their pervasive feelings of ambivalence; for example, they feared the changes that Bighole would bring to their valued way of life, yet hoped the company would provide more jobs for young locals. Townspeople shared ranchers' frustrations and anxieties over the fact that the company's optimistic announcements were not followed by reliable information about what kinds of growth to expect, when it would come, nor even absolute assurance that the development would actually occur—even though research for the Environmental Impact Statement was under way and applications for required state and federal permits were being submitted. The company seemed no more adept than the locals at preventing or closing the gap between the need for expanding the community's capacity to provide essential services for their proposed development and the time, money, and expertise which would be required to do so. Meanwhile, various federal and state land agency personnel, along with others in the private sector, appeared ready to rubberstamp whatever the company wanted, with virtually no interest in seriously considering local opinion.

Feeling overwhelmed by the magnitude of the proposed project and a sense of inevitability, many residents cynically conceded, "You can't stop progress." Others believed they should have an active part in how this "progress" should be defined and in what ways it should proceed; for example, a marginal rancher stated: "We're going to stand together. Maybe we can get something out of it. You can't run night guard all the time." In both cases the impact of anticipated development prompted the community to respond by tightening the established social circles and restricting membership to longtimers. In the anticipatory stage at Sagebrush, the tightening of social circles entailed taking the following measures, all of them, but in various ways and sequences:

1. Reducing participation in areas of outer structure where paths crossed readily with those who appeared to be agents of intervention and with most other nonmembers of the community. This meant that the connections among these parts of outer structure and between them and inner structure were not likely to be used much or at all for the duration of the perceived disruptive impingements on these traditional protectors of inner structure.
2. Increasing participation in areas of outer structure where paths did not cross readily with nonmembers of the community. (At this time, some people in Sagebrush joked nervously about how they might have to form an oldtimers' club to ensure having such a refuge.) This meant that, probably for the duration, the locals chose to strengthen and use connections among these parts of outer structure and between them and inner structure to concentrate their activities where outer structure was functioning best in its basic role of shielding, fronting for, and otherwise protecting inner structure.
3. Creating parts of outer structure not previously present which would provide additional safeguards for inner structure and/or other parts of outer structure, for example, establishing the Rangeland Protective Association.
4. Maintaining connections between and among intimate social circles as a way of helping to tune out actual and potential threats to community culture and social organization and to tune in on and use more exclusively, demonstrably, and unguardedly the values and social relationships which made up the core of community life, the inner structure.

My reflections on instances of tightening social circles raised some questions and led toward some answers: Do all social circles/groups have inner- and outer-structural components? The Sagebrush evidence indicates that they do. For example, when a family turns inward on itself, does it then present itself to others in outer-structural ways as part of trying to ward off potential and actual threat of which it has become especially fearful? If so, is this behavior indicative of an outer-structural component in an otherwise essentially inner-structural human organization? As just suggested, when larger networks of relationships languish, familial social circles tend to turn inward on themselves. Doing this functions to keep *Gemeinschaft* alive, much as tightening of larger social circles does when the community's outer structure undergoes rapid change.

Noting the beginning of this process of tightening established social circles, a middle-aged housewife commented: "Our daughters don't play pool at the bar anymore and my husband and I don't eat out at the cafés. We take the camper and grandma and meet a few friends up on Trout Creek." While this tendency was not necessarily conscious and deliberate in every case of gravitating toward one's own kind to safeguard and perpetuate the core of community life, it was symbolic of the natural resistance to the forces of change which were expected to reshape much of the community's physical appearance and many of its relatively symbiotic and secondary relationships, that is, its outer structure.

The process of holding public hearings and doing research for the Environmental Impact Statement (EIS) on the proposed coal development was itself a source of anticipatory impact on Sagebrush and a revealer of still other aspects of the community's vulnerability to outside intervention. Accordingly, an examination of the EIS process is in order.

The Environmental Impact Statement

An EIS was required by federal and state law to ensure that research would be done on likely effects of Bighole's proposed project on natural and human aspects of the environment. As part of the process of doing an EIS, the proponent of the project, Bighole, would agree to take whatever steps were needed to make certain that these effects would be kept within certain environmentally acceptable limits. The public too—especially those residing in the vicinity of the proposed project site—would have a voice in the preparation of the EIS so that its views on likely environmental consequences of the proposed project would be given due consideration.

What follows is a brief sketch of the process of doing an EIS on Bighole's proposed project. The sketch aims to explain why the very process of doing the EIS as it was done turned out to have substantial anticipatory and actual impacts on the people of Sagebrush and to account for an initial step the locals took to begin making new connections between inner and outer structure to deal with these and other new threats to their way of life.

Since most of the project would be done on federal land administered by the Bureau of Land Management (BLM), it was decided in discussions between BLM and the counterpart state agency for this project, the Department of Natural Resources (DNR), that BLM would be the "lead" agency in working with the project's proponent, Bighole, and whatever environmental consulting firm would be employed to do the research required to meet federal and state regulations for doing an EIS. After Bighole submitted a formal proposal to BLM and DNR for a coal mining and power plant project near Sagebrush, representatives of the company and the agencies met to discuss getting the EIS process under way and hiring an environmental research firm to do the necessary research. In due course, these representatives selected a Denver-based firm, Apex Consultants, whose reputation, cost estimate, and availability most appealed to them. Bighole then turned over to the lead agency, BLM, enough money to enter into a formal contract with Apex to do the research and write the comprehensive draft and final EISs on the proposed project in accordance with pertinent federal and state laws. Shortly after receiving the contract, Apex put research crews into the Sagebrush area to begin gathering data on current environmental conditions in order to assess the likely effects of Bighole's project on them. At about this time, too, BLM began taking steps to solicit public comment on the proposed project as part of fulfilling its legal obligation to encourage the public to become involved in the process of designing and doing an EIS on probably impactful resource development projects such as this and to indicate their views on likely environmental effects and ways of "mitigating" (i.e. avoiding, minimizing, or otherwise coping with) them.

To get its public involvement program going, BLM sent letters to all residences in the area to invite people to comment by letter on what they expected to be noteworthy impacts on natural and human aspects of the environment if the project went forward as proposed. Although composing letters for publication in a draft EIS was not a congenial and suitable mode of "input" for the average concerned citizen in the area, many residents took pains to write thoughtful letters to BLM about expected impacts. For its part, BLM asked for this kind of public input only because the EIS guidelines required them to do so. Letters from residents poured in; they came from ranchers and others who were knowledgeable and concerned about water supplies, land reclamation, wildlife habitat, etc. The issue most eloquently addressed in nearly every letter was the importance of keeping the area primarily agricultural in order to safeguard a way of life that had been cherished for a century. BLM simply did not know what to do with this qualitative data, however empirically sound, well-presented, and illuminating it may have been. BLM quickly disposed of the problem of what to do with this material by classifying most of it as too subjective to be used in its planning and decision making. Thus, although this public input was retained by placing copies of the letters in an appendix of the draft EIS, the letters were disregarded in all other respects pertaining to the EIS process.

A similar fate befell the locals' input into the many public meetings to which BLM invited them. If letters were difficult for area residents to deal with, getting up in front of an audience and speaking into a voice amplifier so intimidated them that few dared attempt that kind of performance. Even though most of these meetings were held in Junction City or the state capital, the people from Sagebrush usually were well represented. Their attendance at these distant and inconvenient meeting places dwindled as they learned that the eloquence of their better public speakers and the presence of many of the other concerned and attentive Sagebrushians made absolutely no difference in the level of BLM's official understanding of their views as revealed in BLM's unwavering ability to take their views out of account. Predictably, Sagebrushians eventually became so discouraged with this disregard for public input that only a handful continued to attend BLM's public meetings. BLM then cited their lack of attendance as evidence that they did not care enough about their professed interests and convictions to represent them at meetings now attended almost solely by public agency representatives, Bighole's public relations staff, and the technical experts they paid handsomely to assure the world that no harm would come to the natural or human environment if Bighole were permitted to do the proposed project.

The locals' cynicism about BLM's entire public involvement program was intensified when they learned that Apex's researchers also found their letters and the statements they made at public meetings too subjective and unrepresentative for inclusion in Apex's data. Apex preferred to involve the public in its social impact research in a less emotional, more controlled, and allegedly more scientific way by putting together a questionnaire based on previous community surveys, pretesting it in telephone interviews, and administering it by telephone to a random sample of Sagebrushians listed in the telephone directory. All these phone calls were made from Apex's Denver office, as its social impact researchers saw no need to spend any more time in Sagebrush than it took to reconnoiter the area, snap some pictures of it, and have lunch with some city and county officials on whom they later pretested the questionnaire. These researchers used available demographic information and statistics on health, crime, and business conditions supplied by state and federal agencies that regularly obtained such data. Locals were dismayed to find that Apex's social (and economic) researchers were no more inclined than BLM's regular staff to find out what life was about at Sagebrush, what the people's values were and why, what held the community together, why the members found it to be so attractive in its present state, what the members' environmental concerns were and why, what was already impacting the community's culture and social structure, and therefore what difference the project was apt to make in their lives if it went ahead as proposed.

Apex's telephone interviews were conducted at a time when the people were already very frustrated and disillusioned by BLM's public involvement program. Being asked to reply off-handedly and tersely to questionnaire items struck the locals as another instance of a lost opportunity to be heard in a way which was germane to their interests and concerns. The questionnaire asked them to talk about a future they as yet had no good way of visualizing and about the present in a strangely glossing and obtuse way which did not allow them to give their own portrayal of their way of life and their concerns about it.

Accordingly, the people of Sagebrush felt a growing frustration about the superficial and fruitless manner in which they were allowed to participate in BLM's public involvement program and Apex's social impact research. Already distressingly aware that the project-related information they were getting from Bighole and the news media was often inaccurate, undependable, and misleading, the people were further distressed with the dearth of useful and reliable information coming out of BLM and Apex. This frustration was a sort of last straw among the impacts which predisposed ranchers in the area to do something about their situation. To help meet the need to clear up rumors, check out project-related news reports, learn better how to define and safeguard local interests, decrease their individual and collective vulnerabilities to the forces of change, become more adept at representing local views and happenings to the news media, and become more skillful at participating in the politics of natural resource development, ranchers in the Sagebrush area created the Rangeland Protective Association (RPA). They promptly affiliated their new organization with the Mountain State Resource Council, a landowners' organization designed to protect the interests of locals when faced with such intrusive natural resource development as Bighole's proposed project. No organization in Sagebrush or accessible to it was of much help in meeting the community's project-related needs, so establishment of RPA was an important move not only to improve the adaptability of Sagebrush's outer structure per se but to revitalize the relationships among the members and thus between the community's inner and outer structure.[12]

This action to fill a gap in the formal provisions for local representation in the EIS process becomes even more meaningful when viewed in the larger context of producing the legislation (National Environmental Policy Act of 1969 [NEPA]) which mandated doing EISs in the first place. Schnaiberg (1980, pp. 319-20) points out that NEPA is more than

> an environmental reform piece of legislation. [Indeed,] it seems more accurate to view NEPA as a political response to the social problem claims raised by environmental movement organizations in the 1960s—an attempt to deal with these groups as political claimants. . . . It was drafted, though, with a recognition that conventional public projects providing infrastructure for private investment and economic growth were threatened by "excessive" environmental reforms. . . . Thus, NEPA was an uneasy balancing between two sets of claimants—economic interests, and environmentalists. Overall . . . NEPA has favored economic interests over environmentalists.

Locals were given even less consideration than environmentalists in the original formulation of NEPA. It was not until such politically active organizations as Mountain State Resource Council were established that locals had any clout at all in addressing social and other environmental impacts in NEPA-related resource development projects.

Commenting on the practice of EISs to rely heavily on benefit-cost analyses (and thus to make questionable assumptions about dollar equivalents of environmental impacts), Schnaiberg (1980, p. 324) states:

> Those who see impact assessment as a science are frustrated by the political dimensions and the lack of science. Conversely, those who see the EIS process as a purely political arena are disheartened by the cumbersome rules of the game that are imposed by a facade of science. Confusion and frustration are enhanced by the [political tone and the] false promises that benefit-cost logic has always had. . . . "Benefit-cost analysis cannot answer the most important policy questions associated with . . . fusion-based economy . . . these questions are of a deep ethical character. Benefit-cost analysis . . . may well obscure them (Kneese, 1973:1). . . . How does the 'old economics' of natural resources differ from the 'new economics'? The old economics was mostly economics. The new economics is mostly politics. ([Wildavsky]1967: 1115)"

In fairness to BLM and Apex, it should be noted that both were operating in a manner consistent with the requirements of federal and state law covering doing an EIS. It should also be noted that doing a social impact assessment was (and continues to be) only a minor part of doing an environmental study according to federal and state guidelines. Nearly all the research effort went into studying the nonhuman part of the environment and the likely impacts of the project upon it. These and other agencies involved in the EIS process really did not know what to do about the people's overwhelming concern about impacts on the human aspects of the environment represented by the local community, as neither the legal guidelines for social impact research nor their methods of doing such research did much to enable them to adequately address the people's sociocultural concerns.

Moreover, BLM had long been uncertain about its mandate to relate to and serve those portions of American society located in the vicinity of the land which BLM managed. The agency was given to making platitudinous statements about being there to serve the public, but its actions did little to support these assertions. While some individual employees of BLM sincerely wanted to take the public more into account and serve it better, their work environment continually reminded them that they were part of a bureaucracy which was simply neither organized nor inclined to do that. Rather than being sensitive to the values and circumstances of people local to its many field offices, BLM was more oriented to its own hierarchy and to the more nebulous American public that it purported to serve. The agency's field offices, like the one at Junction City, were usually so out of touch with the locals' values and circumstances that they often made erroneous assumptions about them. For example, BLM personnel at the agency office in Junction City were essentially dead wrong in their belief that Sagebrush ranchers were more interested in selling out at a big profit than in staying put, continuing their struggle to stay economically viable, and doing their utmost to protect their community and its way of life from the damaging forces of rapid industrialization. Understandably, then, it often appeared that BLM's nominal client was whatever category of people it was expedient to designate as such. Not all of this was lost on the people of Sagebrush, but they had a deep and abiding faith in the U.S. government and, willy nilly, BLM was part of what they tried to believe in and trust. With respect to BLM, however, it just was not easy to keep the faith.

When the smoke of the EIS process finally began to clear and the last revision of the EIS was in the hands of the printer, more than a year had been spent on the EIS. This was longer than it would have taken had BLM and Apex paid more attention to the locals' expressed concerns about the proposed project's various effects on the environment. It took many months for the locals to succeed in convincing state and federal permitting agencies of the statutory and scientific merits of their objections to some of Apex's research procedures and findings on aspects of the environment which these agencies were mandated to oversee and protect (e.g. air, water, wildlife) and of their objections to the recommendations BLM was making for "mitigating" expected environmental impact. When the locals finally did get through to the agencies, the latter held up permits needed by the project until convinced that the proponent, Apex, and BLM would satisfy some of the objections which the locals had raised. Having failed repeatedly to get Bighole, Apex, and BLM to satisfactorily answer their questions or address their objections regarding the environmental research, impact mitigation recommendations, and public involvement program, the locals turned to the permitting agencies and finally got action on some of their concerns. All this had the effect of delaying the completion of the EIS and thus the start of the project at considerable monetary cost to Bighole. However, as locals pointed out, Bighole would ultimately recover the cost of this and other blunders by increasing its rates and passing these costs on to the users of its electricity.

Summary

The anticipation of impending chaos, the prospect of an outside take-over of what had been their community, and the idea of being forced to make lifestyle sacrifices of great magnitude so that projected market demands by people elsewhere in the nation could be met really rankled the locals. They suspected that those living in the more populous states probably had no realistic conception of what impact Bighole's efforts to satisfy urban energy desires was already having and would continue to have on the people of Sagebrush. The latter certainly could not outvote these consumers if the issue of the proposed and future development in the area were decided at the polls; such a vote would merely use the trappings of democratic decision making to tyrannize a small minority that had infinitely more at stake in the outcome than the majority did. In response to this recognition, locals began searching for genuinely democratic ways to gain a voice in development-related decisions that would affect their lives as individuals and as members of the community and to keep from being such "sitting ducks."

Sagebrush residents' increasing sense of vulnerability was fueled by the fact that both public and private agencies involved in the proposed development had been giving relatively little weight to the locals' sociocultural concerns compared to that given the technological and economic ones of the corporation and its customers. Also, area residents feared that they would be overrun by people using the national energy shortage as a justification for ripping off the underlying coal to feed operations motivated more by profit than anything else. As such feelings and fears became stronger, they began to have more and more impact on the community's inner and outer structures. For example, some residents worried that openly expressing a particular position regarding development would alienate lifelong friends who held opposite but unspoken views—and so, as such, inner structure suffered. Merchants had difficulty deciding whether to expand their businesses and how to shift their orientations to include new customers they expected would somehow importantly affect the modes and meanings of outer-structural behavior in Sagebrush. The most noteworthy impacts of anticipated development occurred in those aspects of the community's social structure and culture that were particularly vulnerable to impingements of imagined and expected industrial growth. These impingements included both the process of doing the EIS on Bighole's proposed project and the locals' initial reactions to this process.

Notes

1. This behavior had lost some of its potency in recent years but was still very important to the social system.
2. Very few ranchers owned the mineral (coal) rights to their land.
3. Ranchers used this term for speculators who negotiated lease agreements with landowners and then sold them to coal companies.
4. Valuing personal independence, ranchers did not overtly pass judgment on each other's actions or try to proselyte each other for given causes. Such conduct was tabooed.
5. The area was made up of many small societies; some of these "natural communities" gradually revitalized themselves in the face of the coal issue.
6. As indicated in note 4 of chapter 2, this and other such quotes are from the fieldwork files kept by my associates and me.
7. Lease hounds were quick to single out those ranchers who were natural leaders and, in some cases, to use this knowledge to their mutual advantage. One stated: "When ranchers band together against development, someone always steps out—and we can psych that one out. You take each one's values and work with them. We were able to help one family relocate their son in a job."
8. Examples of comparable avoidance behavior are found in Eggan (1955), Homans (1950), and Malinowski (1941).
9. Through this attachment the rancher maintained the feeling of social solidarity with his forebears. Through improving the land he encouraged his offspring to pick up where he left off. In this way the rancher reaffirmed his belief that he was doing right by the land no less than by its caretakers. The cattle he raised and sold provided him with income needed to fulfill his solemn responsibility to maintain this family-centered, man-land relationship.
10. When describing the people of Buffalo Creek in West Virginia, Erikson (1976, p. 77) could have been talking about residents of Sagebrush: "They are . . . resourceful and obdurate, yet they are often overwhelmed by their own vulnerability." On the same page Erikson notes that the communal resemblance between these mountaineers and the Italian-Americans in Gans's study of Boston's West End (1962) is "indeed remarkable." So it is with the people of a variety of *Gemeinschaften*.
11. This part of the West was homesteaded when the federal government's policy was to retain ownership of the mineral estate. Thus, coal leases had to be obtained from the Bureau of Land Management, and the permission to act on these leases had to be obtained from those who held deeds to the land surface overlying the coal. This permission ordinarily took the form of a leasing agreement between coal proponents and surface owners, for example, ranchers.

12. As will be noted in chapter 5, this revitalization was not in itself enough to keep community *Gemeinschaft* from waning. It took a substantial slowdown in the scope and rate of community change, i.e., an end to the intrusive construction period, to create conditions needed for generally revitalizing the community's *Gemeinschaft*.

4

Impacts Experienced at the Outset of Development and During Construction

Ranchers' Views at the Outset of Development

From the time of the first announcements concerning development near Sagebrush through the onset of actual mining activities, locals felt a great deal of uncertainty about what was going to happen and a great deal of dissatisfaction concerning Bighole's actions. Their larger uncertainties pertained to the company's project-related statements and actions, as experience had shown them that the company was given to engaging in deceptive practices. Locals noted that Bighole had said it "didn't know" when later it was revealed that in fact plans had been made. The company also reportedly lied about its intentions for development; for example, only later were power line placement plans and subsequent industrial commitments revealed. As one rancher stated: "This company is making fools of us. They have lied about what they're intending to do and how much of it they intend to do. They are sneaky and deceptive. They get you to sign easements through lying and then it's too late to get a fair deal."[1] Bighole's statements of intentions, no matter how viewed, were just not believable. Dealing with this kind of situation may not have been totally unfamiliar to local residents, but it was nearly so. Certainly it was distressing to them to feel it necessary to operate on the assumption that project representatives could not be believed or trusted.

There were other, more specific uncertainties which surfaced at the outset of development. Even if water sources went undisturbed by coal mining, they and the air might become so polluted by the proposed industrial complex that cattle raising would be jeopardized. Further, the success of land reclamation efforts had yet to be demonstrated to the satisfaction of most informants. Announcements that only a small amount of acreage would be disturbed were misleading in that the disturbance could divide a ranch, whether it was due to mining itself or to the installation of power lines or rail spurs. Also the portion of land affected could turn out to be located right over a spring. The company's offer to drill wells to replace any springs that went dry on its account was unacceptable to locals because wells were not a reliable source of water (e.g. they could go dry suddenly or freeze up in winter). Ranchers reported that such deceptive announcements and offers were typical of Bighole.

Accustomed to conflict with competitors, customers, regulatory agencies, and legislatures, the company drew on a repertoire of business strategies to expedite its plans. As locals became more organized and informed and thus less gullible and manipulable, Bighole tended to view them as "the enemy" not only of the project but of the "progress" it was designed to achieve. The company had already been expending a tremendous amount of effort to get ranchers to do what it wanted and needed to facilitate project development. Any questioning of, or other evidence of resistance to, this great effort only intensified the company's resolve to have its way. Thus rigidified, the company's approach to doing this project left very little room for negotiation and accommodation of differences with locals. In a sense, the battle was joined well before locals comprehended the scope and intensity of Bighole's determination to do the project.[2]

Taking advantage of this situation, some lease hounds were able to breech inner structure by cultivating relationships of mutual trust with certain landowners they perceived as having the requisite potential (greed, principally) for breaking ranks with their fellows. Other locals, observing what ensued, began to learn some valuable lessons about avoiding such penetrations. Valuing trust, credibility, and honesty, the ranchers found themselves greatly handicapped in their situation of not being able to trust and believe most who sought to do coal-related business with them. It was difficult for the landowners to shed these values and to adopt industry-wise ones they needed to defend themselves, and the constant frustrations made it increasingly difficult to make any plans or decisions.

Because ranchers could control very few of the manifold aspects of coal development, they had little or no assurance of any return on their investments which needed to be expanded regularly to keep their cattle operations economically viable. In fact, failure to improve and expand them was synonymous with failure to keep up and be competitive. If ranchers knew for sure that development would go only so far and no further, they could make certain commitments and take certain stands. Much of their initial information had been based on rumors rather than on confirmed or official statements, and it took close to a year for the newly formed protective association to assemble definitive materials on what was proposed and to familiarize landowners with the kinds of formal and bureaucratic procedures they would need to employ to protect their interests. Meanwhile, positions continued to form.

Those who favored development constituted a divergent group. There was some evidence that they usually did not have the same family ties to the area as did their neighbors. Some were reportedly poor managers who were trying to regain their losses or who were getting back at unproductive soil. Those favoring development were optimistic about being able to continue to ranch and to lease back their land or buy it back after mining had taken place, which they figured would require a relatively short period, and believed that the land would not be totally and irrevocably destroyed. They said: "If we can send people to the moon we can figure out how to reclaim the land. We could improve it by putting coal money into leveling and irrigating it. In the long run, I believe, coal development is good for the land. In the short run, it will certainly mess things up and some damage will be irreparable, but we should be able to live with it." One informant contended that this closing of eyes to the future made it easier for pro-development ranchers to "justify their greediness" in getting money from coal.

Because much of this part of the West was homesteaded after the federal government had adopted the policy of deeding ownership of the surface of the land to the settlers but retaining ownership of whatever minerals might be beneath the surface, most of the ranchers in the Sagebrush area did not own the coal and other "minerals" in their land. The federal government's Bureau of Land Management was (and is) responsible for determining what coal fields could be mined throughout most of the West; the railroads owned much of the remainder; some Indian tribes also owned significant amounts of coal; and individual landowners wound up with rights to relatively little of the region's coal. It should be noted, however, that since the mid-1970s federal policy has given the landowner a significant voice in what happens to the minerals in his land even when he owns only the surface and the federal government owns the minerals. In Sagebrush, who was for and who was against development was not simply a matter of who had fee coal (i.e., coal which belonged to the surface owner) under his property.

Although the presence of coal may well have been a factor, it did not fully explain ranchers' views, since several who were opposed to development did have fee coal and had been offered a great deal of money for it. A partial explanation was that those who tended toward being predominantly pro-development[3] usually defended their view in the publicly acceptable terms of being obliged or duty bound to help the nation deal with its energy crisis. Others were willing to go part-way: "If they get the coal that's all we should have to sacrifice. Let them build plants at the load centers [i.e., at the cities which will use the electricity]. Those in urban areas enjoy their lifestyle and we enjoy ours. We shouldn't [have to] give ours up for them." Antidevelopment people did not accept the assumption that it was necessary to strip-mine the area's coal, pointing out that mining could be continued in established places closer to the source of demand (e.g. in Appalachia), that deep mining could be done instead and the coal exported to appropriate metropolitan centers, and that solar or wind power could be developed to meet energy needs—all without requiring people like themselves to pay such disruptive and irrevocable social costs for short-run energy benefits. Acting on these sharply divergent views on coal development tended to polarize the ranching community, severely strain many lifelong relationships, and thus make the ranchers keenly aware of vulnerabilities in their social system.

The ranchers' social system was vulnerable because in a number of respects it seemed to be more nominal than real. It was more alive and idealized in the memory of what it used to be than in the apparent actuality of the loose and uncertain social ties which formed the basis for claiming that these landowners were members of a community. The ranchers' idealized or fictionalized community was maintained by acting as if the relatively latent, quiescent, and little-used *Gemeinschaft* were much more manifest, active, and used than was in fact the case; relatively inactive *Gemeinschaft* had been kept going through sporadic efforts to lessen differences between their actual and their ideal community.[4] Although they continued to share a ranching way of life, Sagebrush area cattlemen had been doing so in smaller and smaller groups, such as is done by urban dwellers in their particular way of life. The obvious great reluctance and seeming inability of ranchers to effectively band their small family groups together in the face of an enormous, commonly experienced threat to their way of life had the initial effect of making them easy prey to the industrial intruders. The fictionalized aspects of their lifestyle, preference for handling things informally, and antipathy to collective planning and action all contributed to the cattlemen's great vulnerability.

Coal development and its "people pollution" specifically threatened the freedom, absence of regimentation, isolation, and quiet that ranch life offered, as well as the aesthetics of the area. Ranchers found that, with the exception of former natives attracted back to Sagebrush by the new job and business opportunities, their fears about so many people coming in were entirely justified. It was already evident that newcomers subscribed to a substantially different set of values. For example, they did not have the same respect for the land as did the landowners, who were bewildered as well as angry about abuses to which their property was being subjected by the influx of thoughtless trespassers. Many newcomers did not understand that a large piece of land was just as private as a 50-foot lot and acted as if these ranches were public playgrounds.[5] Informants angrily reported finding gates left open and cattle being chased by motorcyclists, who left ruts and other damage to the land. In general, most ranchers felt that a demented value system was being imposed on them, that their Western hospitality and trust were being violated, and that they—like their land—were considered expendable. These feelings came from the *Gemeinschaft/Gesellschaft* struggle between the lifestyle of the economically and politically powerful interventionists and that of the economically and politically reactive, socioeconomically subordinate locals.

Committed ranchers were beset by other concerns related to development. Of major consequence was whether the newly formed protective association could really keep their highly interdependent social system from collapsing if any more ranchers "sold out." Commenting on the fragility of the situation, one informant stated: "That sums it all up. . . . We need each other in order to survive. Until this coal business entered our lives, we had been acting as though we were good neighbors but we had actually been drifting apart. Now we have to really be good neighbors again or we are going to be easy pickings for the industrialists." Another cattleman explained: "Tearing up one's roots to allow rootless people in is not a solitary act. It has a big impact on one's neighbors, on their water, on their ability to live as they wish, and on their ability to be a community. How can anyone justify selling out to industrialists as anything but an antisocial act?"

But the situation was not as cut and dried as it might have been. For example, some ranchers felt driven to sell or lease to coal developers because of the almost chronically poor cattle market and the pressure created by the sudden increase in land prices, which made expansion almost impossible.[6] Also, a few who had leased land (primarily from federal and state agencies or from the railroad) found that their leases were being taken away on short notice. Most ranchers depended on such land for grazing, because they did not have enough deeded property to support their livestock. As a consequence, competition for replacement land quickly accelerated as leases were withdrawn, making it increasingly difficult for ranchers to afford the gradual expansion of land holdings needed to maintain economically sound operations. What was viewed as antisocial "selling out" was often simply a matter of trying to keep going rather than a revelation of latent greediness or abandonment of all one had once valued. Most of the relatively prodevelopment ranchers (about 15 percent of the landowners) who had not yet leased or sold land for development resented being made to feel that they should give up the income they could make from coal to preserve a neighbor's feelings, sensitivities, and way of life; they were willing to pay big social costs to obtain big money. Being unwilling in this respect, the neighbors got nothing positive in return for the big social costs such unilateral land development forced them to pay.

Ranchers who saw in coal an opportunity to make a lot of money for themselves became estranged from the local scene in the way that boomers were. The latter enjoyed the novel experiences and strangeness which were part of being highly itinerant and mobile and had no interest in getting involved in local organizations or affairs or in developing social ties. Their ranching counterparts tended to become inordinately loyal to themselves and acted as though they, like boomers, were rootless and therefore not responsible for the effects of their actions on those who had been their friends and neighbors. Such estrangement, temporary though it may be, can function as a way of absolving oneself from feeling responsible for doing something about the social problems one may or does create.

Other problems and concerns were voiced. Many focused on taxes, which were rising due to conditions beyond the locals' control; and landowners feared a heavy tax burden when the coal boom was over. "We are paying for development" and "we are paying for our own destruction" were common expressions of dismay about the situation. Ranchers also recognized that, because they were so highly specialized in their work, so deeply attached to the land, and so committed to their way of life, they were not in a position to readily adjust to the unfamiliar changes threatened by development. Most were having a very difficult time imagining the future. Such possible industrial problems as air pollution were still considered abstractions for they were simply outside the ranchers' experience. In addition to these uncertainties, the cattlemen felt that they had no say in the decisions being made which were so fatefully affecting them and that they were powerless to influence what was happening. In the face of such ominous and sweeping change, they stood to lose everything they had and were.

Being outnumbered by prodevelopment businessmen, industrialists, and a host of new construction workers, antidevelopment ranchers sensed that they were being herded into the status of persecuted minority. For years these cattlemen had been considered prototypical Americans, the backbone of the country—and of Sagebrush's economy; now, suddenly, they were being accused of standing in the way of "progress" and being made to feel guilty for trying to protect their rural way of life from the impacts of a coal development project which would result in substantial monetary gain for the developers and enable the users of the project's electricity, who resided in urban areas elsewhere in the nation, to maintain their energy-intensive lifestyles. Such a radical change in status was both befuddling and outrageous. Ranchers were caught in what appeared to be a losing battle:

the nation's alleged need for Western coal versus the lifestyle of a few. Commenting on the general feeling that industrialization of the area's coal resources was inevitable, one rancher said: "The very best that industrialization can offer is some extra money, which is too bad because, for people like me, land guarantees happiness, dollars don't."

A commitment to a chosen lifestyle or to one's home ground which took priority over the money which could have been made by selling to a coal company was totally baffling to most of the industrialists, who could not understand why anyone would forfeit a sizable sum of money to maintain what to them had no particular personal value or appeal. Still, the values of most cattlemen in Rangeland County inclined them—even those who took an extreme position against development—to want to accommodate industrial wishes. Ironically, the latter were considered radicals by Sagebrush businessmen and by their prodevelopment neighbors, even though the alleged radicals were actually traditionalists who were acting entirely in character when trying to protect their prototypical capitalistic way of life. Efforts to be obliging were continually rebuffed; the landowners ran head-on into industrial values which were based on conflict models of behavior and to which they did not subscribe. One rancher commented, "Isn't it a terrible way to live, not to be able to trust anyone?" The prevailing situation generated an abundance of scapegoating behavior directed at Bighole, the county commissioners, and other likely targets as ranchers' concerns and aggravations continued to mount without resolution. Similar pressures and problems were also felt in town.

Impact in Town on the Eve of Construction

Experience had shown people in the Sagebrush area that neither the news media nor the coal and power companies could be relied upon to give accurate, truthful, or believable information concerning coal development. Unlike the ranchers, the residents of the city of Sagebrush did not have an organization such as the Rangeland Protective Association to turn to for current and reliable development-related materials and assistance. A few residents who were close to and especially sympathetic with the ranchers' situation joined the association as a gesture of support. Their nominal membership in an organization oriented to the rural sector of the area had little effect at this time on their ability to understand and handle social impacts in town. Later on, after the association was more established, it was able to take into account and deal with the project's effects on the town as well as on the ranches. However, the association's primary concerns continued to be with the rural situation.

With a few exceptions, the people in and around Sagebrush had been independent to a fault and could not or would not get together to take collective action to handle long-range implications and ramifications of rapid growth and change. For example, they had little interest in public or land-use planning, because they had always managed their affairs individually and informally through the operation of natural community forces. Understandable then was the feeling of many locals that the new city-county planning board had been set up for show and that there was really no strong inclination to give the board much power to engage in land classification or land-use planning and zoning which would be binding on the area's residents. In light of this reluctance, it was not surprising that trailer courts of various degrees of unsightliness began to spring up haphazardly all around in order to provide housing for arriving newcomers, as the few houses to rent or buy had already been taken.

Builders in Sagebrush feared there would be a short boom followed by a bust in the community. Skilled labor was not available in town for large-scale construction of houses or apartments, a factor which further discouraged builders from putting up new dwelling units even though there already was a market for them. Older locals who ordinarily would have sold their homes for smaller ones more suitable for their later years were dismayed to find that, quite suddenly, smaller houses were no longer available; hence, while the demand for larger homes was already very great, only those willing and able to relocate felt they could put their places up for sale. Some older farming and ranching couples who had been looking foward to retiring to Sagebrush feared that even after the boom peaked out the cost of housing would probably remain high due to the anticipation of booms resulting from future development and that this situation would tend to price them out of the Sagebrush market for the foreseeable future.[7]

The economic picture looked good to area merchants, who found increased sales and profits a welcome change from the past. They believed the economic benefits of the boom outweighed the various social costs, which had not yet come into full view. Local workers—and some ranch-hands—were of a similar mind. Noteworthy exceptions were those in work situations which were personally satisfying and fulfilling, security-minded public employees with vested interests in pension schemes, and traditionalists who opposed big changes on sociocultural grounds; they wanted no part in a venture which might damage their valued way of life. However, full employment at higher than predevelopment wages so appealed to the less skilled, less professionalized, and less culturally committed workers that they tended to downplay the social impacts of industrialization. Some with this tendency could be found among the many females who were part of informal life-support systems which supplemented formal ones (e.g. the Home Health Care program run by the county nurse) and which would have to be neglected or disrupted if they went to work. A number of these women sought employment anyway, and in certain instances women not in the labor force, for example, wives of merchants and professionals, helped to fill the support gaps left by the former; others chose not to work in order to maintain their established social arrangements. Locals' increased incomes were tempered by rising expenses, however.

Predevelopment residents[8] resented cost-of-living increases due to the influx of newcomers, whose presence required immediate expansion and renovation of the city's aging water and sewage systems. Realizing that construction workers would be there a relatively short time and thus would help pay for only a fraction of the cost of such major improvements, locals foresaw that the long-term balances would have to be picked up almost exclusively by them. Taxes had already risen to cover other expanding needs, e.g. the city-county law enforcement staff had to be increased and additional school personnel hired. Having to pay all these unanticipated costs of externally conceived and uninvited development was most irritating. It also put inordinate pressure on those on low and fixed or slowly rising incomes. Retired persons, who made up a large (almost 30 percent) proportion of the area's population, were shocked to find that their financial outlook was becoming unexpectedly bleak.

Other aggravations included the observation that coal and power companies ordinarily received preferential treatment from various public agencies; for example, people in Sagebrush generally complained that big companies paid proportionately less for utilities than small ones or individuals did, although some persons felt that this situation was defensible. Locals also observed that Bighole gave the appearance of paying less than its fair share of taxes, and it certainly had made no provision to put up any "front-end" money. For example, Bighole was bringing about school crowding problems but apparently felt no obligation to do anything to forestall or solve them. The two schools at Sagebrush could absorb a few new pupils, but were unprepared to assimilate the anticipated fall enrollment. Locals feared that educational programs would be adversely affected, that established social circles would be disrupted, that control of the school district would be taken over by newcomers, and that taxes to support the construction of extra classrooms and the addition of required services (e.g. facilities and staff for special education, as required by state law) would escalate excessively. Demands for other local services, such as medical care, were also overwhelming; and in many cases locals felt crowded out.[9] As one informant stated, "We pay the costs and the company reaps the benefits."

Social costs became more evident in other ways as time passed. The impact of newcomers on recreation sites at Sagebrush caused considerable strain in their relationship with locals. The construction workers tended very quickly to displace the established residents from their accustomed places in taverns and, in the words of the predevelopment locals, to "take over" these social centers. This development was significant and from the standpoint of those concerned, very memorable. In response, many Sagebrushians began to flee to the country club as the one place where they could still control things and not risk any kind of unpleasantness or altercation with the lusty young construction workers. Outdoor recreation sites were likewise rapidly appropriated by large numbers of newcomers. Favorite hunting and fishing spots were invaded by people whose accustomed ways of entering and using such places (e.g. treating them as if they were expendable) were very different from those locals employed. As a result, many of the established residents decided to abandon these spots while the newcomers were around, seeking instead to do their hunting, fishing, and picnicking outside the likely recreational travel radius of the newcomers. The takeover of both indoor and outdoor recreation sites made it difficult for all but the most prodevelopment residents to continue unqualified support for further industrial activity at Sagebrush, and it opened locals' eyes to the annoyances and stresses which they had previously chosen to disregard.

One of the major strains created concerned the relationship between merchants and ranchers and resulted from a confrontation between those who were socially distant enough to view the development largely in economic cost-benefit (outer-structural) terms and those who were so close that they had to view it almost entirely in sociocultural (inner-structural) ways. From the standpoint of the former, there were several enclaves (e.g. informal social circles, the country club, the courthouse—which newcomers seldom used) available for weathering the influx of new people. It evidently was important to these locals to put up with the newcomers— even giving them priority treatment—in order to make money off them. This they were able to do through using such enclaves so long as they believed that their fundamental way of life was *not* endangered by Bighole's project. From the standpoint of the ranchers, however, industrialization *was* endangering their essential way of life—and the damage could not possibly be forestalled or "mitigated" by money alone.

The Construction Period

As time went on, the various impacts and social costs of development became even more evident. Social alienation and disruption grew as Sagebrush residents found themselves surrounded by newcomers in the stores and on the streets and by the sights, sounds, and smells of construction itself. For example, locals increasingly saw themselves being turned into strangers in a place which, before development, they had naturally considered their own community. Less obvious social costs included the anxieties of local businessmen about having to face chain store competition or even having to expand and thus lose their family orientation should development stimulate further growth of their community. An increasing number of established residents felt that now, for the first time, they must be sure to lock up their homes and automobiles, keep their daughters off the streets at night, and otherwise be continually on their guard. Another less obvious cost stemmed from the residents' growing realization that, because so much of the energy to be generated at Sagebrush would be sent to urban centers out of the state, the desires and values of these urbanites were evidently considered superior to local ones.

A major and particularly upsetting impact of development fell on Sagebrush's two schools, which had always been the focal point and center of activity in this community. The district had great difficulty trying to get reliable data on incoming and outgoing population from Bighole and its associates, which made it impossible to predict and plan for a fluctuating enrollment. As a result of some misleading data which were finally obtained, both schools wound up with too many teachers during the first year of the boom, a needless expense which was borne by the district's landowners.[10] The following years saw just the opposite problem. According to the school personnel interviewed, the subsequent extensive overcrowding persisted because the financing needed to alleviate the problem came too late. This impact became more noticeable as the Sagebrush population continued to increase.

Related impacts took on various forms. Locals feared that the overcrowding and the athletically (more than academically) oriented children of the newcomers were affecting, i.e. lowering, the quality of education offered. Teachers' relationships with students were reportedly not as satisfactory as they had been when classes were smaller. Newcomers were questioning the assumptions and values of the locals, and teachers shared the sense of uncertainty and insecurity felt by the ranchers' children. Some landowners feared that the longtimers would be voted off the school board and that the newcomers would then increase the bonded indebtedness, with which ranchers and other landowners would be stuck. Further, newcomers who were not yet paying taxes to help support the school system had already made various demands on its facilities for adult recreational and religious instructional purposes, and these unprecedented requests both puzzled and annoyed the locals. As a consequence of all these problems, and as newcomers came and went, the pride longtimers once felt in the two schools steadily waned.

Predevelopment parents believed that what had been a compatible student body had rapidly and dramatically changed into a much bigger and less congenial one, although both new and old students reported that the two groups were getting along quite well. Previously there had been only a small number of school-age children living in town, given the relatively small proportion of younger married couples in Sagebrush proper, hence "old" students were predominantly rural youngsters. They shared many interests, such as 4-H and ranching activities. In contrast, the children of newcomers lived in town and had little to do during out-of-school hours and few places to go. In this respect, they were like some of the construction workers' wives who found life here to be frustrating, boring, and essentially demoralizing (Moen et al. 1981). However, many new students did share the locals' enthusiasm for sports and found that they had more in common with each other than did their parents; indeed they were already in process of fitting into the schools' inner structure.

In contrast, it was almost impossible to avoid unpleasant impingements upon community structure at such events as basketball games. In this community, where all who tried out for the team knew they would get a chance to play and would have encouragement and appreciation from spectators even on off days, predevelopment parents and friends suddenly found themselves sharing the bleachers with newcomers inclined to hurl insults and put-downs at the local players. Such violations of the unspoken and sacred taboo against deriding, insulting, or otherwise deliberately embarrassing the members of either team could not be stopped or prevented without first fitting the newcomers into the local way of life. The basketball games revealed the inability of longtimers to control the behavior of the new spectators so as to protect the locals' roles, selves, positions, and norms publicly represented and displayed in these games via widely familiar outer-structural veneers. Longtime residents found this situation discouraging and demoralizing.

The construction period spawned other changes. For example, disturbances in ranching operations, such as those resulting from increases in road and off-road traffic, erection of power lines and waterlines, and the sale or leasing of ranches, which were part of social and economic interdependency networks in given rural neighborhoods, created the need for continual reassessments and readjustments; and almost all residents were disturbed by the constant visual and auditory pollution, for example, the extremely bright blinking lights on the power plant's smokestack[11] and the noise from heavy construction machinery. As she talked about having to spend so much time and effort trying to protect individual and collective interests which appeared to be threatened by developmental interventions, one elderly ranch woman (who had survived hostile Indians, drought, and the deaths of her husband and a child) said: "It's such a cloud hanging over us all the time that we can't enjoy life like we used to."

Meanwhile merchants and other small businessmen were altering their views. In the past, both groups—along with farmers and ranchers in the study area—had strongly identified politically, economically, and ideologically with big business; but as power plant construction began, their various and continual disenchantments with it led them to redefine industrialists as the enemy. For example, local merchants and contractors were encouraged by company spokesmen to "gear up" to provide goods and services to the project, but as the pace of construction accelerated and schedules became strained, expedience won out over the company's commitment to favor local suppliers. A spokesman for the business community explained: "We were given a lot of promises but, for many of us, nothing has resulted. Some small contractors bought new equipment, and now big outfits from out of state are getting the work. Two local stores bought big inventories of special clothes that the construction work requires, and now the company is selling such clothes for wholesale at the project site." The previously positive indentification was superseded by a conflict relationship as more and more locals realized that big business was putting them into a passive, reactive, and dependent position which they could not accept, given their traditional values of self-reliance, self-direction, and independence.

The positive aspects of development were few. Some ranchers and townspeople welcomed the employment opportunities which power plant construction made available to close relatives as well as to themselves at wages which local employers could not match. As some high-school graduates began to earn seven dollars an hour for janitorial work at the mine site, friends worked for minimum wages at similar jobs in town. A motel maid whose sister was hired to drive a truck at the mine bewailed her plight: "I want to get drunk and be somebody too." A few locals availed themselves of other living benefits offered by the industrialization process; for example, a more interesting social life was enjoyed by the few on both sides of the coal development issue who mixed with some of the construction, coal, and power company officials. There was also a certain excitement in opposing coal development, including contacts made by some ranchers and their wives with state and national figures sympathetic with local opposition to turning the area into an industrial park. A few cattlemen made a lot money leasing and/or selling surface and/or coal rights, a few made a modest amount this way, and most merchants prospered in some degree. However, what the majority of landowners and townspeople got were feelings of disorientation and estrangement, anxiety about the viability of the community and their place in it, and a compelling need to learn how to cope with the industrial process and its consequences.

Those working for the company generally felt it would be improper to openly oppose industrial development, but privately they did what they could to safeguard their valued way of life. As part of the coping process, locals turned inward and tightened their social circles.[12] This process entailed deliberately revivifying relationships with old friends and relatives, membership in established voluntary associations, and other commitments to the community's traditional way of life. It also involved reaffirming one's social and self-identities, and thus included interacting with significant others more and with outsiders less than before the boom. Structurally, it entailed taking extraordinary steps to protect and preserve inner structure and its outer-structural connections and veneers.[13] For example, as a family-oriented store became busier and busier, the members took pains to keep this busyness from getting out of hand and requiring great expansion and thus basic change in the form and functions of their economic unit. They worked hard at keeping a tradition-oriented, acceptable balance between the socioeconomic commitments they had made to each other and to the community.

Accordingly, tightening of social circles was a response to a morale problem brought about by decreasing ability of members of the community to act together in pursuit of their collective goals. Through this tightening of social circles, the larger community parceled out to its constituent units responsibility for keeping morale, values, etc. from waning out of existence until conditions became more favorable for revitalizing *Gemeinschaft* behavior on a community-wide scale. In this sense, there was a temporary waxing of *Gemeinschaft* in the community's social circles as *Gemeinschaft* waned more generally in response to growth forces which inhibited predevelopment kinds of interactions between inner- and outer-structural behavior. Being a member of the community was more of a mixed bag than it had been (i.e., life was more inhibited in outer structure and more fulfilling in inner structure), and it appeared destined to remain this way throughout the construction period.

A net effect of these circle-tightening actions was to insulate longtimers from the new majority.[14] The old tradition of reaching out to newcomers did not apply now, given their overwhelming numbers.[15] Even the churches did not make a concerted effort to assimilate the newcomers, although this fact was not exclusively a matter of deliberately keeping the newcomers at arm's length. A number of the construction workers were from fundamental Southern churches, and many of the miners were Mormons. Religious and organizational differences kept these religious groups from even considering joining the existing congregations at Sagebrush, so they gradually formed their own. Most newcomers were socially very distant from the locals and were not all that interested in being accepted into Sagebrush's inner circles. Additionally, the many highly itinerant workers on short assignments there frequently remained morally unconcerned if not unaware of how they and their work impacted permanent residents of the area.

With so many people coming and going as sociological strangers to each other as well as to the locals, the construction period brought to Sagebrush not only single categories of "we" and "they" but subcategories as well. The social stucture during construction was in this regard a hodgepodge of ad hoc and relatively permanent social categories, a phenomenon which itself contributed to the general impression that much of Sagebrush was then more a mere settlement than a town. Indeed, it was then a strange mixture of way stations and a deeply rooted community.

Summary

Impacts of the preconstruction forces of alteration and displacement which had led to many structural strains in the lives of rural people in the vicinity of Sagebrush, were much in evidence during the two years it took for power plant construction activities to reach their peak. Some ranchers, including well-established ones, lost hired hands; land prices went up so rapidly that cattlemen could no longer afford to plan on continually acquiring land; the ranchers' work load increased owing to lack of help and trespassing by newcomers whose motorcycles and other vehicles disturbed both cattle and land; the landowners and their wives spent a lot of their own time going to public hearings in hopes of finding out what was going on in coal development in the area; they suffered from uncertainties regarding their ability to continue their valued way of life here or any place else and to remain unchallenged in their attachment to the land; they devoted much more time and effort than previously trying to get service from vehicle and equipment dealers, craftsmen, and other skilled artisans who were now less inclined to give them accustomed first-priority treatment; and they became sensitive to and anxious about actual and potential water rights issues when previously they had just taken for granted that good water would be available as and when needed.

Townspeople experienced similar concerns and irritations. Taxes on land went up, putting an unexpected financial drain on locals. The sudden jump in the local cost of living was particularly felt by the elderly, who now found themselves trapped in what appeared to them to be an exceptionally high-cost town. In addition, Sagebrush area residents felt they were losing control of the schools and that the educational standards they had worked to achieve were being lowered; they experienced noise, visual, traffic, and "people" pollution; they suffered from anomie and future shock; and they worried about regaining control over their lives, fearing a permanent take-over by outsiders. Nowhere was the construction worker takeover more evident than in the bars, only a few of which were still thought to be congenial places for predevelopment residents. Some locals went so far as to forego all the town bars for the duration of the boom, going instead to those in Junction City for relaxation. Notable exceptions to the many who feared a permanent takeover were the several merchants and ranchers who convinced themselves that potential economic gains would outweigh potential social risks and that undertaking the project would help both the community and the nation to achieve desired "progress." While a few ranchers, merchants, and others were enthusiastic about the new opportunities development provided and, as a consequence, shifted their lifestyle orientations in inner- and outer-structural ways, most locals responded by tightening their social circles against the newcomers. Tightened social circles helped to maintain morale and other aspects of *Gemeinschaft* while community outer structure became increasingly oriented to the growing proportion of newcomers in Sagebrush.

Notes

1. As indicated in note 4 of chapter 2, this and other such quotes are from the fieldwork files kept by my associates and me.
2. There were a few significant exceptions of ranchers who correctly sized up Bighole's determination from the very beginning of the project, but, by and large, it took many months for ranchers in the area to gain such insight.
3. The labels "prodevelopment" and "antidevelopment" indicated only what one's "druthers" were, not necessarily how one would act toward offers to use one's land for strip-mining or related activities. Some ranchers who had initially tried to accommodate to coal development and who still tended to favor some form of it were now actively fighting it, and some who opposed it were hedging against an uncertain future by leasing to the industrialists. Correlations between attitudes and actions are always uncertain.
4. The actual began moving close to the ideal as a consequence of the social impact of development, which brought the ranchers' views of community organization and culture into much sharper focus than before. As these landowners began to make the idealizations of their communities more real, they reduced their vulnerability to predatory invasions. Thus, for example, the protective association they created strengthened the ability of community outer structure to avoid and fend off many actual and potential threats to inner structure as well as to itself.
5. There were a few newcomers who wanted to earn enough money to be able to live here the way the ranchers did, and some people who came to the area fairly recently had adopted the local attitudes. Most of these people were from similar rural areas or, if not, had consciously learned how to make themselves a place in a small community. However, they represented a small portion of the newcomers. Other persons were also interested in preserving the area. In the words of one rural informant: "When Easterners buy places out here, they tend to be more resistant to industrialization than we oldtimers are."
6. The new land evaluations going on in the county had already recorded an eightfold increase in land values.

7. A similar observation is reported by Swanson, Cohen, and Swanson (1979, pp. 143-44): "Industrialization imposes many costs on a community, often in excess of the benefits it brings. Who bears the burden of those costs? Who receives the benefits? New industrial development may boost a town's tax base and increase local payrolls, indicators of *community* prosperity. These same economic improvements, however, may totally ignore the plight of the town's poorest residents, its low-income or welfare population. . . . [Accordingly, not] everyone benefits equally from community economic development. It is important therefore to exercise caution in selecting measures of success and prosperity. What might be good progress for the *community* (a high multiplier, for example) might not help or might even adversely affect many individuals."
8. Predevelopment residents are persons who have lived in the community and vicinity since before the recent industrialization of the area.
9. Efforts to recruit additional doctors resulted in no lasting success.
10. State figures indicated that enrollment increased 38 percent in Sagebrush during the first year of power plant construction. The teaching staff doubled during this period.
11. The power plant smokestack was in place months before the plant was ready to operate. Powerful strobe lights were attached to the stack and blinked incessantly to warn aircraft of its presence. The continuous blinking was highly visible for miles around and greatly annoyed the ranchers, particularly because the blinking interfered with their ability to do routine visual checks of their cattle and for possible trespassers at night.
12. The few exceptions included uptown merchants who showed a willingness to compete in ways which threatened to seriously strain or destroy the traditionally cordial, controlled, and competitive relationship with other local businessmen and their associates. They were comparable to business-oriented ranchers.
13. Insight into what can happen to make tightened social circles a standard feature of a community comes from Suttles's (1968, p. 93) observation about an ethnic area of Chicago: "Small sections of the inner city are regularly displaced through the processes of ethnic succession, urban renewal, and rezoning. The narrow reach of each resident's associations and trust assures that he will not be too disturbed by these excisions."
14. Our fieldwork was not adversely affected by this tightening of social circles, because my fellow researchers and I were able to maintain our relationships of mutual trust and respect with residents who participated in a cross-section of these informal groups. We therefore had no difficulty staying in touch with what was happening in the inner circles while they were becoming increasingly sheltered from the newer, more threatening aspects of outer-structural life.
15. The area had grown from 1,300 to over twice that number in less than two years.

5

After Construction: The First Year

Although my colleagues and I are continuing to do research on community changes resulting from energy and other natural resource development projects in the rural West, our data on Sagebrush cover only a 5-year period which ended one year after Bighole's mine and associated power plant became operational. In focusing on this first year of operations, the present chapter will describe the principal physical changes which occurred in town since the project began, and the postconstruction situations of longtimers and newcomers in town and of ranchers in the surrounding rural neighborhoods which were part of the community of Sagebrush.

Physical Changes in Town

After locals had endured more than a year of feeling intimidated by announcements, meetings, trespasses, rumors and other uncertainties, vulnerability and powerlessness, future shock, and disenchantment with big industry, followed by three years of various kinds and levels of construction chaos which kept locals in a highly reactive state, Bighole's project finally became operational. At the end of the fourth summer after the first project rumors had begun, the last temporary workers had left Sagebrush. Oldtime residents, who had often assured each other that "after the construction workers leave we can get back to normal," began to redefine "normal" to allow for some changes that were acceptable—and even desirable, for example, improvement of the town's water system—and others that were irreversible, such as imprint of the boomtown experience on the local way of life. Even the most optimistic agreed that Sagebrush would never *look* the same as it had four years ago (e.g. see description of a 60-unit "suburb" below). The "temporary" trailer parks were not dismantled, but continued to provide housing for families of lower-paid workers, single workers who did not want to buy homes, and job-seekers who continued to flow through town. Designed for short-term use, these trailer parks did not easily accommodate amenities like lawns, sidewalks, and landscaping; consequently they had begun to look seedy and unkempt as weeds grew everywhere and trailers deteriorated.

Other temporary structures around town, which had been hastily set in place to serve as classrooms, a clinic addition, and offices for subcontractors during the period of highest employment at the project, were converted to permanent storage buildings, the office of a used-car dealer, and a real estate office. Other more elegant-looking additions to Sagebrush were an addition to the county courthouse, which was nearing completion with the help of a federal grant, a new restaurant/bar, and a supermarket-style grocery store complete with a connecting laundromat and game-room complex, the latter chock-full of electronic playthings for habitués of all ages.

In general, the established residential areas of town would not have looked much different now in photographs than they had about four years ago. The houses were in somewhat better repair than they had been, and the lots that had been vacant were now occupied by homes, all but two of which were mobile. The only striking difference was the prevalence of late-model automobiles and recreation vehicles. Most had been purchased at Junction City, as Sagebrush still had no new-car dealer. Nearly all of the remainder had been bought from Sagebrush's two used-car dealers, both of whom also sold a variety of recreation vehicles. To Sagebrushians, a "car" almost always meant a pickup truck, the vehicle of choice for these dedicated outdoor recreationists. At any rate, as their incomes increased, their initial tendency was to update and add to their rolling stock, which they regarded as essential for realizing their version of the American Dream.

The main business district had a few new stores, and some of the old ones had new façades, but otherwise its appearance had not changed much either. The most visible change would be the addition to the county courthouse, scheduled for completion a few months from now. More new businesses were located on the edges of town along the highway than in the downtown area. And there were the aforementioned used-car dealers, which were flanked by auto repair shops, a concrete ready-mix plant, gasoline bulk plants, a bowling alley, two fast-food drive-ins, a veterinary clinic, and Sagebrush's newest and finest motel. The town's airport was about a mile beyond these businesses. Its runway had been lengthened and strengthened to accommodate company jets, a convenience paid for by taxes on local property.

A 60-unit "suburb" of attractive new houses had been built on the edge of town and was occupied mainly by managers, professionals, and supervisors from the project. This development looked very different from adjacent blocks of some of Sagebrush's better old homes with spacious yards and large front porches which faced toward the streets and sidewalks (and were generally open to the neighborhood). In the new section, houses were built closer together with minimal front yards and unobstrusive windows and entrances on the street side. Their more spacious back yards were fenced to screen patios and picture windows from neighbors and passersby, providing privacy for the family as well as for gatherings of invited co-workers and other friends.

The Longtimers' Situation in Town

It was no longer practical for "everyone" to be welcome at informal get-togethers in the community because, although the town's population count had for a long time been stabilized at less than 1,000 when Bighole's project had begun, nearly 1,800 people now resided in and around town[1] and even the best-informed Sagebrushians no longer knew who everyone was nor how one should be relating to them. Oldtimers who had said, "if too many strangers come to Sagebrush, I'll just move somewhere else," were still around. These outbursts were more an expression of their need to control life than a declaration of intent to leave. Other gloomy predictions of dire consequences if the coal project went ahead were not borne out—at least the more overt and dramatic of these predictions, like rape in the streets and total incompatability of the project with ranching. There was less active participation in the Rangeland Protective Association, a general loosening of the social circles recently tightened to the point of being highly exclusive, a renewed tendency to greet all manner of people on the street and in other public places and, overall, a growing certainty that the community was still "country" and that it was noticeably starting to get itself together again. Some newcomers and longtimers were starting to make exploratory and tentative gestures toward fraternizing with each other although, by and large, many Sagebrushians agreed with the veteran local shopper who said:

> During the past few years, when I walked downtown and through the grocery store, I didn't automatically greet everyone the way I used to. I found that I even passed up some people I had always spoken to, and only greeted and visited with relatives and my closest friends. Now I find myself starting to make a point of greeting people again, but I still have a ways to go before I do this as completely automatically as I used to.[2]

School records provided the most reliable measure of short-term population changes. Having peaked at 983 during the last year of construction, enrollment gradually dropped until, on opening day of the first school year after the project became operational, 692 students were registered. Trustees had previously notified nine teachers that their contracts would not be renewed, bringing to an end a new foreign-language program and the year-old services of a school psychologist who had never "fit in." Contrary to early fears, control of the schools never did get out of local hands and, with few exceptions, the permanent newcomers who were active in school affairs clearly wanted to build upon their mutually cooperative and productive relationships with those in control. Changes in the school's social system had come with little conflict. The previous spring, students had elected a first-year junior boy as prom king, and a senior girl, the fourth generation on one of the largest ranches, was engaged to the son of a Bighole electrical foreman. When football season began, two newcomer girls were chosen for coveted cheerleader assignments. Not every boy could depend on making the football team anymore, but the teams were more apt to win a few games, although the record was not expected to be as good as during the construction period when more experienced players from urban areas had given Sagebrush its most winning seasons.

The proportion of elderly to the total population had dropped sharply in the past three years, since virtually all newcomers were of working age or younger. Sagebrush's new reputation for high living costs and limited housing made it an inappropriate choice for potentially incoming retirees. The elderly who were longtime residents managed to meet their basic needs with the help of old friends and family, some of whom had prospered in business or were getting relatively high wages as a result of the Bighole project. They were more apt to be taken on shopping trips or to the doctor by young women who were not related to them but were fulfilling a commitment made by a "service sorority" to which they belonged. Many of the women who had constituted the informal helping networks in predevelopment Sagebrush had gone to work full time during the boom and were unwilling to give up the personal fulfillment and lifestyle advantages they had found in employment. Consequently, the helping networks which evolved in postconstruction Sagebrush became more outer-structural as newcomers and oldtimers began to establish formally organized groups to provide helping services.

In some cases, oldtimers found new interests by becoming involved in organizations started by newcomers, e.g. a Weight Watchers group and a Miners' Wives club. Sagebrush's many pinochle clubs were almost entirely made up of oldtimers, but a few longtime residents who preferred serious bridge games found new challenges in card clubs whose members included Bighole personnel. A sure sign of progress toward membership in the community was for an oldtimer (of any age) to take a new friend to his favorite, and usually secret, fishing hole. Newcomers had taken over the most accessible and popular fishing and hunting spots, and started their own sportsmen's club. But the old rod and gun club members and other long-time sportsmen who represented generations of hunters and fishermen were able to keep secluded some favorite, remote, and most desirable sites.

Although newcomers did not "take over" as had been feared, positions of leadership in the community were no longer a litany of old family names. As newcomers gradually gained recognition for being "doers," signs of leadership emerged from people who had lived in the area two to four years. During the last year of construction, the wife of a Bighole manager was appointed to the hospital board and, in fall elections, a mine foreman, who had been serving as a volunteer fireman, was elected to the city council. However, little change was apparent in the capability of local governing bodies to deal with the area's continuing problems with land-use planning, health and safety services, and other growth-impacted services. Oldtimers, who were still the majority of the various boards and councils, had little spirit or skill for getting and using professional help or technical assistance, and showed no disposition to hire a city or county administrator. Elected officials still tried to handle matters through traditional rural practices, although their constituents were beginning to demand a different level of accountability, especially with regard to what had been happening to Sagebrush's outer structure. But there was no route for directing that pressure to upgrade the community's land-use planning capability, because plans had not been formalized to legally control undesirable subdivisions, haphazard location of businesses in and around town, inappropriate creekside trailer courts, and the like. The county commissioners, who had been accustomed to conducting business in almost complete privacy, were irritated and even threatened by the audiences that began to appear at meetings. Newcomers from more urban areas took for granted that commission meetings should be attended by civic-minded citizens, but to the longtime rural commissioners, such monitoring implied suspicion or disapproval of how they were managing county affairs. Officials, newcomers, and oldtimers alike, despaired that taxes would ever catch up with the host of expanding county services despite increases in revenue each budget year.[3]

Some of the Bighole personnel had the kinds of administrative and technical skills that the city and county desperately needed, but there was so much fear that Sagebrush might become a de facto company town that locals resisted Bighole's offers to make such help available at no cost. The company's reputation for deceiving, "muscling in," and "taking over," which had been earned again and again throughout the previous stages of the project, made it difficult for locals to seriously consider Bighole's offers for use of its equipment to improve the public parks.

Despite the local inclination to continue to distrust and act guardedly toward Bighole, most longtime residents really tried not to allow this inclination to color their relationships with Bighole employees. (Likewise, most newcomers tried to take locals as they found them, rather than simply classify and act toward them as enemies of Bighole's version of industrial progress.) Exceptions were a handful of middle-management people on site and upper-management people at the home office whom locals generally viewed as the policy and decision makers behind most of Bighole's "devilries."

One of the cluster of "civic improvements" instituted toward the end of the construction period was the appointment of a dog control officer (a newcomer with interest in and talent for such work), the establishment of a "pound," and the enactment of related ordinances. When she left to follow her construction-engineer husband to his new job, the program was abandoned, and local dogs (which had rarely been confined but had caused their owners to be fined) roamed again without risk. In other areas of law enforcement, it was more difficult to reverse formal controls instituted during the time when locals were worried that construction workers would be disruptive and violent. The sheriff's force protected their mandate and budget by continuing traffic control and curfew policies initiated during the construction years. Like other service agencies, they resisted reducing staff who were devoting an increasing portion of their time and effort to formal record-keeping and other paperwork.

According to the statistical records, crime rates in the county had increased more than 300 percent in three years and were dropping only slightly now that construction workers were gone. Such reports made for spectacular headlines in the Junction City paper and were used to justify the sheriff's manpower and equipment requests. But it was clear that the dramatic increases were more a function of changes in the record system than of Bighole's project. For years, the sheriff's office had recorded and then reported to the state crime commission only the most public and flagrant of the crimes committed by locals. Such crimes were relative rarities, but they did occur and were officially acknowledged. Not recorded were the cases of spouse and child abuse, incest, theft, etc., because the community preferred to handle such matters informally unless they got out of hand and became too public and/or flagrant to continue being exempted from official notice and intervention. Crimes of any sort perpetrated by transients had always been fully recorded and then reported to the state crime commission. Consequently, comparisons of recent formal records (which were essential for claiming desirable state and federal funds) with less formal records of the years when these outside funds were not sought were of no use in understanding how the community's growth had affected crime rates. Newcomers, many of whom had come from more urban areas, were pleased to live in an area that seemed safe and quiet.

Predevelopment residents observed that the sheriff was too busy to stop and offer them a ride when he saw them walking with a heavy load; but they acknowledged that the community had not become violent and unstable as they had feared. A businessman observed: "There are more bar fights because there are more people. But Sagebrush has always had bar fights." Nevertheless, it was now common practice to lock cars and houses, and locals accepted (not without complaint) the loss of predevelopment courtesies from law officers. It had been common practice for a deputy to personally deliver an inebriated teenager to his parents and tell only them that the youngster had tried to break into a filling station. But there was no inclination to do the same for unfamiliar youngsters whose families were not personal acquaintances of the officer, so in the past few years such events had become crime statistics no matter whose child was involved.

Similarly, local merchants generally did not reinstitute charge accounts or unlimited check-cashing privileges for well-known customers even after the construction workers left. Exceptions were the few doggedly traditional merchants who had never wavered from these hallowed practices even during the busiest part of the construction period. The local bank, which had begun to stay open until 6:00 P.M. on Fridays during the last year of construction, continued that service. And the bars could always be depended on to cash payroll checks. But locals were disappointed that many of the personalized services which had disappeared during the construction period still showed no signs of reappearing. What had been a downtown made up of neighborhood stores which were both in and of the community was now a downtown where, other than a few exceptions just noted, the stores were now clearly less of the community than they had been before outer structure boomed. Nobody was certain how to induce merchants and service providers to return to more informal and "country" ways of doing business, and not all of these businessmen were sure that they were so disposed. This slowness and uncertainty about returning community outer structure to something approximating what it had been before construction made the people of Sagebrush begin to realize that some basic changes had occurred in connections between inner and outer structure. The values and related behavioral practices of the one (e.g. unqualified trust, informality, satisfying social place) were not now meshing well with those of the other (limited, credit-card type of trust; being treated categorically as a customer more than personally as a community member).

The plain truth about Sagebrush's merchants is that nearly all of them got "boom fever" at some point or other during the construction period, and now, even though this contagious situation no longer obtained, about half of them had not yet shaken its effects. To be sure, business had slowed down in the months immediately following the end of the construction period, but it was still far better than it had been before construction started and thus was nothing like the bust that many locals had feared might now occur. Still, about half of the storekeepers were continuing to view the boom as a fine dose of economic progress which more than compensated for attendant social disruptions, and they made no secret of their hope for another such dose in the near future. They were willing to risk more lifestyle disruptions and possible chain store competition for another crack at making a lot of money in just a few years. The other half of the merchants were relieved to have gotten through the boom with nice profits and their lifestyles largely intact and had no stomach for another boom any time soon. They felt that another large influx of people would greatly increase the likelihood of attracting chain store competition that Sagebrush was not quite large enough to attract at this time. They also feared that next time they might suffer greater and more permanent damage to their way of life, a risk which they, unlike their more feverish colleagues, were unable to justify. Aside from the few businessmen who were totally for or against another spurt of growth, there was considerable ambivalence in the boom-related feelings of businessmen in both of these categories. That is to say, at bottom, few merchants had no mixed feelings about the possibility of further industrial development near Sagebrush, just as few had had no mixed feelings about Bighole's project when first proposed.

The end of the construction boom left a few businessmen with more inventory and debts than they could manage comfortably, but most local merchants had been cautious about overextending their resources, especially those who had not wanted expansion to endanger their relaxed way of life. Competition from the new supermarket helped to stabilize escalating food prices, and one longtime grocery store proprietor, who had successfully gouged locals and newcomers alike during the construction period, was able to take his profits and leave town. Another businessman, who had come from a neighboring state to start a fabric and gift store to make quick profits during the construction boom, was happy to sell to a partnership of two wives of Bighole supervisors and move on to the next boomtown.

Unlike the few who sold out and left town, the great majority of local businessmen really had no intention of doing anything of the sort. Rather, nearly all of the latter were in Sagebrush to stay, and all made a point of trying to accommodate to the wishes and needs of the newcomers while holding on to as many of their longtime customers as they could. Being accommodative was evidently what even the most scrupulously traditional merchant had in common with the most opportunistic of storekeepers. But there were also some notable differences, as shown in the following sketch of two such local businessmen.

A good example of a merchant who tried to keep the appearance and activities of his business "country" is that of a man I shall call Walter. Even with modern merchandise, Walter's store had that unmistakable look of having been there for many years and of having continued to use seemingly indestructible display cases, racks, and counters, because he (and his wife who worked with him most of the time) and his customers had gotten used to them and saw no purpose in replacing them with unfamiliar, current designs. Although he was an unabashed traditionalist—out of the store, as well as in—Walter decided early in the construction period that it would be decent and proper for him to develop a style of doing business which suited the itinerants and other newcomers who could not or would not fit in with his folksy, relationship-oriented style of interaction. He developed this more urban style to get through the construction period, but found that it was still needed for relating to the many permanent employees of Bighole who were more comfortable if treated by him as though they were at K-Mart or Sears, Roebuck in Junction City. These were people whose motto seemed to be, "Let the merchant beware." Accordingly, he found that he could not safely give them credit; allow them to browse through the store without watching to see that they did not shoplift; permit himself to interact with them in his natural, personalized manner; introduce these perpetual strangers to longtime customers who happened to be in the store at the same time; discuss new local happenings with them; make any but strictly economic assumptions about them; expect them to appreciate his brand of humor; or do anything else a K-Mart clerk would not do. Being who he was, he could not completely resist the temptation to occasionally try to socialize some of these customers to fit in, but these efforts were usually unsuccessful. Then he would return to just being courteous, polite, and not too obviously watchful until the next time this temptation got the better of him.

During the work day, his wife would always be in the store when she knew it was time for him to walk down to the town's oldest restaurant where he would share a large pitcher of coffee with some old friends. These coffee breaks were so important to him and the other participants that they rarely missed them. Although informal and unscheduled, they were held so regularly that "you could almost set your watch by them," Walter observed. A core of the same participants was sure to be there, joined now and then by other townspeople and by ranchers and other county friends who happened to be in town and who made a point of joining the group when they knew the coffee-breakers would be together. More than half were men and, in the man's world that Sagebrush was, the conversation was decidedly masculine; but this was definitely a gathering of men and women who were old friends—a coming together of people who wanted to stay abreast of the latest community news, check out rumors, exchange business notes, talk about their latest outdoor recreational experiences, and generally reaffirm for themselves and each other their social identities, self-conceptions, cultural values, and thus their sense of community.

These were people that Walter saw frequently in other social circles at night and on Sunday, when his store was closed. A good family man and member of a large Sagebrush-based kin group, Walter devoted much of his nonwork time to maintaining relationships with his many kinfolk. Most of his wife's close kin lived on ranches elsewhere in the county, but they were not neglected either. In addition, Walter always found time to keep up his contacts at the various lodges and card clubs he belonged to and, in recent years, at the Rangeland Protective Association. Many of his longtime customers and lifelong friends were stalwarts in the association, and Walter naturally did what he could to involve himself and other townspeople in this essentially landowners' association. Such involvement helped to keep the association functioning as a link between the community's inner and outer structure; his own involvement helped to keep his store functioning this way, too.

Among Walter's extensive contacts with locals of all description were those with nearly all who were employed by Bighole. He was well aware that most of these men and women were like him in that they had kept their traditional values intact, continued to treat work as a means to traditional lifestyle ends, kept active in established relationships, and were on cordial terms with newcomer workers without having much occasion to socialize with them off the job. On a couple such occasions, Walter was pleased to meet a newcomer who seemed to be much more interested in what was going on in the community than in what was happening on the job. These were newcomers who evidently were trying to learn about the community and become accepted as part of it. Otherwise, like Walter, the traditional locals employed by Bighole saw little of the newcomers off the job. It was not that these locals had deliberately avoided having work associates over for dinner (although a few had), it was just that it had not yet seriously occurred to them to initate such gatherings.

At the other extreme were a few locals employed by Bighole that Walter knew were on the way to becoming "company men." They had been associating so much with newcomers that they had become isolated from many old friends. Walter and other longtimers viewed them as becoming estranged from the local way of life, in that they were making their work a focal and pivotal point in their lives. Nominally still locals, while internalizing company values and seeking the status of full-fledged members of their work organization, these employees were at this time marginal to both the old and the new.

Also characterized by such marginality was a fellow merchant named Ronald. Unlike the local variety of company men, Ronald did not seek to become a cultural convert, and still thought himself to be as much a local as ever, considering that he had bought his store from an old local couple about nine years before the beginning of the Bighole project, having operated a similar store in a smaller town elsewhere in the state for several years previously. He had looked at this purchase as an opportunity to get ahead. After selling his other store and moving his wife and teenage son to Sagebrush, he and his family had settled in Sagebrush so completely that it had taken them only a few years to consider Sagebrush their hometown and another few for longtimers to begin accepting them as members.

Ronald's recent and current problem was that his economic opportunism and related social curiosity had caused him to lose so much of his perspective on the new and the old that, increasingly, he had allowed the pursuit of the Almighty Dollar to take precedence over just about everything. With nearly all of his eggs in that basket, he found himself more and more estranged from the old while still neither very familiar nor comfortable with the new.

It all started when Ronald decided to get ready for the influx of construction workers by modernizing his store and expanding his inventory. While most of the other businessmen on Main Street were wondering how to handle the construction period, Ronald was already investing thousands of dollars in drastic changes in the appearance and mode of operation of his store. Before long, the changes were made, and he had the town's most modern-looking store, complete with clerks whose uniform jackets enabled anyone to distinguish them from the customers, no matter how crowded the place became. Throughout the construction period, Ronald and his staff worked diligently to meet their new customers' wishes for quick and efficient service and succeeded handsomely. Ronald tried not to neglect his old customers but simply did not have the time needed to interact with them in accustomed ways. The store was always busy, if not crowded, and there was money to be made while the free-spending construction workers were in town. Things continued that way for over three years.

Now that Bighole's project was operational and its much smaller, albeit permanent, work force was in place, the pace of business in Ronald's store had slowed down substantially, but he was still doing well—and still using his modern, formal, dollar-oriented way of running the store. His past and present efforts to socialize locals to fit in to his kind of operation were totally futile. Locals still patronized his store, but felt they were in a branch of a Junction City chain store every time they did. Now that Ronald had made his fortune (he could have retired comfortably over a year earlier), he was losing his zest for meeting the challenges and handling the personnel management headaches of his modern business.

Local eyebrows were raised recently when Ronald sold his modest house and moved into a fine new one in the "suburb" occupied chiefly by Bighole executives and supervisors. This move, when added to the steps he had taken to make his store the most profitable one in town, had the effect of disconnecting, or at least loosening, him, his family, and his business from old friends, relationships, and values. True, he occasionally gathered former fishing buddies and other old cronies around him and attempted to act like one of the "good old local boys," but their gatherings were about as satisfying to the participants as trying to get past the second couple of hours (the first were full of reminiscences) of a reunion with old army buddies after a separation of over twenty years. Ronald was, to most outward appearances, still a community member in good standing, but such occurrences as the following had made his membership more apparent than real: the shift in his values, his actions as a change agent in the local business community, his severance of most of the ties between his business and the parts of Sagebrush's inner structure in which he and his family had participated and which the dwindling number of longtimers who still patronized his store vainly tried to carry with them into interactions with his personnel (only the bookkeeper, his sister-in-law, was a longtimer, and she was in the back office most of the time), and so on. He found himself well past the point of no return and reckoned he would try to keep the business going for a bit longer before selling out (his only son was soon to become a veterinarian and was not likely to be interested in taking over the business). Would he want to remain in Sagebrush or follow the paths of those who had made "fast bucks" during construction and departed? If he remained, where would his place in the community be? Could he revitalize his membership by cultivating relationships with some of the older Sagebrushians who were quite well-to-do? How well would he and his wife fit in with that crowd? Would he and his wife not want to continue associating with the managers and professionals employed by Bighole? These new people were pretty nice, he felt, but how much did he and his wife really have in common with them? Could he really ever again be one of the boys in Sagebrush, even if welcomed back with open arms by those who used to be his closest friends and recreation companions? As Ronald pondered these questions, a bunch of well-dressed newcomers entered the store, and he could fairly hear the cash register ring as he hurried to help part them from some of their cash. There would be another time to worry about membership. Now was the time to go after more of the big money which Bighole's employees had brought within his grasp.[4]

Thus, in the town of Sagebrush, the activities of traditional residents like Walter and more dollar-oriented ones like Ronald had at least this much in common: they contributed (Walter because of himself, Ronald in spite of himself) to reestablishing community by reconnecting the façades of outer structure, which appeared to have changed much, to the inner structure which had changed little. Reestablishment of these connections facilitated the loosening of social circles and the lowering of community growth-induced inhibitions to members' pursuit of traditional communal objectives; thus it fostered a general waxing of *Gemeinschaft* and, with it, a general increase in morale.

Compared to what the longtimers had expected the sociocultural consequences of the project would be, the actual consequences at this time were more subtle, less visible, and perhaps more telling for maintaining quality of inner-structural life and for general ability to control the community's socialization processes and resultant way of life. Regarding quality of life, some gnawing questions remained. Would going shopping and otherwise doing business ever be the enjoyable and satisfying social act it had always been before Bighole's project intervened? Would law enforcement be humanized again? Would who you were begin to make a difference again when dealing with the city council? Would the tendency to bureaucratize outer-structural interaction ever be reversed? Some oldtimers had the uneasy feeling that the "good old days" of predevelopment Sagebrush might be awfully slow to return as long as Bighole's people were around. However, others pointed to the continuing practice of businessmen to provide part-time jobs for all teenagers who sought work as an indication that downtown continued to be more a part of the community than some folks realized it was. Even while thus engaged in keeping their community going, most longtimers perceived that life in Sagebrush was still scrambled and confused, and that it was still too soon after construction to be sure of whether and how the various loosened, disconnected, and new pieces of the town would fit together as an integrated community. They, with the help of newcomers who were trying to put down roots, simply needed more time to sort out the temporary from the long-term changes in community structure and way of life.

The Newcomers' Situation in Town

Some of the Bighole families that came during the construction period and were expected to remain as permanent workers were unable to fit into a place where they felt isolated from friends and family, and they returned to the company's urban headquarters; some had coping skills and family support that made it possible to survive and even enjoy the new setting; but others who remained in Sagebrush struggled with various emotional and/or physical abuse problems. Spouse and child abuse were hard to hide among the newcomers because there were no grandparents or other relatives to help cushion or divert the impact of such family problems. Having no informal helping network to turn to, victims of these and other personal abuses became far more visible than such victims in predevelopment Sagebrush had been. By the end of the first year of the operations period, the community had begun to welcome workshops, films, seminars, and other forums for public discussion of these problems. One result was that some longtime Sagebrush family members who were closet drug abusers (e.g. high school students experimenting with "pot" or housewives covering up chronic depression with solitary drinking) or who had other chronic abuse problems became less fearful of being found out; it became more appropriate to discuss their behavior with and accept help from "outsiders." Other personal, familial, and more socially visible problems, like vandalism (a rarity before the boom), also began to receive more public attention. In response to these pressures, the town's human services professionals, consultants from Junction City, and a local service club began to lay plans for a "hot line" for crisis calls, and a group of Bighole employees formed a "friends to youth" support group. Such response recognized that personal and social disorganization, created or worsened by the boom, somehow touched everybody, even those who chose to remain sociological strangers.

Some of Bighole's permanent employees considered their assignment in Sagebrush akin to "foreign duty" and therefore maintained separate social circles and their status as outsiders. They were here for the duration of the project only if no transfer occurred to advance their careers in another project by Bighole or another company. They may or may not have been enjoying living in Sagebrush; what really mattered to them was how satisfied they were with the conditions and rewards of the job. They fit in to Sagebrush's outer structure if they fit in any place at all in the local community. Some of them had learned where and how to shop in Sagebrush; who the good cooks in the local restaurants were; what shifts they were on and what their particular cooking strengths were; how to get things done at City Hall and at the county courthouse; whom to call when a pipe was leaking; and so forth. An example of learning to shop in Sagebrush was given by this newcomer: "I was irritated by the proprietor of the building-supply concern because he seemed too inquisitive about what I was going to do with the stuff I was buying. But I learned that he wasn't just being nosy, nor even overfriendly. He was just trying to give me better service by learning about my particular interests and needs." Newcomers may on occasion have espoused certain civic improvements, but were not inclined to become part of the action needed to effect them. These newcomers established some relationships and even some social circles with each other and tended to let their participation in the social life in town go at that, as they regarded themselves as temporary or otherwise mobile and just passing through. The fact that some newcomers clung to their sociological stranger traditions and did not consider themselves candidates for the status of locals, whereas others wanted to put down roots and thus did consider themselves candidates, made for a certain social differentation between the two which affected their relationships with each other and their respective places in the town's social stratification system. Those who chose to remain sociological strangers or who could not or would not fit into the community of Sagebrush nevertheless had a membership of sorts in their work organization and/or their occupational group (engineer, mechanic, etc.).

Other newcomers, who hoped to remain in Sagebrush regardless of what happened to the project or to their jobs, began to seek membership in the community. They had sought work here to live in a rural Western setting, and they conceived of job satisfaction largely in terms of making it possible for them to raise their families in this kind of community. Their values were already much like those of oldtime Sagebrushians. Some were urban refugees; others had come from rural areas where they had wanted to live but could not find work. They began to fit into the outer structure of the community with a view to eventually putting down roots and attaining membership. Merchants, who had survived by catering to the special requirements of cowboys and other outdoorsmen, were willing to take the time to special-order supplies for newcomers who pursued handicraft or other home-entertainment interests. Newcomers who had joined local organizations as transfers, e.g. through previous membership in the Masons or Lions, gained some access to intimacy with oldtimers by fitting into these organizations through universally accepted and expected behavior, such as displaying their expertise in Masonic rituals. During the first winter of the postconstruction period, a manager at the Bighole project died from a heart attack. In response to sentiments he had expressed to his family, he was laid to rest in the old Sagebrush cemetery following full Masonic burial rites—performed by oldtime Sagebrushians for the survivors and friends of their new lodge brother.

The Ranchers' Situation

In the surrounding ranch neighborhoods, where the project's impacts had been felt earliest and continued to be largely unmitigable, the process of "getting back to normal" was more difficult. After all, because the merchants were more able than the ranchers to disconnect the inner-structural from the outer-structural aspects of their lives, the merchants experienced much less social impact. The merchants therefore had more to gain economically and less to lose socially in the event of further industrialization of the area. These factors help to account for their willingness, if not eagerness, to acquiesce to the demands of the Bighole project and to be tempted by the prospect of further coal development in the area. It is understandable that relationships between most merchants and most ranchers were strained by all this, just as were relationships between the latter and the several ranchers who had been identifying with Bighole and flirting with prospective industrial purchases of their land. Although these several ranchers and many of the merchants shared a tendency to accommodate to industry, the merchants had treated them as indifferently as they had all other ranchers when their stores had been filled with free-spending construction personnel. Resultant relational strains lingered on. One rancher, angered by some merchants' construction-period practice of keeping him waiting while giving Bighole contractors preferential treatment, had begun to do all of his buying in Junction City and had not yet returned to Sagebrush to shop. Another rancher, who had not joined his neighbors when they first organized the local protective association, discovered that the mine development was definitely damaging his land and water and consequently the health of some of his cattle. At this point he publicly denounced the mine and spoke out against any further development in the area. He thus joined forces with one of the most active antidevelopment ranchers (I shall call this activist Tom) who had vowed never to be "run off" by the industrialists. As an expression of that determination and defiance, Tom had built a fine new house on the creek downstream from the plant's settling pond.[5] On several occasions, Tom unhesitatingly ran off the railroad surveyors who wanted to identify potential paths across his land for a spur line which would make further coal mining in the area more attractive to developers. The disappointed surveyors regularly failed when attempting to intimidate him with talk of the railroad condemning his land; his invariable response was to tell them to "get your butts off my land and go to hell." He made a point of staying in touch with his neighbors, all of them, the ones who were struggling to survive and needed his neighborly assistance a lot more than he needed theirs, the ones who were active with him in the RPA, and even the ones who had convinced themselves that coal development in the area would somehow increase the quality of their ranching way of life. Tom felt inwardly that the latter were just rationalizing their greed, but he tried not to reveal this feeling in the interest of maintaining cordial relations with them when their paths crossed in town or at neighborhood parties and picnics, when they needed to collaborate in maintaining common fences, or when any other neighborhood matter brought them together. In this regard, he simply wanted to act responsibly to help keep their neighborhood society intact. Tom was likewise mindful of the desirability of not interfering with the mutual inclinations of their children to associate with each other at school and at home and of their wives to visit with each other on the telephone (a vital mode of contact for widely dispersed neighbors, especially during long periods of inclement weather) and in person, notably when taking turns driving each other's children to and from the school bus stop. Like most Sagebrush ranchers, Tom was physically close enough to Bighole's mining and power plant operations to see, hear, smell, and/or feel (ground tremors) the project during the course of the day and night. (These continual sensory reminders of this industrial intrusion were mainly a rural experience, as the town of Sagebrush was far enough away to be spared virtually all of them.)

Tom continued to perform as a public speaker to environmental groups and to groups of industrialists. He preached antidevelopment to his own children (and to others in the community) along with the stories he told about their great-grandfather's pioneer experiences in Rangeland County. He organized hunting trips on his ranch for Bighole executives and then used the occasions to demonstrate the nature and consequences of Bighole's trespasses. He refused to accept that the project was a social and economic defeat for the ranchers and continued to fight by talking to statewide and national audiences about the Bighole project. Tom not only retained full membership for himself and his family but became a marginal member in Bighole's social circles where he delighted in responding to the inevitable newcomers' question: "And how long have you been here?" with "nearly a hundred years."

While these ranchers and some of the protective association's charter members continued to try to fight industrialization in the area, others were disillusioned by their failure to stop the "ultimate trespass"[6] intrinsic to such industrial interventions as Bighole's. They were inclined to turn the fight over to more formally organized, broader-based organizations which had emerged and withdraw to activities confined to their ranches and families. One of these had been a close partner in Tom's "dog and pony shows" during the preconstruction and construction period hearings. These performances had been difficult for Tom's friend, and losing the fight was too painful to permit him to continue after the operations period began. He was a scrapper, accustomed to winning. Now he had lost much of his way of life, especially those parts which had been the victims of various trespasses and whose loss had eroded his sense of place and thus of membership in the community. He withdrew to his small corner of the world made up of family and its ranching way of life. Less aggressive than Tom and inclined to express his idealism differently, he was cynical about future developments and unwilling to invest so much of his life in another protracted fight that he did not expect to win. He and other combat-weary ranchers, who had been trucking their cattle from summer pastures to winter ranges to avoid construction traffic and equipment, began to join together for cattle drives on horseback, complete with chuckwagon. Such picturesque drives were harder on the cattle and consequently not profitable, but they were a way to affirm that ranchers were no less "country" than before.

At Christmas time it was learned that a prosperous, third-generation rancher in the community who had been one of the antidevelopment leaders had sold his entire operation to a Bighole competitor and was moving out of the state. He had abandoned all efforts to prevent trespass and preserve membership, taken the considerable sum he had received, and withdrawn to a society of affluent racehorse-breeding ranchers. Some locals tried to account for his betrayal of their idealized community by asserting that family problems which contributed to his dramatic move were caused by Bighole (for example, his 19-year-old son had run off with the 30-year-old wife of a construction worker). But some others thought the project was a scapegoat for the family's domestic problems. A few others even speculated that the rancher was so offended by the changes brought about by the industrial project that he struck back at Bighole with the only weapon he had left. Whatever the reason, the sale set up a proposal for another large-scale coal development project in the vicinity of Sagebrush.

As this possibility emerged, the protective association, which had been almost exclusively run by local ranchmen, began to expand and gain momentum under the direction of a few determined ranch wives who were less cynical than their husbands about the inevitability of another industrial project. These women, along with other oldtimers who had the spirit and energy to try to stop the new proposal, found some strengths that were not available during their efforts four years earlier: they profited from expensive lessons learned during the Bighole conflict; e.g. by withholding trust from the industry representatives and declining to "wait and see." They took advantage of recent progressive state and federal legislation that regulated industrial developments, and they sought information and support from their state's resource council, from established environmental organizations, and from other nationally known activist groups.

By the end of the winter, as the implications of another round of industrial intervention became clear, another antidevelopment movement emerged. Newcomers, some employed by Bighole, others representing new service professionals and other "cultural converts," who had begun to put down roots and try to become members of the community of Sagebrush, began to take steps to band together to resist a project that they felt would bring unacceptable disruption to the community they were trying to put together with the one the longtimers were trying to keep together.

The aggregate effect of all this loosening and intersecting of social circles and revitalizing of connections between inner and outer structure was itself sufficient to stop the lifestyle waning cycle and restart the movement of *Gemeinschaft* activities toward *Gemeinschaft* ideals. Additional impetus to this movement came as a result of banding together to fend off feared impacts of another prospective coal development project that would threaten the hard-won sociocultural gains shared by old residents and the many new ones who were putting down roots. And so, within a year after Bighole's project became operational, *Gemeinschaft* in Sagebrush once again began to wax.

Summary and Comment

Superficially, the physical appearance of the predevelopment sections of Sagebrush had not changed much since the Bighole project began. Automobiles and homes had been upgraded, mobile homes had been placed on vacant lots in and around town, a cluster of sixty houses had been added, and several new businesses had moved into the approaches to town along the highway. The most obvious difference in the town's appearance was the addition of the new 60-unit "suburb." Other changes were less obvious.

Social circles, which had become more exclusive in reaction to the flood of construction workers, generally remained tight but were beginning to loosen up in response to explorations in fraternization now going on between old and new residents. Some newcomers were definitely trying to put down roots and prepare to take an active part in community affairs (a prospect which most longtimers found acceptable), for example, in various service organizations.

The formalization of helping services which had begun during construction continued afterwards, although there were signs that informal helping networks were being restored or created anew to aid in dealing with personal abuses and other consequences of rapid and encompassing community change. The costs of these and other public services were still being borne mainly by local property owners, notwithstanding the tax contributions of Bighole's project. That there was no certain tax relief in sight was worrisome even to those locals who had been staunch advocates of the kind of progress brought by the project. More annoying than worrisome were changes in their longtime expectations of service providers.

The sheriff's staff was treating even longtimers impersonally and not tailoring the law to them as they had done in predevelopment days, and many of the personalized services which had disappeared from stores still had not been restored or had been only partially restored, noteworthy evidence of loosened and severed connections between inner- and outer-structural behavior. Much obviously remained to be done if inner and outer structure were again to become neatly dovetailed aspects of an encompassing way of life. At least, this was how the situation looked in Sagebrush early in the first year of operations.

Meanwhile, Sagebrush's ranchers had become more sensitive than townspeople to the general waning of *Gemeinschaft* during construction and at the beginning of operations, as most ranchers had greatly reduced their active involvement in the Rangeland Protective Association, had normalized their work schedules, and were seeing and influencing each other much less than they had during the previous few years. In addition, their earlier fear that much of Rangeland County was in process of being turned into a "national sacrifice area" for the benefit of coal developers and their customers had gradually diminished. However, an additional dimension of the waxing cycle for their *Gemeinschaft* seemed imminent as new and very plausible rumors about further coal development in the area started to rekindle this fear and remotivated them to get together to deal with a threat which had greater potential than Bighole's project to destroy their ability to maintain the land as a good, reliable, food-producing area for the nation.

It will be recalled that, in the year or so immediately preceding the construction period, it had been difficult or impossible to check out project-related rumors and that the Rangeland Protective Association had helped greatly to correct this problem. Now, as rumors regarding further development were beginning to spread, the Rangeland Protective Association was again playing an important role in controlling their impact by providing accurate, timely, and credible information concerning this new wave of reports about the imminence of additional industrialization. Another, quite unexpected, source of checking out rumors was Bighole's contacts with the coal industry. These contacts were used by highly placed newcomers to obtain information which was useful for safeguarding both the company's competitive interests and their personal status as residents and potential members of the community. By combining the Rangeland Protective Association's and Bighole's sources of information on future coal development in the area, the community was able to reduce considerably the incidence and impact of rumors about new projects.

The present chapter shows that newcomers were, in many instances, getting into Sagebrush's outer structure as a first significant move toward putting down roots, a move in which they were beginning to develop symbiotic ties of considerable value for all concerned. Further, it shows that some of the newcomers were already starting to get into inner structure as well. Keeping these findings in mind, note that chapter 3 indicated how symbiotic relationships among ranchers had evolved into moral accountabilities as they had formed neighborhood communities. The neighborhood fabric consisted of interwoven social and symbiotic ties. Sagebrush's permanent newcomers who were starting to become members were in process of replicating what had happened in the interaction of the symbiotic and the social to create ranching neighborhoods in the first place. In time, in such situations, the social (and the cultural) supersedes the symbiotic as the fundamental interdependency to the extent that those concerned become morally accountable to each other and thus become a community. The process of fitting in newcomers is, in this sense, one of teaching, motivating, and otherwise helping them to be morally accountable to the community in the same ways that longtimers are. In this process, outer-structural (symbiotic) tics become interlaced with inner-structural (social) ties; outer- and inner-structural considerations are tempered by each other as rationality is brought into working balance with sentiment in ways which make acceptable sense to the community.[7]

As locals had expected, Bighole's project did inject new life into the town's economy during the construction period. Unexpectedly, it had also had the effect of injecting new life into some aspects of the community's *Gemeinschaft*. However, this particularized revitalization of *Gemeinschaft* was costly in so many individual and communal respects that locals generally felt that the quality of their lives was lower during construction than it had been in the preceding years. Now, in the first year after construction, it was not as much lower as they had expected it to be, and it was higher than it had been during construction. These findings suggest that there is a direct relationship between waxing and waning of *Gemeinschaft* and how those concerned evaluate the quality of their lives.

Notes

1. An additional couple hundred people associated with the project resided more in the vicinity of the power plant than of Sagebrush.
2. As indicated in note 4 of chapter 2, this and other such quotes are from the fieldwork files kept by my associates and me.
3. Even when the Bighole project was added to the tax rolls, expenses continued to exceed revenues, partly because the company received tax credits under a state law designed to attract new industry.
4. What happened to Ronald's store brings to mind Suttles's (1968, p. 49) account of a typical invasion of an ethnic store by members of another ethnic group: "In the long run, no comfortable resolution can be found; as the old habitués withdraw, the business place either loses all ethnic characteristics or takes on the ethnicity of the newcomers." Encouraged by Ronald, his store took on the K-Mart ethnicity of the newcomers.
5. The settling pond was used to collect ashes and other noncombustibles channeled to it by air pollution control devices in the huge smoke stack in Bighole's coal-fired, steam-generating power plant.
6. Strip-mining without the affected surface owners' blessings constitutes "the ultimate trespass."
7. This discussion is reminiscent of Whitehead's (1933, p. 127) observation: "Ideas arise as explanatory of customs and they end up by founding novel methods and novel institutions."

6

Conceptualization and Analysis

The advent of large-scale industrialization in Sagebrush produced massive changes in the area's way of life.[1] The impacts were similar to those which Hughes (1943) found in the French-Canadian city of Cantonville over forty years ago, even though the latter resulted from much slower growth and development. The sociological composition of both communities bore a marked resemblance to the one in the racially and ethnically mixed section of Detroit called "Poletown" (City of Detroit 1980), whose residents were about to be forcibly relocated and who therefore faced devastating impacts from a bust rather than a boom. This chapter uses a comparative perspective to help place the discussion of the preceding chapters into an analytical and conceptual framework that draws together the basic elements in the sheer persistence as well as in the cyclical functioning of *Gemeinschaft*.

Gemeinschaft and *Gesellschaft*

Wherever there is a natural disaster, *Gemeinschaft* invariably surfaces above *Gesellschaft* organizations and relationships. For example, people in the United States identified with the hostages in Iran and their families and were deeply touched by what transpired during 1980 and 1981. After an outpouring of personalized, warm offerings of help, in and through which *Gemeinschaft* showed, *Gesellschaft* was resumed as the dominant façade. Such occurrences, which are familiar to all of us, constitute further evidence that the latter is a much more rationally contrived and culturally stylized mode of organization and lifestyle than the former. Such occurrences also help to reveal that, in the *Gesellschaft*, formalization and impersonalization have the effect of placing standardizing façades on the ways people are naturally inclined to act in their ongoing efforts to maintain and develop their essential personal and human qualities.

People organize themselves to become and remain human essentially by inventing and utilizing culture to socialize their young and each other. The socialization process operates on both affective and cognitive levels and is sentimental and personal in many respects, just as it is categoric and normative in other respects. The humanizing aspects of this process are those which foster initial and continuing development of self in the child to enable him to control his impulses to perceive, think, feel, and act and to do so in the framework of the expectations, rules, norms, and other behavior-shaping, behavior-regularizing influences to which he is more or less regularly and even methodically exposed. Learning to control one's behavior in the framework of the culture being used to socialize—and to be recognized, accepted, and appreciated by significant and important others as one who fits in and belongs to the community they represent—is at once a humanizing experience (through transforming a mere member of the species into a member of human social groups) and a personal and social developmental experience (through fostering growth of self, personality, interaction abilities, role behaviors, careers, etc.). It is in and through the socialization process that individuals become and remain human. When the process is made exclusively rational and impersonal, as in the *Gesellschaft*, those concerned have to find ways of making it more sentimental and personal—hence the inevitable informal creation of personalized, humanizing opportunities for interaction in even the most bureaucratic of organizations and urbanized of communities. Clearly, then, even with its cultural brilliance, *Gesellschaft* inhibits the ways people organize themselves to become and remain human; it offers no fundamental and enduring contribution to what people need to maintain, enhance, or expand the bases of their humanity. Accordingly, *Gesellschaft* is always rationally staged, formally negotiated, seemingly artificial, and much more subject to impersonal rules and pretense in comparison to *Gemeinschaft*.

Rules, mechanisms, and procedures which support and maintain formal organization are, in a sense, ways of trying to keep *Gemeinschaft* from making sentimental, informal, folksy assaults upon *Gesellschaft*; i.e., methods of treating people categorically are designed to control natural tendencies of people to interact personally. For example, *Gesellschaft* has far greater potential than *Gemeinschaft* for setting up and using procedures for incorporating lots of new people into an organization and turning them into members in a short period of time through setting forth highly explicit and impersonal bureaucratic rules for membership and behavior, thus functioning to minimize expression of natural tendencies to interact informally, "pair off," form inner structures, and, in effect, trespass upon *Gesellschaft* to create a *Gemeinschaft* within it. These tendencies naturally occur where industrial and communal circles intersect, because everywhere and always in such situations people are striving to establish or maintain a balance between community and bureaucratic (or other organizational) membership and thus between inner- and outer-structural behavior. However, as shown in the case of Bighole's project at Sagebrush, an industrial representative of *Gesellschaft* puts its veneer on everything it touches because it is poorly equipped by design as well as predilection to relate to less formal structures in less formal ways: it insists that others speak its language and use its norms and, in this sense, is overbearing and ethnocentric. A large, complex organization tolerates cliques and the like so long as they do not threaten the formal rules; as such, elements of *Gesellschaft* and *Gemeinschaft* can and do intertwine within it and thus increase its potential for relating to a rural community.

There are also rules, mechanisms, and procedures which support and maintain *Gemeinschaft* and which ward off the potential or actual impacts of *Gesellschaft*. For example, the rural community has a double standard of behavior, one for members and one for nonmembers, which functions to safeguard and maintain the local way of life by keeping potential and actual sociocultural intrusions and disruptions from getting out of hand. Thus, when substantially isolated from the urban-industrial world and in relatively full control of its socialization processes, the rural community requires new residents to fit in socially and culturally and, in these respects, pay their membership dues before they may exercise the privilege of being openly critical of the community. This double standard becomes more difficult to enforce in circumstances of rapid growth. So, until growth slows down enough for the process of socializing newcomers to work effectively and manageably once more, the established members consciously and unconsciously tighten their social circles (in the way this was done at Sagebrush) to fend off and take *Gesellschaft* forces out of account and thus protect and perpetuate their social circles as inner-structural repositories of the community's organizational and cultural essences. Even when socially impacted as Sagebrush was, an unshakable commitment to the ideal qualities and characteristics of *Gemeinschaft* enables this form of collective life to persist. These sociocultural attributes of the *Gemeinschaft* include:

1. Shared traditions and values.
2. Members' taken-for-granted ability to realize their values—to bring the actual into congruence with the ideal.
3. An emphasis on local social and cultural values rather than on monetary ones. These include having control over one's own destiny (self-reliance), a commitment to family and friends, informal social networks—especially through kinship and church, fitting in, and participation in neighboring (informal helping networks).
4. Mutual trust. While not extended automatically to strangers, mutual trust is assumed and expected of members.

5. Friendliness toward others. Reaching out to newcomers implies initiating a process of giving or considering giving them membership. Residents who do not make an effort to learn how to fit into the established way of life are disliked, distrusted, or both.

6. A slow, predictable, orderly pace of life. Members find it difficult to anticipate or cope with rapid and/or far-reaching change, that is, with anything that preempts, usurps, or otherwise intrudes upon traditional control of local socialization processes.

7. Informality in social controls, organizational procedures, business dealings, and personal relationships. For example, in preboom Sagebrush, a longtime resident who appeared before the city council for a land-use permit was quickly accommodated. Sometimes such action was requested in absentia, in which case word was sent orally through a representative (rather than in writing). Agreement was by consensus; e.g. council members looked around the table and nodded to one another. A distaste for the bureaucratic and preference for the informal was thus evident in the official meetings of local government.

8. Family-centered life.

9. A sense of membership and roots in the community. Referred to here are such aspects of identifying with and belonging to a social world as these: a deep sense of being an integral part of one's community, a certainty that one's place in the community is well known and secure, a feeling that one's values and worldview are natural and right because they are essentially the same as those held by the rest of one's community, an assurance that one is known and cared about by the community at large as well as by one's intimates, and, that, should calamity befall one, others in the community will quickly and quietly come to one's aid in all ways needed to bring the event under control; and thus a contentment which comes from believing that life in one's community is well ordered, meaningfully controlled, acceptably sensible, and good. Residents have little, if any, desire to live elsewhere.

10. A predominance of inner structure. Members feel little need to conceal or disguise their basic human sentiments, their selves, and the social activities, relational ties, and other aspects of community life which they value.

11. Ties to the land. Locals are committed to maintaining for future generations of gardeners and agriculturalists the land of their forefathers.

12. Family-owned and -operated businesses. Almost all local businesses are family enterprises, and their owners prefer that they remain that way. In Sagebrush, fear of chain store competition, the prospect of a new commercial center developing away from the established one, and loss of family orientation and of associated personal contact with customers tempered hopes for a sounder economic base for the local enterprise. A Sagebrush proprietor commented: "The fun of operating this little business is starting to go out of it. I spend so much time in the

store that I have no time for fishing. All this defeats the purpose of living and being in business here."[2]

13. A vulnerable elderly population. Most older persons do not want to risk destruction of the social circles they have nurtured much or all of their lives, nor do they relish being forced to test their ability to cope with drastically changed and probably uncongenial living circumstances.

14. A tendency to "wait and see" (passive reaction) when change is threatened rather than to engage in immediate and agressive counteraction and/or protective action. Reactive attitudes of "you can't stop progress" and "we'll just roll with the punches" were accompanied by feelings of fatalism and cynicism in Sagebrush.

15. A sense of powerlessness and resignation in the face of prospective industrialization or other large-scale intervention.

16. A perceived need for collective organization and action to safeguard local values threatened by the anticipated community change. These efforts were slow to develop in Sagebrush. At best, members were able to mitigate industrial impacts, not prevent them. For example, various rural spokesmen became skilled at circuit-riding to meetings and other public forums to present their case, and nationally organized environmental groups (previously spurned by ranchers and other small businessmen) were persuaded to become their allies.

17. A sense that a foreign—even demented—value system is being imposed upon economically and politically reactive and socioeconomically subordinated locals by economically and politically powerful interventionists for the benefit of outside investors and consumers.

18. A sense of being turned into a minority. Locals in Sagebrush felt they were losing control of their lives to invading forces.

19. Scapegoating behavior. Sagebrush parents, who were tolerant of juvenile drinking, feared that construction workers would bring an influx of drug problems.[3] However, locals self-consciously reminded each other that water, sewer, and other infrastructural problems, which they were also inclined to blame on Bighole-related growth, were problems that they had been unable to resolve before development began.

20. A readiness to "fight fire with fire." Locals often try to use legal leverage to resist—or at least bring under control—colonialistic attempts to displace them (Gold 1978, Cornerstone 1980a). Sagebrushians' pervasive feeling of being trespassed and trampled upon in the name of "progress" led them to become active in the Rangeland Protective Association.

In contrast, the *Gesellschaft* is characterized by such sociocultural attributes as the following:

1. Interaction according to formalized organizational roles, rules, and schedules. Members have less in common than do their *Gemeinschaft*

counterparts; hence they shy away from informal dealings at most levels, feeling more comfortable with legalized controls and procedures.

2. Behavior which is generally rationalistic and calculative and hence impersonal.
3. Loose or weak ties to the community in spite of length of residence in the area. Developing sociocultural roots is not a primary interest.
4. Minimal participation in local events. Residents prefer to be spectators rather than get personally involved; they are more inclined to observe the community than to participate in it. In many respects, therefore, they are sociological strangers to each other in what is nominally their community. And, in fact, each resident knowingly shares with very few others a sense of what it means and should mean to be a member of the community.
5. A lifestyle characterized by diversity, growth, and change.
6. Restraint toward others. Residents prefer to be helpful to newcomers in ways which are relatively devoid of membership implications or which favor anonymity. For example, they would rather give money to the Salvation Army than be of direct, personal assistance to the needy.
7. A predominance of outer structure. Members ordinarily present themselves in guarded and categoric terms. This façade serves to protect the individual from revealing his vulnerabilities and feelings—both as a community member and as an individual.
8. A taste for the bureaucratic and preference for the formal in business and government.
9. An emphasis on monetary values, external appearance, fashion, front.
10. An instrumental relationship to the land.

Although *Gesellschaft* situations are heavily based upon outer structure, they still have elements of inner structure present. Similarly, while inner structure predominates in the *Gemeinschaft*, evidence of outer structure is readily visible. In many respects the two structures are conceptually and empirically distinct entities, but they are also so intertwined that neither can exist or be understood without the other. The fact that *Gemeinschaft* and *Gesellschaft* each needs infusions of the other to survive does not necessarily give rise to problems. What does create problems is the ways these infusions are handled—that is, *mis*handled. At Sagebrush, for example, the mishandling typically took the form of incursions and trespasses by those acting on the (erroneous) Bighole assumption that a more accommodative way of handling the industrialization and thus the infusions would not be in the company's interest. In the course of surviving, *Gemeinschaft* waxes and wanes in response to social processes within it as well as to such forces (e.g. Bighole's project) as those set in motion by the local and national economies.[4] These cyclical aspects of *Gemeinschaft* will be discussed next.

Waxing and Waning of *Gemeinschaft*

A discussion of waxing and waning of *Gemeinschaft* requires a conceptual distinction between this form of organization and the members whose behavior patterns take on this form. For this purpose it will be useful to focus analysis of *Gemeinschaft* on the more structural or static aspects of this form of community and to focus analysis of membership on its more processual or dynamic aspects. As analytic perspectives and as actual human organizational phenomena, membership and *Gemeinschaft* are so closely intertwined that each is a function of the other. It follows, then, that quality and size of active membership and degree of coherence, integrity, and viability of *Gemeinschaft* are functions of each other. In this sense, *Gemeinschaft* waxes as a result of social forces which boost membership, and it wanes in their absence—or when the impact of the forces of community change on membership is negligible or inconsequential, or disruptive or destructive. Ordinarily, the bolstering forces are social occurrences and processes which function as rites of affirmation and reaffirmation regarding who the members are, what they mean to each other, what life for them is and should be about. On a mundane level, people continually get together to perform these rites in relatively informal, unobtrusive, spontaneous ways; for example, they have gatherings of friends in their homes, drop in on neighbors, chat with relatives on the telephone, and otherwise pursue and renew relationships. Various voluntary associations perform similar functions in relatively formal, overt, planned, and continuing ways which are similarly integrative for the community or parts of it. Examples of such associations in small towns like Sagebrush are the local historical society, the rod and gun club, the voluntary emergency medical technicians (EMTs), the volunteer fire department, the local landowners' association, and organized boosters of the local high school's ball teams. In the rural areas of the Sagebrush community, *Gemeinschaft* waxes when ranchers get together in an ad hoc, folk way to fight a fire, and when they bury one of their own without hiring coffin makers, gravediggers, or other such workers. What may be regarded as informal and *Gemeinschaft*-affirming in town may be eschewed by ranchers as too formal, externally controlled, and professionally orchestrated to serve them as a rite of (re)affirmation. In both town and country, *Gemeinschaft* waxes in the face of and in response to drastic or dramatic change. Natural and man-made disasters tend to stimulate such waxing; so do more welcome changes of considerable magnitude and impact. An example of the latter is an industrial intervention which the locals invite but which nevertheless makes outer structure grow in size and complexity more strikingly than expected and which impacts the community's inner structure enough to lead to some tightening of social circles and other defensive reactions which, as the story of Sagebrush has shown, have the immediate effect of getting the *Gemeinschaft* act together. Responses of the community to rapid and massive intervention tend to have an ad hoc and spontaneous quality, no matter how well prepared its emergency and other formal organizations may be to handle that sort of occurrence. Most other community-wide occurrences which function as rites of reaffirmation are well organized and take place with annual or other periodic regularity; examples are the county fair and the 4th of July parade and picnic in town, and roundup and branding of cattle in the rural areas. These events function to cause a short-term waxing of *Gemeinschaft* and to do something equally felicitous for the town's relatively *Gesellschaft*-like outer structure.

The socialization process can be viewed as a relatively open-ended and continuing rite of affirmation and reaffirmation of what life in the community is and should be about. The very act of teaching social values and behavior enables the teacher to do this reaffirming while helping the learner to incorporate into his behavior the social knowledge and sensitivity needed to affirm membership in the community. Looking at the community as a whole, the relatively organized and readily observed aspects of this process are outer-structural and thus formal, such as the socialization which occurs in school, at church, or at work. However, the bulk of social teaching and learning is informal and is done in mundane relationships in a continual, rather subtle, and low-profile way; as such, it functions for the community as a highly effective rite of affirmation and reaffirmation and thus as the most continuous and pervasive builder and maintainer of *Gemeinschaft*. For the individuals engaged in this process of forming social perspectives, roles, selves, and relationships, the *Gemeinschaft* consequences are profound and enduring. The socialization process leads the participants to identify with each other as well as with shared symbols, to care about and for each other—and thus to regard each other as persons who really count, to develop a common commitment to maintaining their values and relationships, to feel a consciousness of kind with each other that is integral to their sense of social and personal place in the community, and hence to be bonded socially in the *Gemeinschaft* manner. The rites of affirmation and reaffirmation of what people stand for, of who they are, and of what they want to do with their lives with and through one another are indispensable for forming and maintaining *Gemeinschaft*. *Gemeinschaft* waxes when these rites are present in relatively full measure and adequacy, and it wanes when the opposite condition obtains.[5]

Why exactly does *Gemeinschaft* wane? Why does it require routine, periodic, occasional, and even extraordinary affirmative and reaffirmative acts to counter its apparently intrinsic tendency to deteriorate, atrophy, wane? Is this mainly because *Gemeinschaft* (unlike *Gesellschaft*) depends for its existence on sentimental ties, goodwill, a certain amount of selfless devotion to the common good, artful interpersonal sensitivities designed to maintain the relationships which make up *Gemeinschaft*, providing members a secure sense of social place and personal well-being, and so on? *Gemeinschaft*'s social fabric is woven of many thin and delicate threads into intricate patterns which begin to lose their body, fade, and come loose at the seams as a result of life's ordinary vicissitudes and so need to be sewn back together, ironed out, and otherwise revitalized more or less continually. But even all this is not enough to keep *Gemeinschaft* from becoming musty and stale and more alive in the members' idealizations of it than in its actualities, so contrived or fortuitous revitalizations are needed from time to time to keep *Gemeinschaft* from becoming such a fanciful and pretended community that it loses its ability to serve its essential purposes for its members.

While fieldwork on industrial intervention at Sagebrush gave me some important answers to the question of why *Gemeinschaft* wanes, I still lacked the explanatory insight which comes from comparing one's data with that on a more ideal-typical case of the same sort of phenomenon. Kai Erikson's (1976) study of a disaster at Buffalo Creek provided the kind of comparative data I needed.

Erikson's report on the survivors of a devastating flash flood resulting from the collapse of an earthen dam at Buffalo Creek in West Virginia describes an extreme case of waning of *Gemeinschaft*. The tiny settlements along several miles of the hollow through which Buffalo Creek flowed had been highly integrated neighborhoods of a community of coal miners when, without warning, an earthen dam which had impounded a settling pond containing muck and scrap and various other waste materials collapsed and sent a mountain of this mixture cascading down the narrow hollow. The flood had the effect of scouring and reaming out the first several miles of settlements so that the damage to property in that area was almost total, there was much loss of life, and the emotional aftershock left the survivors just barely hanging on as persons and as human beings. As Erikson is keenly aware, the social and psychological sciences have no satisfactory explanation for such great collective and individual trauma, particularly when even that wonderful healer, time, seems unable to bring the victims back to anything resembling "normal." As I read about this profoundly puzzling event, many questions came to mind: Is this a case of where people were so dispersed and segmented that they did not have a group (other than some members of their immediate family) to turn inward with, so (a) they turned inward on themselves and rendered themselves largely incapable of making society with any but themselves and, as a result, (b) they made their *Gemeinschaft* wane in the extreme? Did this last-ditch protecting of self lead the survivors to keep inner structure within themselves to such an extent that interaction with spouses, children, old friends, and others who had been their intimates was largely reduced to the relatively psychologically safe level of outer-structural interaction? Could they no longer bear to risk intimacy and all the self-exposure it entails? Were they fearful of what they most needed to be fully human again? How were these self-concerns related to the widespread feelings of alienation and aloneness which Erikson found among the survivors? Then, as I compared this extreme case of a waning of *Gemeinschaft* with what I had observed during the construction period at Sagebrush, I began to see more clearly the outlines of a pattern. A significant aspect of waning of *Gemeinschaft* appears to be a general withdrawal to smaller units of interaction (to self-interaction in the extreme case). This withdrawal has the effect of weakening and even severing connections among these units, for example, families, and starts a chain reaction of deterioration of inner structure, of connections between inner and outer structure, and thus of the general *Gemeinschaft* quality of life. Close inspection of this withdrawal enabled me to discriminate between different degrees of tightening of social circles and their consequences for quality of *Gemeinschaft*. For example, an initial tightening of social circles may have entailed merely an intensification of interaction among and within social circles, with the immediate effect of causing *Gemeinschaft* to wax. However, a further tightening (in response to further, continuing threat to way of life) may have entailed an intensification of interaction within family units to the relative exclusion of what had been the remainder of the associated social circles, with the immediate effect of causing *Gemeinschaft* to wane. The limiting case may well be what Erikson found at Buffalo Creek, where what seems to have been *Gemeinschaft*-destroying mass trauma may yet turn out to have been the bottoming of a tragic waning period.[6]

In light of the foregoing analysis, I should like now to recapitulate and restate highlights of waxing and waning of *Gemeinschaft* at Sagebrush.[7]

1. The immediate reaction to construction was a tightening of social circles without disrupting connections among them and between inner and outer structure. As an aggregate effect, *Gemeinschaft* waxed.
2. The general *Gemeinschaft* waned, as people increasingly retreated to and tightened their social circles and as many of the established connections between inner and outer structure were severed, mothballed, or were operating less effectively than they had been prior to Bighole's entry.
3. The tightened social circles in both inner and outer structure (recurrent

courthouse and restaurant contacts are examples of the latter) were cultural and structural shelters. On the positive side, family and friendship groups were more vibrant and alive than they had been, as people poured their *Gemeinschaft* energies into these restricted social enclaves for the duration of the boom. On the negative side, further tightening of social circles had the effect of disrupting long-established connections among the social circles which constituted inner structure and between inner and outer structure, thus lowering morale by inhibiting members' ability to act together in pursuit of many traditional communal objectives and reducing the pervasiveness and flavor of *Gemeinschaft* as the community's dominant sociocultural motif.

4. A really important waxing of *Gemeinschaft* occurred primarily among landowners when they got organized (e.g. as a local protective association) to become better informed and better able to look out for themselves as both an interest group and a collection of neighbors.

5. On balance, therefore, what happened during the boom and thus during the period when general *Gemeinschaft* waned in reaction to widespread sociocultural threat, was that the several components of the *Gemeinschaft* became like variously coiled springs waiting for the threat to subside. In this sense, even as overall *Gemeinschaft* waned, it was building up potential for waxing on a community-wide scale as soon as the construction dust settled.

6. What waxing of *Gemeinschaft* there was during the boom period occurred primarily in relatively small social circles and at some short-run cost to the larger community.

7. After construction, the ties between inner and outer structure which had been weakened or severed began to be reestablished and enabled the community to safely resume being more openly a *Gemeinschaft* in outer- as well as inner-structural ways, whereupon *Gemeinschaft*, and with it, morale, began to wax on a community-wide scale.

8. What happened at Sagebrush was that construction impacts led to rearranging the elements of *Gemeinschaft* and to changing the balance between *Gemeinschaft* and *Gesellschaft*. There was a greater variety of mixtures of both than there had been and there were also more elements of *Gesellschaft* in town. Although this was not a simple case of displacement of *Gemeinschaft* by *Gesellschaft*, these changes contributed noticeably to the waning of *Gemeinschaft* as the community's general form. On surface, at least, Sagebrush was less "country" than it had been. As the sociocultural threats of construction abated, the townspeople gradually began to feel that it was again safe to risk routine, everyday, public displays and affirmations of *Gemeinschaft*. Accordingly, in the first year after the end of construction, they began to loosen their social circles, to restore connections among them and between inner and outer structure, and, generally, to allow the community's suppressed "country" character to surface once again as its dominant motif. This

waxing of *Gemeinschaft* was well under way as our fieldwork came to an end about twelve months after Bighole's project had become operational.

A further discussion of the differences and connections between *Gemeinschaft* and *Gesellschaft* will help to develop a deeper sense of how they are interrelated. It will also show that the survival of inner structure is what accounts for the ability of *Gemeinschaft* to persist in spite of the impinging forces of *Gesellschaft*.

Inner and Outer Structure

Inner structure concerns sentimental and traditional bonds and behavior, while outer structure consists of so-called infrastructure and other readily observed organizations and conduct. The term *infrastructure* is misleading because it denotes the underlying foundation of the community and thus the relatively hard-to-see and hard-to-change rock upon which the social structure is built. Contrary to this denotation, outer structure is relatively easy to see and change. Inner structure is the actual foundation of community life, and is relatively hard to see and change without explicit effort.

A major reason why so many sociologists see and portray community largely or entirely in outer-structural terms is that they prefer to study it at a distance;[8] they gain little or none of the intimate knowledge of inner structure needed to do justice to it in their reports. Another reason is that, wittingly or unwittingly, community informants continually use outer structure to protect inner structure[9] from undesired and untoward scrutiny, judgment, and impingement. Residents tend to portray their community in idealized or "what ought to be" terms when asked to talk about it, and their accounts of the actual, as well as of the ideal, tend to reveal much more about the local inner structure's outer-structural veneers than about inner structure as such.

For example, ask a man why he is so committed to living in Sagebrush and he will say, "It's a great place to raise kids." Ask why, and he will point to the fine school, the good law enforcement, the great recreational opportunities, and the like. However, when the questioner is able to probe beneath these outer-structural veneers, he will find that the man knows full well that his children are continually under the watchful eye of friends and neighbors all over town, are in a community situation which fosters learning to interact easily and skillfully with residents in all age groups and other social categories, are becoming the sorts of persons he wants them to become, and in other respects are benefiting personally and socially from the good things such a community has going for it. Small wonder that his gentle, cordial manner of interacting with visitors and other strangers in town functions to help keep them at arm's length socially and therefore is itself part of the community's outer-structural veneer.

Other ways of protecting inner structure include maintaining connections between inner and outer structure,[10] contriving glossed versions of the community, deliberately making errors of omission and commission about it, dwelling unabashedly on outer-structural matters when questions and concerns about inner structure are raised (e.g. dwelling on the local economy, the natural environment, and the town's physical appearance when asked about community values), and so on. In so doing, these informants are using a tried and true folk procedure for guarding, sheltering, and otherwise protecting the foundation and basis for much of their selfhood.[11]

Even when the fieldworker does an effective job of taking these protective actions into account, the informants' situation may militate against achieving a desired balance in his presentation of inner and outer structure. For example, Erikson's (1976) account of the disaster experience at Buffalo Creek tells little about what outer structure was like before it was destroyed by the flood or what happened to it afterwards, except to note that Housing and Urban Development's lack of regard for what had been natural social units led to bureaucratically convenient and therefore socially nonrational placement of the survivors in temporary dwellings. As there was not much else in outer structure to tell about, Erikson told about the outer-structural *behavior* of the survivors in the months following the disaster, when they were capable of only minimal inner-structural interaction. As a point of contrast, note that outer structure was the arena for much of the industrial "disaster" experience at Sagebrush, whereas the flood disaster experience occurred largely on a mass basis in the context of nuclear family segments of what had been natural social units consisting of neighbors, friends, and extended-family members. This experience so disintegrated these constituent social units of the Buffalo Creek area that the survivors felt they were no longer members of a community, that their inner-structural bonds had been destroyed, and that the physical manifestations of outer structure had simply been washed away. Erikson's sociological portrayal of this situation shows respect for these empirical facts by concentrating on the survivors' inner- and outer-structural façades—which were virtually all that remained of the area's once well-integrated *Gemeinschaft.*

Other community researchers would also do well to use methods which enable them to perceive and analyze the connections, relationships, and interactions between inner and outer structure.[12] Unfortunately the common sociological disinclination to utilize probing participant-observation procedures[13] accounts for the discipline's general tendency to address little more than outer-structural matters and consequently to make various unfounded, incorrect, or misleading inferences concerning what life is really about in the community under study.[14] To do community research which produces sociologically sound descriptions and explanations, both inner and outer structure must be addressed so that their interrelationships[15] can be inspected and associated pretenses taken into account.

Pretenses

Inner and outer structure are used in mutually protective ways, largely through pretense (including tact, caution, exaggeration, and fictionalization). Pretense functions to minimize interactional risk, protect cherished relationships, reaffirm value commitments, and the like. Examples of such use are legion: using outer-structural veneers to guardedly display (show but tell little or nothing about) inner structure; using a safe, communal universe of discourse to talk about and around sensitive inner-structural topics and concerns, such as talk about natural environmental and economic impacts as the most feared effects of a proposed energy project, when the basic, underlying concerns are its social and cultural effects; exaggerating how great the relationships between neighbors are, what a great place this is for retirees, how wonderful the local schools are, and the like; and using fictionalized accounts to bridge the actual with the ideal, particularly when they have taken sharply divergent courses and the bridging makes it appear that sluggish, inactive, or malfunctioning aspects of the structure in question are alive and well. The last-mentioned fictionalization warrants further discussion as an example of the functional importance, and perhaps necessity, of such pretense for maintaining the structural integrity of a *Gemeinschaft* type of community.

As explained earlier in this chapter, *Gemeinschaft* naturally waxes and wanes. At Sagebrush it was in a waning period when the coal developers appeared. Fictionalizing of relationships among Sagebrush ranchers was helping to keep relatively inactive parts of *Gemeinschaft* alive through coloring the actual with the ideal. Fictional accounts gave the feeling to those concerned, and the impression to nonmembers, that the ranchers were doing a lot of neighboring when, in fact, they were doing precious little. Such stretching of the facts helps to keep the relatively inactive parts of inner structure bridged with the relatively active ones during periods when connections between the two are more latent and symbiotic than active and social.

A *Gemeinschaft* is not the best place in the world to go in heavily for pretense. Such a place thrives on its ability to take sentiments into account and to encourage its members to present themselves as whole persons rather than mere role players and to do so under conditions of minimal self-risk. In addition to the pretending associated with coloring and sustaining the actual with the ideal, the only other kind that makes sense in a community where members know each other intimately and secrets are few and far between is that which is designed, for the most part, to try to take out of account words and deeds which might disrupt valued relationships and/or do violence to associated sentiments. Being polite, gracious, tactful, considerate, and/or diplomatic usually suffices to nip such disruptive behavior in the bud. At times, however, careful steps must be taken to inhibit or suppress utterances and actions which appear to have an unmanageable potential for hurting feelings, damaging reputations, alienating members, and otherwise doing grievous harm to personal and communal integrity. In short, pretense of any sort makes sense in a *Gemeinschaft* only when, in the view of the members, it is needed to help keep their relationships going and, while doing so, to help safeguard their relationships' inner-structural character.

Pretense is better suited in a *Gesellschaft*, where outer structure predominates, i.e., where the name of the game is to act guardedly in accordance with the community's broadly defined status and role expectations. Such cautious, calculative action serves to protect one's position in outer structure, to keep self shielded, and to insulate inner structure from the relatively nonsentimental, untrusting, and impersonal character of outer-structural behavior. Acting guardedly lends itself to handling situations where a person is unsure of how to foster desirable and acceptable evaluations of his behavior—where he depends heavily upon outer-structural veneers to deal with perceived risks to role, self, and position. It also lends itself to making a practice of using versions of reality which are calculated to meet the perceived expectations of one's associates (e.g. telling people what they want to hear); project to them certain desired images of role, self, and position; and, in such ways, reach the essentially rational, instrumental, and other nonsentimental objectives of outer-structural interaction. For example, when shopping in situations consciously governed by impersonal rules of interaction, most persons have no other recourse than to act *as if* they trust the person(s) with whom they find themselves doing business, even though they may not really trust them but do not know what else to do to obtain the services or goods offered. This behavior is an extreme instance of the pretense or veneer of outer-structural behavior.

Like other ways of packaging and presenting behavior, pretense does not always manage to serve the purpose for which it was intended. There is always a certain risk that an attempt to use "little white lies" to protect feelings will boomerang, that a perceptive stranger will break the linguistic code being used to talk about inner-structural matters in his presence, or that people will begin to believe their exaggerations about the community and thus fail to heed early warning signs of emerging community problems. Worse still, some pretense that has become dysfunctional for the community may be so grounded in local values and so self-righteously defended by the community at large as to get in the way of achieving important community objectives. An example is pretending that it is defensible to maintain the traditional belief that what a man does with his land is nobody's business but his, even when the community is growing rapidly. What happens then is that the community continues to avoid public land-use planning and control.[16] This avoidance has the effect of continually throwing community development up for grabs and results in crazy-quilt growth patterns which leave everybody shaking their heads in consternation. In this example, outer-structural needs to do "something" about the glaring land-use mess are entrapped in a cultural web. An inner-structural value is kept going by longtimers pretending it is too sacred to touch, at least so long as they are running the local government. Some, meanwhile, are quietly hoping that newcomers will soon take over and assume responsibility for getting the community out of this dismaying bind in which interaction between inner and outer structure is encumbered by pretense.

When in the throes of rapid change, people rely not only on pretense but on many other social tactics to modify their behavior so that it is in keeping with evolving changes in interfaces and working balances between inner and outer structure.

Behavior Related to Inner and Outer Structure

To bring together instances of such modifications, the following chart presents a number of examples of locality-wide shifts from inner- to outer-structural behavior as the community's manifest interactional motif. In these examples, cultural aspects of inner structure are paired with their outer-structural counterparts for Sagebrush, and for Sagebrush and two other communities.

Examples of Contrasts between Inner- and Outer-Structural Behavior

Inner	Outer
Sagebrush	
The supervisor of the nearby U.S. forest wanted "hard" data from the EIS on Bighole's project to justify resource decisions that he "knew" and "felt" were right. Lo-	The forest supervisor wanted a cookbook of "rational, objective, hard" data. He had to have numerical evidence of objectivity to support the resource decision he

Inner	Outer
cal sentiment was for these decisions.	was inclined to make. Without such evidence he could not justify to his organization the "sentimental" judgments he personally wished to justify.
Wedding guests were close relatives and intimate friends only, all invited in casual conversation.	Formal invitations to weddings and receptions were mailed to all guests. No RSVPs were requested since everyone knew who could or could not come.
Wedding guests included persons only slightly known to the bride and groom but who were important to one or more of the parents.	Guests were invited to the wedding reception selectively and RSVPs were required since no one knew who would feel it important to come.
In predevelopment Rangeland County, everyone knew what to do when smoke was sighted.	Later ranchers felt it necessary to organize a volunteer fire department.
A rancher said to a coal developer, "You'll always be $3.65 short of what it would cost to lease my land for strip-mining."	A rancher responded to a coal developer's offer by initiating lease action with his lawyer because "when a dog is after you, you climb the best tree."
A café operator closed on Thursday to go fishing.	The owner put up a sign stating "Gone Fishing—Back Friday."
In predevelopment Rangeland County, the oldest males in the families related to a deceased relative would go the cemetery to "open the grave," i.e., they were the gravediggers. Even if too old to dig, the men went to show respect for the occasion. Family members cared for the plot and for plots of deceased who had no relatives in the area.	Later it became necessary to hire a gravedigger who also cared for the cemetery plots.

Inner	Outer
As a *Gemeinschaft*, the division of labor was so simple that outer structure had few work places and thus provided few job opportunities. Even though connections between inner and outer structure were solid and known widely by the locals, they were so few that many young adults had to leave town to find jobs.	As an emerging *Gesellschaft*, the division of labor was becoming so complex that outer structure had many work places and thus provided many job opportunities for young adults. Even though connections between inner and outer structure were generally fragmentary and not well known (connections among components of outer structure were relatively more solid and better known), job opportunities were so ample that few young adults had to leave town to find jobs (i.e., leaving town to work was becoming more a matter of choice than of necessity).
Informality prevailed in city and county governmental transactions.	Later it became necessary for *every* person who wished to ask something of the city council or board of county commissioners to prepare written materials and requests, which were then made into formal recommendations, following which a self-conscious, formal vote was taken.
Dogs in Sagebrush ran at will.	Later a dog ordinance was passed, an animal control officer employed, and fines levied for offenses. Longtimers, who were fined repeatedly but did not confine their pets, remained valued members of their inner circles.
Sagebrush and other Communities[17] Everybody knew everybody.	Most looked like strangers to most.
Who you were counted more heavily than what you were.	What you were counted more heavily than who you were.

Inner	Outer
Fronts, pretenses, formal politeness, and other guarded behavior were used sparingly and self-consciously.	Façades of these sorts were used so much and so expertly that they were more the norm than was relatively uncontrived, spontaneous behavior.
Relationships with kinfolk, friends, neighbors, and work associates were no less ends in themselves than means to ends.	These relationships were much less ends in themselves than means to ends.
In time of emergency or crisis at the individual or family level, everyone did what came naturally to help those directly affected to handle these problems.	In such cases, few felt it natural and right to initiate personal interaction without fear of the consequences of "getting involved" and/or getting in the way of professionals who were paid to deal routinely with the emergencies and crises of individuals and families.
In time of community-wide disaster, conflagration, or calamity, everyone automatically pitched in to help everyone else.	In time of community-wide disaster, conflagration, or calamity, many dropped their outer-structural inhibitions and interacted in unaccustomed inner-structural ways to help and be helped by others in getting through the occasion.
Relationships of commitment to kin and childhood friends prevailed.	Relationships of convenience to neighborhood friends and work friends emerged as optional interaction patterns.
Everywhere and always, people knew who they were, what their place was, where they stood, and what they should/should not, could/could not, and must/must not say and do.	Outside of their most intimate circles and their most formalized and ritualized interactions, people were relatively uncertain of who they were and what to expect of themselves and each other. To play it safe, therefore, they tended to keep each other socially at arm's length in these situations.

Inner	**Outer**
Connections between inner and outer structure were relatively clearly defined and understood.	Connections between inner and outer structure were relatively difficult to define and understand.
Interaction between and among the generations was relatively free, easy, and unself-conscious, as generational differences were minimized by overriding commitments to keep relationships viable, reaffirm everyone's sense of social and personal place, respect everyone's attempts to display community membership in accordance with pertinent norms, and thus safeguard the structural integrity and value system of the community.	Such interaction was often strained and hampered by conflicting values, incongruous expectations, and other generation-gap problems peculiar to a community with limited and weak connections between and among its inner structures, such as those made up of people who shared age-related values and lifestyles.
The dominant character of the community was inner-structural, even in outer-structural interaction, where informality, candor, sentimentality, ingenuousness, trust, etc. were more in evidence than called for by the rules for outer-structural interaction.	The dominant character of the community was outer-structural, even in inner-structural interaction, where formality, guardedness, rationality, etc. were more in evidence than called for by their rules for inner-structural interaction.
Working to earn money was a means to a local lifestyle end.	Working to earn money was a means to achieving career objectives which bore no necessary relationship to a local lifestyle.

Sagebrush locals whose overt behavior seemed to evidence a change of values or an impending disintegration of *Gemeinschaft* often were simply taking advantage of project-related, money-making opportunities—which also entailed certain risks for the community's existing social structure. These locals did not see the latter implications, firmly believing that their actions would just net them more money, strengthen their businesses, and ultimately help safeguard their valued traditional way of life. Such behavior can be understood in terms of certain interactions between inner and outer structure.

For example, the owner of a Sagebrush family business had enjoyed having a hand in all its basic work. As development neared, he deliberately expanded his operations into a highly competitive, money-making outfit that, as such, intersected much less than its predecessor with inner-structural circles of the community. Through various and regular gatherings of locals (who were generally inclined toward adopting an accommodative philosophy), this individual maintained connections between his business and personal ties to the community while taking big, nontraditional (but not antitraditional) risks by going after extensive contracts related to construction of the new power plant. However, as disillusionment with the company became widespread and antidevelopment traditionalists more outspoken, the perceived benefits of those risks waned considerably and tempered his desires to pursue further work with Bighole.

Meanwhile, one of the more prosperous landowners in the area was also taking big risks by adopting the position that he could use coal lease and coal production money to expand his ranch and make it more secure and enduring for generations to come. By fomenting contentious resource development and becoming an outspoken member of a dissident group of ranchers, this individual contributed substantially to splintering the local community. His was an antitraditional way of relating outer to inner structure in that he traded off, and risked further trading off, some of the inner structure for outer-structural gain, thus violating a traditional taboo. In the process, he and his fellow dissidents pretended to themselves and others that mixing ranching and coal development was both a feasible and a desirable way of protecting inner structure and making it more durable and viable. This was a case of de facto change of values. These landowners posited a new ideal—a mixture of coal development and ranching—and invented ways of bridging it with the actual, much as all ranchers had long done to color actual with ideal *Gemeinschaft* when parts of it were languishing, atrophying, etc. In contrast, several neighboring ranchers risked outer-structural change—and thus impingements on inner structure—*not* to make money, expand their ranches, and thus economically benefit their grandchildren, but by doing their best under the circumstances to keep coal development from destroying their ranching way of life.

The lifestyle in Sagebrush revealed that inner structure predominated, as evidenced by the everyday social occasions found in going to the post office, grocery store, or courthouse; the folksy way local boards and commissions ran public meetings; the personal consideration given people who sought or solicited certain city council actions; and the like. The town's outer structure served and was otherwise connected with ranchers as well as townspeople. For example, the board of county commissioners was long dominated by ranchers, who were the biggest local taxpayers; and landowners typically received preferential treatment at equipment repair shops and were valued customers at other places offering goods and/or services. Sagebrush's family businesses revealed how outer structure fronted for inner: they provided a means (making money) for inner-structural ends (family togetherness, time for fishing, personal contacts, etc.). "Success" was in the *Gemeinschaft* terms of keeping the business going well enough to secure what income the family needed to get by, not in the *Gesellschaft* terms of building up inventories, acquiring more floor space, increasing the number of employees, improving the business's competitive position, and otherwise preoccupying oneself with expansion and profits or other outer-structural concerns.

In these ways, Sagebrush's businessmen had long ago found a satisfactory solution to a problem inherent in capitalistic enterprise: "the contradictions of capitalism. . . have to do with the disjunction between the kind of organization and the norms demanded in the economic realm, and the norms of self-realization that are now central in the culture" (Bell 1976, p. 15). Then, when the rapid change of the construction period strained or severed connections between inner and outer structure, Sagebrush's businessmen, like the economist Power (1980), found that there is no necessary relationship between economic development and quality of life.

In general, Sagebrush locals managed to protect inner structure, but they were not prepared for the huge social and personal adjustments they had to make in doing so. For example, they were not accustomed to the necessity of tightening their social circles, i.e., intensifying interactions with their "own kind" when threatened by forces of change. Protecting outer structure was more difficult; for example, outside interests (e.g. from Junction City) saw to it that stores and services catering to newcomers' needs sprang up almost overnight, attracting a certain amount of trade away from established, locally owned businesses in the process. All concerned had to make adjustments to these and to such other impacts on community structure as higher incidences of crime, spouse and child abuse, mental illness, and the like. Involved in these problems were both longtimers and newcomers, who, for various reasons of social circumstance and personal character, were already among the principal victims and/or victimizers of rapid change. Moreover, rumors contributed to keeping the community off balance by kindling uncertainty about the course and consequences of Bighole's project, stirring up such deep emotional reactions as fear and suspicion, making it bewilderingly difficult to know what to think, feel, and do about the many friends and strangers continually reported to be the instigators of this or the victims of that, and thus, variously, and often unpredictably, upsetting normal interactions and relationships between inner and outer structure. Established residents of Sagebrush found that the various trespasses and other externally initiated and directed forces of

Gesellschaft hit all aspects of their community (see Hughes 1943; Shibutani 1978).

Predominant Areas

Even though inner and outer structure are intertwined, there are many instances in which one rather than the other is predominantly affected by externally induced impacts. The following chart presents some examples and accompanying analyses of these structural phenomena:

Phenomenon	Discussion
Inner-structural	
Feelings of vulnerability and subsequent tightening of social circles. The Sagebrush newspaper reported that some oldtimers were "trying [during the construction period] to maintain the status quo by living by the old rules, by not altering their way of doing their jobs, by running the community in customary ways . . . and hoping that, after the construction period, everything will return to 'normal.'"	Feelings of vulnerability are largely fears that inner structure may be penetrated and/or made nonviable by uncontrollable external impacts, since the latter invariably affect the connections between inner structure and its outer component. Many of these feelings come from fear of loss of place in and control of one's community, a sense of alienation and estrangement, perceptions of trespass, anxiety about one's continuing ability to safeguard and realize social and cultural values, etc.
Caring for elderly and handicapped members through a personal support network rather than through formalized agency services. "He's not a relative—he's a neighbor and very old and just needs someone to stand beside him" (a Sagebrush housewife).	Evidence of the kinds and severity of external impacts on a community is found in what happens to connections between and within inner and outer structure. Informal helping networks in process of complementing and supplementing formal ones (e.g. human service agencies) are examples of connections between inner and outer.
Three other logical possibilities of functional relationships between inner and outer structure are also	Allowing compassion and other sentiments to lead to preferential treatment of longtime, loyal, and

Phenomenon	Discussion
commonly found in human communities. Like the much-discussed relationship, the other three can also be spotted readily in rapid-change situations such as the one Sagebrush was in. These three are: (1) using inner structure to buttress and strengthen outer structure; (2) using outer structure to buttress and protect itself; and (3) using inner structure to buttress and safeguard itself.	dedicated employees of a big company ("the company takes care of its own") is another example of connections between inner and outer structure—and also an example of the tradeoffs which evolve between inner and outer structure. In this case, loyalty and hard work are exchanged for special personal and/or career considerations. These examples also reveal that inner structure is sometimes used to buttress or protect outer structure. The work of a chamber of commerce likewise reveals that outer structure is used to affirm, enhance, and protect itself, just as a regular Wednesday night poker or bridge game with old friends whose conversations affirm, enchance, and protect their relationships, values, worldview, reveals that inner structure likewise uses internal connections for its own sake. Even the management of communication among these old friends provides an example of using inner-structural considerations to protect inner structure—as when one of the friends avoids saying something which might damage valued relationships with the others.
Feeling off balance. "We really haven't done very well at handling the changes which have occurred. We're all sitting on pins and needles waiting for things to happen. We feel inadequate at trying to predict and handle what's going to happen" (a Sagebrush native).	When connections between and within community structures are not functioning well or in desired and accustomed ways—or, perhaps temporarily are not functioning at all—the main parts of community social structure may get so out of sync with each other

Phenomenon

Discussion

that the community may be said to have been thrown off balance, such as in the experience of a boom. Which connections are affected tell what kind of upset is in process and where, and the nature and extent of these effects tell about the intensity or magnitude of the impact on the community.

Newcomers accepted by established residents. "[Oldtimers] advocate a narrowly acceptable way to live if we want to fit in" (a construction worker).

"Fitting in" entails making suitable connections between new and established inner structures so that the new ones become *of* the community as well as *in* it. In a broad sense, it also entails making connections between new and established outer structures (e.g. between the new welfare office and the established offices which represent law enforcement) and between the changing inner and outer structures of the community.

Anxiety about the human and other environmental costs of operating Bighole's coal-fired power plant. A rancher who lived downwind from the plant, wrote a poem about the pain he felt from loss of a way of life he loved. It said: "Why does the flavor of gold in the air taste so of ashes and dust?"

As the power plant construction neared completion, Sagebrush ranchers wondered anxiously what socioenvironmental costs their community would have to pay for the economic "progress" the energy project would bring to it. They especially feared that industrialization would destroy the community's dominant inner-structural character.

Loss of sense of community as longtimers were suddenly outnumbered by newcomers. The Sagebrush newspaper reported: "[Oldtimers] feel that Sagebrush may be becoming a company town—in fact, if not the name. They are worried that Bighole's ca-

The feeling that one's community has been taken over is a conclusion which comes from actually perceived changes in outer structure, e.g., strange faces about town, many more vehicles on the street, lots of new children in school, many new mobile homes,

Phenomenon	Discussion
pability and resources for solving problems, e.g., related to water, sewer, and other services, will result in loss of [local] control to a benevolent paternalism."	much evidence of change in the town's appearance, etc. The conclusion is part of a fear that inner structure may be damaged or breached by the forces of change which appear to be in process of transforming the community's outer-structural buffer and altering the traditional functional relationship between outer and inner structure.
Rural helping networks respond to crises without formalized organization and rules. "When a member of the community dies, we don't have to get organized to help the family. Everyone knows what to do, and what others will do" (a Sagebrush mother of three).	Everyone felt certain unspoken inner-structural responsibilities. Natural and customary help was given to those in distress, facing crises, or experiencing emergencies on an individual or familial level.
Communal stability. If your family had ancestral roots in Sagebrush you could leave for a 30-year career and return to find that your place in the commmunity was still assured.	Many townspeople were related to each other and to the landowners in the vicinity, and everybody knew everybody. A widely shared, well-known, and secure sense of social place and continual reaffirmation of who one is and what life is and should be about are easily recognized manifestations of the dominant inner-structural character of the community.
Outer-structural Seeking personal profit from opportunities provided by the boom or bust. Energy development was, in the view of some in Sagebrush, their first chance to get a real mouthful of the American pie.	The few who became preoccupied with the prospect of making money on the deal offered them revealed a certain predilection for greed and, as such, a predisposition for individual (as opposed to communal) action which exploits the potential for outer-structural development without considering

Phenomenon	Discussion
	or being willing to be influenced by communal opinions regarding the action's likely effects on the established inner structure.
Formalizing social controls. "I'd rather pay an occasional fine than keep Shep tied up all the time. This new dog ordinance was Bighole's idea, not ours" (mood of Sagebrush locals).	Deviance was handled so as to protect inner-structural integrity and keep vital status relationships going amidst newcomer threats, i.e., situations irritating to newcomers were managed in outer-structural ways with minimal effect on the inner structure of the community.

The last two examples, taken from Hughes (1943), apply as well to Sagebrush:

Status positions. "In our community it is evident that French Canadians as a group do not enjoy that full confidence of industrial directors and executives which would admit them easily to the inner and higher circles of the fraternity—and fraternity it is—of men who run industry" (Hughes 1943, p. 53).	Community status determined principally by the job one held represented a new emphasis on outer-structural matters.
Locals seeking work that was foreign (or even threatening) to their way of life. "The system demands the departure [from the family farm] of all children but one son" (Hughes 1943, p. 8).	The fact that most young people had to go elsewhere to establish themselves economically was a consequence of insufficient connections between inner and outer structure.

Rather than address the kinds of phenomena just presented, most attention of social impact and other community change research is directed to obvious and relatively easy-to-quantify impingements and changes. As a consequence, the existing social structure's strengths and weaknesses are seldom identified or discussed in more than superficial ways.[18] Understanding these aspects of social structure is central to understanding how a community functions, ordinarily as well as in a period of rapid change.

The study of Sagebrush has shown that another important dimension of community structure is its vulnerability to the forces of industrialization. I have drawn from Sagebrush's experience to compile lists of outer- and inner-structural vulnerabilities of such an industrially impacted community. These lists are presented in the following section.

Vulnerabilities and Invulnerabilities

A *Gemeinschaft*'s outer structure is essentially reactive, rather than prone to initiate action, in the face of industrial (or other) interventions in the infrastructural and other aspects of the socioeconomy. For example, as the industrial project begins to materialize, many landowners are inundated by offers to allocate parcels of land for housing or commerical development, some for oil exploration, others for coal leasing, and the like. Merchants are intimidated by the multifarious possibilities for expanding their physical plants and/or inventories and otherwise gearing up for actual and expected sharp increases in business. Government officials are likewise under pressure to provide more space and staff to all community and county service agencies and to add new ones. None of these representatives of local outer structure is more than minimally certain of how and when to respond to the urban-industrial forces set in motion by the project, and much hand-wringing, frustration, and uncoordinated growth activity ensues. As a result of such threatening and bewildering impingements as these, people in rural communities ordinarily experience a sense of powerlessness and resignation when confronted by imagined, expected, and actual impacts of industrial intervention in their lives; consequently, they are inclined to wait for the interventionists to make their next move. This reactive stance, particularly of local government, is a vulnerability of the rural community's tradition-bound, change-resistant, *Gemeinschaft*-oriented outer structure. There are many other outer-structural vulnerabilities in an industrially impacted community like Sagebrush:

1. The presence of merchants willing to try competing in ways which might seriously strain or destroy the controlled competitive relationships they have long had with fellow businessmen in town.
2. The tradition of business activities being more a means to lifestyle ends than ends in themselves. (Vulnerable, too, was the valued inner-structural interaction with the many customers who were friends and neighbors.)
3. The potential of greed to upset traditional cooperative relationships and also create money/lifestyle issues new to the community.
4. A long history of getting by with marginal and submarginal community services.
5. Informal government. Locals are accustomed to running the com-

munity more on the basis of informal consensus than with formal rules and organizations, are disinclined to learn about bureaucracies and bureaucrats, and have an antipathy to public or other collective planning.

6. A tradition of handling differences, problems, issues, informally and accommodatively so as not to risk destruction of social relationships in any part of the community's social structure. Accordingly, locals eschew contentious, adversarial, formal, legalistic ways of settling these matters.

7. Politically naive elected officials and administratively weak appointed ones.

8. Ranchers' lack of control of the mineral rights to their land.

9. Local defenselessness against being overrun by people using the national energy shortage as an excuse to rip off the country's coal.

10. Uncertain continued availability of leased land and/or permits for grazing cattle on federal and/or state land. Ranchers with insufficient deeded acreage are at the mercy of bureaucrats who control such leasing and permitting.

11. The way of life. A large number of people with "different" values moving into town would foster much unwanted change. Industry, too, fears having to deal with unwanted change but is powerful enough to see to it that the locals make the principal lifestyle concessions—at least on an outer-structural level.

12. Lack of job opportunities for young adults. Few of those without project-related jobs can afford the economic cost of the social benefits to be gained by continuing to live in Sagebrush.

13. Indoor and outdoor recreation areas which are wide open to trespass, invasion, and succession.

14. The open land, nutritious vegetation, and pristine air and water. Various pollutants which come from coal-related industrial projects could damage these or otherwise seriously interfere with ranchers' dependence on the existing environment.

15. Lack of information, which fosters socially disruptive rumors and makes people susceptible to severe reactions of all sorts.

16. Population size. Locals are readily "Indianized" and otherwise elbowed into an ethnic status by large numbers of newcomers.

Inner structure has its own set of vulnerabilities to the forces of *Gesellschaft*:

1. Fictionalized and romanticized lifestyles (e.g., being so involved in ranching and family matters that ranchers are closer to neighbors culturally than socially). The most damaging externally induced impingements are those which impair locals' ability to idealize and otherwise imagine (to themselves as well as to outsiders) the positive aspects of life in their community.

2. As at Sagebrush, initial awareness of rural vulnerability to industrial interventions is usually a concurrence of uncommunicated individual experiences and is thus more a mass than a group phenomenon. It takes time and effort to modify the value of going it alone so that this awareness can be shared and dealt with communally.
3. A site-specific status and lifestyle. For some, it would be more correct to say they have a community-specific status and a lifestyle which depends on the community remaining small and changing slowly.
4. Surfacing of business-oriented ranchers which has the effect of disrupting the long-established inner circles to which, until then, they had belonged.
5. Valued ways of living which run counter to the larger society's notions of progress.
6. An insular and ethnocentric viewpoint.
7. A "fitting-in" process which can handle only a small number of newcomers at a time. Ordinarily it takes years to turn a newcomer into a sociological member of the community.
8. The fact that few ranchers own the mineral rights to their land jeopardizes their ability to control resource development disruptions of their attachment to the land and their associated family-centered way of life.

A certain arbitrariness is inherent in making the preceding lists, because the many connections between inner and outer structure inevitably make the vulnerability of one more or less the vulnerability of the other. Accordingly, these lists should be regarded as indicative of the vulnerabilities which occur more usually, prominently, and tellingly in one structure or the other. I shall conclude this enumeration by linking together two examples of relative vulnerabilities of inner and outer structure to such forces of change as those which occurred at Sagebrush.

1. It is axiomatic that concepts are usually more durable than associated structures and that people's values are among the most durable, hence most invulnerable, of concepts. Take the institution of outdoor recreation, for example. Sagebrushians value their concept of hunting, fishing, camping, hiking, and other outdoor recreation as highly as just about anything else in life, and have passed this value from one generation to the next. The process of realizing this value contributes much to the friendship of hunting partners, to one's ability to tell and appreciate stories about fishing, to one's general status as a member of the community, to the livelihood of the family that operates the local sporting goods store, to the overall quality of life at Sagebrush, and so on. The places where the outdoor recreation occurs are highly vulnerable to invasions by newcomers, and the social structures used in preparing for, engaging in, and recounting these activities are relatively vulnerable to such community changes. For example, residents who went to work for Bighole are on the job during much of the

hunting season and thus are in the unenviable position of having less recreational freedom than lifelong friends who have continued in jobs and businesses which permit taking off as much time as deemed natural and right for enjoying the season's outdoor recreational opportunities.[19] The value is preserved even though the individual's ability to continue organizing his life to realize the value may be sharply curtailed by changing community circumstances. In one extreme case, an individual decided that changes in local structure were interfering so much with his ability to achieve the recreational objectives intrinsic to this value that he packed up and moved to a remote part of Alaska, with the declared intention of returning after the dust of rapid growth had settled long enough for connections between concept and structure of outdoor recreation to be meaningfully and acceptably restored.

2. Community membership, once granted, is almost never withdrawn. The socialization process, which turns the newborn local or the older newcomer into a person who subscribes to the community's basic way of life and becomes an integral part of its social system, works continually to shape residents into Sagebrushians and to keep them that way. Young adults who had to go to bigger communities in the state to find employment (rarely would they venture out of state for this purpose) commonly returned to Sagebrush on weekends to reaffirm their continuing membership in the one place where they really fit in. When work opportunities opened up with the Bighole project, many of them took whatever Bighole job they could in order to return home permanently for their own sake and in order to rear their children where their own roots were.

When the big impacts of the construction phase of Bighole's project occurred, the relative invulnerability of community membership was more difficult than usual to maintain, and extreme measures were taken when deemed necessary to maintain it. Thus, when customary outdoor recreation sites were overrun by newcomers, temporary new ones were found. Likewise, when favorite bars and other indoor hangouts were similarly invaded and "taken over," locals found substitutes, such as the country club, to be sure they could continue making society with each other in accustomed ways for the duration of the construction intervention. In such ways, the locals rearranged their social circles, reaffirmed who they were and wanted to be as sociological beings, and thus safeguarded the core of their way of life and of their community and their membership in it.

All of us who have had occasion to spend some time in Las Vegas, to drive around its established residential areas, and to do a little chatting with the locals there are aware that, for these locals, "the duration" of impingements by itinerants on community outer structure is thought to be pretty open-ended. Consequently the locals have created and maintained neighborhoods in the city which are, in the kinds of respects just noted, tight little communities where they and their families can enjoy membership in *Gemeinschaften* which stand in sharp contrast to the dominant indoor recreational industry for which Las Vegas is so well known—and where so many of the locals work. Here, as in Sagebrush when Bighole intervened, the relative invulnerability of community membership has to be really worked at, particularly when community outer structure is functioning in some respects as a threat to inner structure and not so much as a buffer for and protector of it. It takes no great stretch of the imagination to see much comparability in the tightening of locals' social circles in these two places: in Sagebrush to keep the community "country" and in Las Vegas to keep the community respectably middle class.

The ability of a community's inner circles to safeguard their structural and functional integrity, to maintain essential connections with each other and with outer structure, and thus to protect and perpetuate the core of the local culture, accounts for much of the persistence of a community's characteristically *Gemeinschaft* way of life. The next section brings together some of the key elements and processes which account for the remarkable ability of *Gemeinschaft* to persist despite its vulnerabilities to internal and external forces of change.

Persistence of Gemeinschaft

One way of thinking about the ability of a *Gemeinschaft* to ride out the urbanizing storm of a boom or the deurbanizing one of a bust, and about its ability to survive in the middle of a metropolis and otherwise to cope with the forces of change, is to take note of the balancing act it performs when handling its relative vulnerability and invulnerability to such impingements. As the story of Sagebrush has shown, difficulties in performing this balancing act can arise from various sources, such as sociocultural tension, normative contradiction, and structural disjunction. While discussing the dynamics of society, Bell (1976) calls attention to the remarkable persistence of established forms of communal life even when the society (or community) in question is superficially unbalanced by forces of change. With regard to analyzing intrinsic forces of change, Bell (p. 14) offers this scheme:

> Within this [conceptual] framework, one can discern the structural sources of tension in the society [or in the community]: between a social structure (primarily techno-economic) which is bureaucratic and hierarchical, and a polity which believes, formally, in equality and participation; between a social structure that is organized fundamentally in terms of roles and specialization, and a culture which is concerned with the enhancement and fulfillment of the self and the "whole" person. In these contradictions, one

perceives many of the latent social conflicts that have been expressed ideologically as alienation, depersonalization, the attack on authority, and the
like. In these adversary relations, one sees the disjunction of realms.

As can be seen, Bell's conceptual scheme shows interrelationships among
what he regards as society's three principal realms, the technoeconomic
structure, the polity, and culture (the first two being roughly what I have
called the *Gesellschaft* aspects, the third the *Gemeinschaft* ones). As such,
his scheme fits well with the analytic framework I have used and may help
to shed further light on what happens in a community during periods of
waxing and waning of *Gemeinschaft* and during those of relatively little
change.

The mode of analysis used by Bell (1976, pp. 7-8) may also be useful for
explaining the essential persistence of society (or community) when impacted by extrinsic forces of change, such as those experienced by
Sagebrush:

> Despite our preoccupation with revelation, and later with revolution, the
> structures of a society—modes of life, social relations, norms and values—
> are not reversed overnight. The structures of power may change quickly: new
> men arrive, new routes of social ascent are opened, new bases of command
> created. Yet such dramatic overturns are largely a circulation of elites. So-
> cietal structures change much more slowly, especially habits, customs, and
> established, traditional ways. . . . If the intention of any science is to show us
> the structures of reality underlying appearances, then we have to understand
> that the time-dimensions of social change are much slower, and the processes
> more complex, than the dramaturgic mode of the apocalyptic vision, re-
> ligious or revolutionary, would have us believe.

At Sagebrush, readily apparent change was largely socioeconomic and
infrastructural, while the underlying *Gemeinschaft* aspects persisted with
relatively less manifest change. This change was more substantial than was
likely to be seen by any but those with intimate familiarity with the community, because the less qualified observer would have little or no awareness and understanding of what was happening to connections and
interactions between inner and outer structure. In Bell's terms, disjunction
occurred between the technoeconomic and the other realms of the community, a problem which calls for a probing analysis, such as the one being
used in this discussion of Sagebrush.

Like Bell, longtime student of development Gunnar Myrdal also reached
some conclusions which pertain to persistence of *Gemeinschaft*. Myrdal's
(1971, pp. 433-34) research led him to realize that social organizations and
ways of life in underdeveloped countries have a way of persisting despite
the best efforts of planners and others to bring economic and technological

stimuli to bear upon them. His reflections on these matters as he observed them in South Asia point out the remarkable persistence of *Gemeinschaft* there and elsewhere in the world and its resistance to efforts to bring about development (i.e. modernization):

> A major part of the work on planning for development in South Asia has been hindered by the assumption that beginning analysis can, be concentrated on the economic conditions—output and incomes, conditions of production, and levels of living—plus those policies that affect only these conditions. Frequently, even levels of living are ignored. There is also the assumption that the chain of causes linking these economic conditions is not affected by attitudes and institutions. Instead, it is often assumed that the latter will automatically be highly responsive to changes in the economic conditions.
>
> In reality, attitudes and institutions are stubborn and not easily changed, least of all indirectly. Policies, on the other hand, represent induced changes in the causal circle, applied to one or several of the economic and social categories; planning means coordination of policies to attain or speed up development.
>
> *Prima facie* the causal interdependence would seem to indicate a highly unstable social system where the force of change in one direction would move other conditions in the same direction. But in sharp contrast to this expectation are not only the common experience of low-level equilibrium in underdeveloped countries and the serious obstacles to development policies, but more generally the astonishing stability of most social systems in history. Balance, instead of being the fortuitous result of an obviously unstable combination of forces, seems to be the rule, not the rare exception. All our evidence suggests that social stability and equilibrium is the norm and all societies, particularly underdeveloped societies, possess institutions of a strongly stabilizing character. In view of these findings the real mystery is how they can escape from equilibrium and can develop.

Some of the features of the persistence of *Gemeinschaft* at Sagebrush, which are listed below, may well be present in all *Gemeinschaften* and may therefore help explain the remarkable "equilibrium," and thus the "mystery" of development, in the social systems on which Myrdal was reflecting.

A community like Sagebrush is far too open, trusting, informal, politically weak, and economically naive for its own good when faced with development which entails rapid, large-scale industrialization. Nevertheless, it manages to compensate for these cultural and structural handicaps in dealing with rapid growth by relying on its relatively invulnerable ability to cope by tuning out much of the change in order to stay tuned to the sights and sounds, thoughts and feelings, and actions and interactions in its traditional ways of making society. Some of the key elements and processes in the ability of people living in a *Gemeinschaft* to "roll with," fend off, or otherwise handle impacts of change and keep their essential way of life intact are the following.

First, *Gemeinschaft* members do remarkably well at taking outer-structural changes out of account by participating minimally in them, during the course of which they deliberately focus attention and behavior on the established and familiar parts of outer structure. Examples of these parts are the post office, the courthouse, the customary tables at local restaurants (which they occupy in such a steady flow that newcomers intuitively shy away from them), and the rod and gun club, country club, or the American Legion hall. As centers of much of Sagebrush's social life, even during the construction period, the local schools also did much to help *Gemeinschaft* to persist.

Second, concurrently, members do remarkably well at taking traditional inner structure into account in consciously, and sometimes deliberately, protective ways. Examples are making one's social circles more exclusive than previously; making an effort to become more sensitive to cultural and interactional concerns of intimates and neighbors; stressing more overtly and more often the words, phrases, behavior patterns, and other symbols of membership in one's family, in other social circles, and in the community as a whole; going out of one's way to reaffirm the social identities and sense of social place of friends and less intimate community acquaintances, and receive such reaffirmation from them in return; using inner structure as a refuge from the interventive effects of the development project or other proximate sources of change.

Third, they become more aware of basic values previously taken for granted. They see more clearly the differences between the ideal and the actual in the local way of life, and make greater effort to bring the actual closer to the ideal, for example through revitalizing relationships with neighboring ranchers. They reaffirm local values and commitments to the common good by minimizing and/or holding in check tendencies to pursue self-interests, exercise free will, and become greedy when such behavior would be incompatible with and/or antithetical to collective interests and community integrity and thus to the general welfare.

Fourth, they react to sociocultural and related impingements of the development project by hanging onto the traditional ways more doggedly and with greater resolve than previously, for example by stubbornly fighting against all manner of rational argument for comprehensive land-use planning; by clinging to the old ways of running the city and county governments, when modernizing and professionalizing them would probably bring the rapid growth and increasing complexity of outer structure under much more administratively desirable and cost-effective control (after a few years, modernization does occur but it is restricted for the most part to relatively negotiable concepts, structures, and behaviors); and by selecting from the present those artifacts, ideas, and modes of social interaction which they believe will fit in with their customs and values.

Fifth, they use established holidays and ad hoc occasions to bring large numbers of community members together to display, commemorate, and reaffirm community sentiments, values, and beliefs. Examples are holding bigger and better 4th of July parades and ceremonies, and putting on pageants to observe local historical events which have previously been given little or no public recognition. These kinds of behavior enable the local *Gemeinschaft* to persist in a remarkably steady way in spite of the impact of forces to which it might otherwise react with a much greater range of waxing and waning.

Summary

In both urban and rural communities, *Gemeinschaft* and *Gesellschaft* are interdependent and interrelated. Neither can exist or be understood without the other. In the course of surviving, *Gemeinschaft* waxes and wanes in response to social processes from within and without. Examples of this waxing are the community membership-reaffirming interaction which occurs when friends come together in homes and voluntary associations, the immediate reactions to industrialization or natural disaster, and what ensues when the impact of industrialization abates or is otherwise brought under locally acceptable control. Examples of waning are the tendency of people to restrict their interaction to smaller and smaller social units and reactions to long construction periods and other prolongations of externally induced impacts on the community.

Other dimensions of waxing and waning of *Gemeinschaft* are examined and a restatement of highlights of the ups and downs of *Gemeinschaft* at Sagebrush is presented. Likewise, additional dimensions of inner and outer structure are indicated and the role of pretense in using inner and outer structure in mutually protective ways is discussed.

Drawing from the data on Sagebrush and from comparisons of Sagebrush with two other socially impacted communities, examples are given of contrasts between inner- and outer-structural behavior. Following these are examples of inner- and outer-structural phenomena which occurred in Sagebrush while it was being industrialized by Bighole's project. These examples are particularly noteworthy because they are important rapid-growth experiences generally given slight attention in community studies which focus on obvious and relatively easy-to-quantify impingements and changes.

Notes

1. These included: shifts in the selection of friends, strains in communicating with friends and neighbors of long standing, the making of social class alignments previously considered unimportant, a shift in the established power structure from the ranchers to the new mining industrialists, the need to live with constant uncertainties for which planning was virtually impossible, a keen interest on the part of some locals in immediate monetary gain, the need to accommodate to the invasions and requirements of newcomers who subscribed to foreign lifestyles and value systems, and loss of a sense of community.

2. As indicated in note 4 of chapter 2, this and other such quotes are from the fieldwork files kept by my associates and me.

3. This attitude prevailed in spite of the belief that a local veteran of Vietnam was the first to introduce "pot" and the rumor that young locals returning from college first introduced other drugs.

4. *Gesellschaft* waxes and wanes for these and related reasons, and, even though attention is here focused on *Gemeinschaft*, many such reasons are revealed in those parts of the present discussion which deal with ties and interactions between *Gemeinschaft* and *Gesellschaft*.

5. In this discussion of waxing and waning of *Gemeinschaft* I am talking in each case about net effect, because not all parts of the *Gemeinschaft* are affected in the same way, and therefore at any given time not all parts are changing in the same direction at the same rate.

6. Or, the surviving shells of the family units and individuals of which the villages of Buffalo Creek had been composed may simply be incapable of functioning again as members of a community. In any event, this case calls attention to the need to account for the various categories of individual casualties of rapid change, invasion, and dislocation, as well as of collective trauma. *Gemeinschaft* certainly does not provide perfect protection for all its members even in a Sagebrush type of situation. As few of the newcomers to such a community have a protective and sustaining network of support available to them, it is likely that many of them pay a high personal price for whatever economic benefits the boom situation may offer.

7. Shibutani's (1978) study of demoralization of Japanese-American enlisted men in "Company K" of the U.S. Army in World War II is full of examples of waxing and waning of *Gemeinschaft* in response to changes in military directives, formal leadership, definitions of the situation, morale, and the like. These changes came thick and fast, and Shibutani's description of them is a veritable treasure trove of insiders' views and interpretations of these roller-coaster impacts of outer upon inner structure and of inner structure upon itself.

8. Like the urban resident Fischer (1982, p. 236) writes about, some of these sociologists may go so far as to personally reconnoiter a neighborhood: "What an urban resident, whether a 'typical American' or the member of a small subculture, sees when he or she walks through urban centers is the public display of a variety of social worlds, each appearing exotic, or distasteful, or even threatening." When such "eyeballing" is done in rural areas, it leads to similar impressions since, in both cases, the observer is seeing displays of outer structure and of outer-structural façades of inner structure.

9. Suttles (1968, pp. 73-80) found this widespread use of outer structure among

the ethnics he studied in Chicago where, as he pointed out, most socializing takes place "on the street" rather than indoors, thus protecting intimate aspects of family life from external examination and evaluation. He also observed (1968, p. 49) that, in some outer-structural settings in this ethnic area of Chicago, inner-structural interaction predominates in order to keep business transactions from diminishing the *Gemeinschaft* quality of residents' lives: "[In the ethnic store,] all economic transactions [with regular customers] are buried in the guise of friendship and sentiment. . . . Among themselves the customers set aside their public face and disclose much of their private life to one another. Their conversations, their exchanges, and their understandings are simply too intimate to be carried out before the general public." For the most part, outer structure fronts for inner structure. Yet as the foregoing indicates, within a *Gemeinschaft's* outer structure, inner-structural interaction is selectively used as a façade to minimize the obvious fact that (in Suttles's example) the customers and the merchant are in the store to engage in an economic transaction which, by its very nature, is essentially outer-structural. Thus business gets done, friendship is maintained, and community membership is reaffirmed in and through such patterns of interaction in the tradition-oriented store.

10. In contrast to Sagebrushians, who moved freely between the community's inner and outer structure, the West Enders in Boston (Gans 1962) restricted themselves largely to "peer group" (inner-structural) activities, leaving it to others to get involved in the affairs of the larger community. The *Gemeinschaft* situation Gans described may well be representative of other big-city *Gemeinschaften* in this respect. A certain ghetto-like insulation from the larger community, one in which we-they contacts occur principally in the marketplace, may be almost essential for controlling socialization and protecting the way of life of the ethnic community.

11. Glossed portrayals may be done deliberately in various other ways for various other reasons (e.g. to display, mathematize, be calculative) by sociologists as well as by members. They may also be done unwittingly as part of a social convention for expressing inner-structural concerns in outer-structural terms. Casper and Wellstone (1981, p. 246) give an example drawn from the experience of a Minnesota farmer who testified against a proposed powerline across his land: "'If, in fact, the issue all along was one of intrusion on the land, then our attempts to address technological questions were at best irrelevant.'"

12. Some years ago, I wrote a review (Gold 1977) of Jack Douglas's (1976) book on investigative social research. Douglas was obviously frustrated by the "fronts" which many of his informants presented to him and his coworkers and advocated doing practically anything which would reveal the truth that his informants were concealing behind their outer-structural responses to his questions about inner structure and inner-structural behavior. Although the research procedures Douglas advocated are technically and morally unacceptable to social science, he was at least more aware than most social scientists appear to be of the tendency of people to present "fronts" even when asked to play the role of informant and thus to be willing to tell the fieldworker all about what goes on in the inner circles of their lives. However, Douglas failed to understand what "fronts" actually are and how they function in relation to the areas of human behavior which are less visible and accessible to social scientists as well as to the more casual observer. The present analysis of outer and inner structure should help to clear up much of the confusion and misrepresentation which pervades Douglas's version of doing social research.

13. The principal partcipant-observation method is ethnography. One of the ethnographer's basic fieldwork objectives is to develop mutual trust and respect with informants, an approach to generating information which lends itself well to tuning in on inner structure. Ethnography functions well as an inner-structural form of interacting and building relationships which quite naturally foster inner-structural telling and showing by informants. As Suttles (1968, p. 11) pointed out, building these relationships can be quite a challenge, for it took him a year to "penetrate" inner structure in his study of the Addams area of Chicago. Erikson (1976, p. 14) noted a similar experience in his study of the flood victims in West Virginia's Buffalo Creek area. When mutual trust finally developed, inner-structural information began to flow (Lofland 1973).

14. As an example, look at virtually any social impact assessment report. The relatively few exceptions are those which relied heavily on ethnographic analysis.

15. The interrelationships and interdependencies between inner and outer structure are good examples of the following insightful generalization offered by Erikson (1976, p. 82): "The identifying motifs of a culture are not just the *core values* to which people pay homage but also the *lines of point* and *counterpoint* along which they diverge. That is, the term 'culture' refers not only to the customary ways in which a people induce conformity in behavior and outlook but the customary ways in which they organize diversity. In this view, every human culture can be visualized, if only in part, as a kind of theater in which certain contrary tendencies are played out."

16. However, as will soon be shown, this avoidance also has a functional side.

17. How far these generalizations go I do not know, but they are based on comparisons I made of Sagebrush with Cantonville (Hughes 1943) and the "Poletown" area of Detroit (City of Detroit 1980) which colleagues and I studied for the social impact statement before this residential area was cleared for an industrial project.

18. To find adequate analyses of community structure, look for social impact assessment reports based largely on ethnographic analysis. See for example, Gold et al. (1974a) and Dixon (1975).

19. Not included in this discussion of outdoor recreation are other important reasons why, in Sagebrush, hunting is an essential part of the community's lifestyle. For example, the recreational aspects of hunting are not separable from its part in supplying food, teaching children the proper use of firearms and hunting sites, and reaffirming man-land relationships.

7

Toward Socially Enlightened Natural Resource Development

Chapters 2 and 3 pointed out many aspects of the process of introducing Bighole's coal development project which locals viewed as leaving a great deal to be desired. The present chapter will bring together some highlights of this sequence of events to make some more general points about how the sequence is ordinarily handled in energy development projects, how it could or should be handled, what the ethical and value issues in the two principal ways of handling the sequence are, and some concluding remarks on theoretical, methodological, practical, and moral implications of what the discussion shows to be the preferred way of handling this sequence of events.

Bighole's Traditional Approach

Bighole's traditional approach to doing a resource development project was grounded in many years of experience in the politics as well as in the other aspects of coal development. Davis's (1982, pp. 56-57) conceptualization of the politics of coal helps to explain this dimension of the tradition of developmental prerogatives which, as we have seen, so strikingly shaped its approach to doing the project at Sagebrush.

> The politics of coal derives first from the *physical properties* of the fuel. The fact that it is solid, found close to the surface, and high in energy for its volume led to its early exploitation by a simple technology. Hence, small, privately owned business set the pattern for later development. The fact that it is found most frequently in the Appalachian Mountains led to its coming to dominate the politics of a few states, such as Pennsylvania, West Virginia, and Kentucky, while their coastal neighbors such as New Jersey, Delaware, and the New England states remained unscarred. The recent discovery that coal may be mined profitably in the Great Plains has brought turmoil to the Big Sky Country, pitting the established ranchers against the interloping coal

companies. Many a cattleman feels suddenly victimized by the black rock buried under his grasslands, for if he is to garner its wealth he must sacrifice his way of life.

If the physical characteristics of coal in part explain its politics, so too do its *market characteristics*. Coal was the quintessential "sick industry." Demand declined relatively (and often absolutely) from the post–World War I year of 1919 until the mid-1970's. This decline cast a pall over the politics of coal. Decreasing need for the fuel caused unemployment in the 1920s and John L. Lewis's backlash in the 1930s, when he found an ally in Franklin D. Roosevelt. The industry's sickness continued, however, even after the New Deal's assistance and still afflicts its politics. The corruption, violence, and criminality plaguing the United Mine Workers could not have been so widespread in a healthy, expanding industry.

The third set of independent variables explaining an arena's policy process relates to its *general political environment*. Since coal has such a long history, it is the product of many transcending issues. As it entered the twentieth century it was firmly rooted in laissez-faire attitudes. Private ownership and the free market held sway. Government regulations had no place. These nineteenth-century attitudes continue to dominate coal to a greater extent than any other form of energy. Yet the arena has not escaped totally the impact of other trends. The New Deal profoundly affected the process, greatly enhancing the role of the union. Today the environmental movement is a predominant influence, but it clashes head-on with the sudden resurgence in demand generated by the energy crisis of the 1970s.

Galbraith (1971, p. xiv) calls attention to another facet of the politics of the large corporation's mode of operations:

> It is central to my case that power in the modern industrial society resides with the large producing organizations—the large corporations. So, far from being safely and resignedly subordinate to the market, as the neoclassical argument holds, they fix prices and go on extensively to accommodate the consumer to their needs. And they also obtain from the state such further action as is needed to insure a benign and stable environment for their operations.

In short, the large corporation has been accustomed to having its way. Bighole's actions at Sagebrush are a good case in point. Initial contacts by Bighole's representatives were not with county or town officials but with ranchers, the landowners who lived where the coal was, whose land would be crossed by water lines serving the future generating plant and by power lines carrying high-voltage electricity from it, and whose signatures on leasing agreements were sought. The ranchers soon learned that these "lease hounds" were devious and untrustworthy and were treating them as adversaries even when pretending to be friendly. These initial contacts with Bighole's personnel were real eye-openers to the ranchers, as they had always identified with and admired big business. Now they found that the people who worked for Bighole were there as exploiters and colonizers, driven almost solely by economic and technical concerns.

Learning that Bighole was not interested in taking into account the locals' growth problems, values, wishes, concerns, traditions, was in itself distressing to the ranchers and, soon afterwards, to others in the community who had occasion to be contacted by Bighole. In addition, the locals were discovering that Bighole was displaying an array of unredeeming and frightening tactics. The community's experience revealed that the company was given to deceiving, bluffing, pressuring, and intimidating the locals; keeping them in a state of uncertainty and capitalizing on knowledge of their vulnerabilities; disseminating inaccurate and unreliable information about the project; keeping the local rumor mills going full blast, thus contributing to keeping the community confused and off balance; allowing locals no voice in plans and decisions regarding the effects of the project on the environment and their way of life; challenging local values by imposing urban industrial values and behavior patterns on the community; contributing nothing to making the public participation part of the EIS process meaningful and worthwhile for the local public; leaving local government to its own resources to plan for and handle the rapid expansion of community services, land-use regulations, etc.; and so on.

Sagebrush felt that it was being colonized and that this exploitation was requiring it to pay exorbitant lifestyle costs for the energy benefit of the nation.[1] Locals became increasingly cynical about the alleged progress [2] which Bighole's project was supposed to exemplify. The community (especially the ranchers) reacted to all this, finally, by organizing the Rangeland Protective Association to secure accurate, reliable, and timely information regarding the project and its impact and to help the residents understand and protect their interests. The RPA affiliated with its state counterpart, the Mountain State Resource Council. Through these organizations, the locals were able to monitor the project, document its failure to comply with certain EIS and permit requirements, file complaints to state and federal permitting agencies (e.g. State Department of Health and U.S. Environmental Protection Agency) regarding these failures, and thus play a role in protracting the EIS study period and delaying approval of various components of the construction, both of which were very costly to the project. These activities contributed to the hardening of the adversarial relationship which Bighole had already established with the locals. The relationship had not changed appreciably even after the first year of operation of the power plant and the coal mine which fueled it.

Just how typical is this sequence of events? How representative of the handling of energy development projects in general and coal development projects in particular is this sketch of Sagebrush's experience with the handling of Bighole's project? Keeping in mind (a) that because Bighole is a traditional company, its project at Sagebrush was handled as most coal and other mining companies and utility companies had "always" handled them (notwithstanding the modifications needed to cope with the requirements of the National Environmental Policy Act of 1969 [and as amended] and the recent requirements of permitting agencies); (b) that coal development projects usually have a much higher impact on the human and other aspects of the environment than oil and gas projects do; and (c) that the present story of Sagebrush is a composite portrayal of community impacts of coal development in the rural West—it is still fair to say that the handling of the Bighole project at Sagebrush is representative of the handling of energy (and of most mining and other natural resource) development projects in the United States.

As Fitch (1968) has pointed out, national development policies are linked to sociopolitical processes which may or may not transcend the interests of the particular groups concerned. Fitch's (1968, p. 287) observations help to make more understandable the broader context in which a tug of war has taken place between narrow self-interest and social enlightenment in development programs—as illustrated by what has been happening in energy development projects:

> A strictly political interpretation of the great national development policies would see them not as expressions of the national will in any meaningful sense, but rather as the vector of forces representing the various groups contending for advantage. In its most extreme form, this interpretation holds that social goals, aiming to promote the general welfare, play no significant part in mobilizing national action; that at best they are formulated by planners and others seeking to advance their own limited perception of the national interest, and that at worst they are perverted by special interests to serve their own purposes. My own view is that this is too cynical and narrow an interpretation of social idealism in general and, in particular, of the great national goals which mobilized generations of effort in such fields as education and public health. To put the matter another way, the forces generated by broadly accepted national goals and concepts of the general welfare generate forces which influence the direction of the national policy vector. Moreover, it would appear that the formulation and pursuit of explicit national goals is increasingly important in the sociopolitical process. The sponsor of the Eisenhower Commission on National Goals was, after all, the least interventionist-minded President of modern times. Daniel Bell points out that the reaching for a rationalistic view that transcends group interests is associated also with the increasing importance in government policy of matters that transcend group interests, such as foreign policy and economic growth [see Bell 1967; Heller 1966].

To do even a rough sorting of sheep from goats as regards the social enlightenment and overall progressiveness embodied in energy companies' economic growth scenarios, close attention must be given to what they actually do versus how they talk about what they do when undertaking development projects. No energy company likes to present itself to the world as "the bad guys," so even the Bigholes among them like to put up a front of acting in the national interest, acting now to meet what they like to think will be the needs of their customers in the next decade or two, and so on. But, like Bighole, they act traditionally. That is to say, energy companies ordinarily make projections of future energy needs in their board rooms; they do so largely in terms of trying to meet their own economic objectives; and they run their projects in the Bighole manner.

Even though more energy companies tend to act in the Bighole manner than not, some of these traditionalists believe that it is good for their public image to appear to be making efforts to right the wrongs of their colonialist past, so they try to act as though they were following the path of righteousness. When doing energy development projects, such companies sometimes spend a lot of money on image-glorifying public relations campaigns, high-priced showcase consultants, and fancy-looking EIS reports. They may even make a show of donating a building or a piece of land to the locally impacted community. Or they may go so far as to arrange to prepay some taxes on their forthcoming physical plant to enable the local community to begin expanding the schools, the police force, etc., in preparation for the large influx of newcomers that their project will attract to town. Understandably, they avoid saying in so many words that they will never make serious efforts to accommodate to the locals because they can always pass along litigative and other project-related costs to their consumers. They usually try to make some gesture of accommodation to the locals mainly because of the pressure they feel from awareness that some of the bigger firms in the industry have recently had experiences whose startling lesson was that "it pays to do the project right" socially and culturally as well as economically and technically. Even a company like Bighole feels such pressure from these significant others in the industry.

But do most companies work with the local community to plan for the rapid growth and get their acts together to minimize the associated impacts? Do these traditional companies see to it that the locals have a significant voice in project-related decisions of interest and concern to the community? Do such companies go out of their way to comply with the spirit as well as the letter of NEPA's requirements? Of course not. Their game is to pretend that they are environmentally and socially concerned while still functioning in the Bighole manner. They invariably give themselves away when faced with tough opposition by environmentalists or with a local community which takes them at their word and insists on getting straight answers to hard questions about community impacts and other-wise insists that the company "do the project right" so as to really soften and make locally acceptable its impact on the community. They give themselves away in these cases because they really do not believe in what they proclaim about their environmental and social enlightenment. To really "do the project right" in these respects would seemingly cost the company much more than top management thinks would be "cost-effective," so the company reverts to type when faced with litigative or community pressures which call its bluff by demanding that it commit itself to substantial expenditures for safeguarding the environmental and community objects of its pretended concern.[3]

Are there *any* energy and/or other natural resource development companies which understand and accept that "it pays to do projects right"? The answer is yes, but they are only few and are still feeling their way along uncharted courses of action in their attempts to redefine traditional economic and technical imperatives in light of their socially enlightened concerns about the effects of their projects on both natural and human aspects of the environment. The going is not easy for them. A principal reason for this is the lack of unanimity among top- and middle-management personnel in even the most vanguardish of these companies regarding what being socially enlightened and progressive really mean. Another important reason is their uncertainty about just how far and how fast it would be in the interest of all concerned for them to deviate from the industry's time-honored, cost-effective, and respected traditions (Gold 1981).

If the traditional definition of cost effectiveness, which is couched solely in terms of maximizing dollar profits, is broadened to give weight to social as well as economic factors, there is a substantially greater likelihood that "doing a project right" will help make it cost-effective. To examine this likelihood, let us turn to situations in which cost effectiveness was defined in terms of managing social impacts of a resource development so as to optimize monetary returns on the project.[4] The several energy and other natural resource development companies which have undertaken such managment have clearly been doing some ground-breaking work in cost-effective community development.

Cost-Effective Community Development

How did natural resource development companies get around to doing this ground breaking? The study of power plant siting done by Johnson and Weil (1977) helps to answer this question by giving some background information on it. They describe the traditional "instrumental orientation" of utility companies in which the environment is seen solely as a means to an economic end and therefore as having no value in itself. After state and federal environmental protection laws forced such companies to complete environmental impact assessments before major projects were approved, the early environmental impact statements were little more than pro forma efforts to fulfill legal and/or bureaucratic requirements, particularly with respect to the constraints that applied to the social environment. The latter were usually addressed in an occasional sentence or two about "quality of life." But as public awareness grew about the implications of such regulations as those that implemented the National Environmental Policy Act (NEPA), and as public interest groups and members of impacted communities became more adept at recognizing and voicing concern about the social costs of rapid growth, the social component of the environment became a major issue in resource development projects.

Considering that a narrow economic conception of cost effectiveness, or efficiency, has long been central to the industrial firm, it is understandable that industry has shown little inclination to make room on the bottom line of resource development for any but its narrowly conceived economic entries.

> The theory of the firm—and one most honored even by the large corporation and its technostructure—is that every firm operates most efficiently when it externalizes . . . negative externalities (and attempts to internalize positive ones, wherever possible). Efficiency is the standard of accountability, the ideological basis, for the industrial system and individual corporations. Other goals must be *forced* politically into the calculus of the firm, directly or indirectly, by governments and organized political forces [Schnaiberg 1980, p. 139].

Such being the case, it is remarkable that even a few resource development firms have been moving toward taking the social component of the environment into account when calculating the cost effectiveness of their projects.

The Cyprus Mining Company's molybdenum mining project at Thompson Creek near Challis, Idaho is a good example of a project which has become part of the cutting edge of the industry's emerging concept of cost effectiveness. The project manager and other key officials of the company valued doing right by the locals as well as by the stockholders; that is, these executives conceived of "doing the project right" as important in and of itself and not just as a means to fattening profits.[5] Because they demonstrated that they were tuned in to the locals' values and concerns and dealt openly with them in the earliest planning stages, residents decided to risk balancing their worries about way-of-life matters with the job benefits that they perceived would result from the project. Consequently, representatives of the community resisted efforts by environmental groups to intercede in the environmental impact statement hearings. Locals, who felt they were aware of and capable of dealing with the social and other risks associated with the project, resented and openly criticized "outsiders'" efforts to question the project's plans with respect to environmental risks.

When the Cyprus–Thompson Creek Project began the process of securing government permits and making environmental impact assessments, it engaged consultants in community and social impact analysis to help the small, isolated community of Challis and the company prevent and minimize the social and socioeconomic impacts of the project. A Los Angeles firm, Resource Assessment, Inc., was charged with planning all aspects of the development (housing, community relations, etc.) other than the mining and milling operations per se. Social Research and Applications, based at Missoula, Montana, sent sociologists to do the social impact assessment for the EIS and monitored social and socioeconomic impacts of the project throughout most of its construction phase. Together, personnel of these two consulting firms helped the company and the community to understand each other's objectives, accommodate differences, develop and maintain mutual trust, prepare realistically for rapid community growth, make certain that locals and near-locals would be given hiring preference to minimize the influx of people not likely to fit into the local way of life and, in general, to keep all concerned in the company and the community informed about what would happen to their complex relationship if certain actions were or were not taken in certain ways within certain time frames.

The history of most resource development companies reveals that they did not begin to address social issues as Cyprus has done until they had already suffered substantial economic loss related to failure to take these issues into account. However, some far-sighted executives have come to recognize that "doing things right" for the people concerned has a desirable economic payoff for the company. One official, addressing an audience of industry representatives, is quoted in the Cornerstone (1980b, p.11) report:

> We can't prove it, but we know that people's needs, when taken into consideration early and sincerely, will save money down the line. Formulate your vision, plan for the high risk, and set your objectives. Don't be afraid to take some chances or try something unusual [to avoid and minimize social impact].

Another observer said:

> The attitude of senior management is crucial. In Calgary Power's Dodds Round Hill project, field people and the assistant vice president accepted the need for community involvement and careful social impact assessment but [other] vice presidents and [the] president rejected the approach. They were authors of their own misfortune and continue to be[6] [Cornerstone 1980b, p. 69].

As in most bureaucracies, decisions made in large resource development companies which affect the local community are often made according to the short-term economic criteria of staff accountants in a distant regional office. The long-term costs of those decisions to the company are rarely evaluated.

Costs of Failure to Manage Social Planning

Companies which fail to incorporate adequate social planning into the design and implementation of their projects pay a number of specific costs. These include: project delays and cancellations, uncertainties affecting the proposed timetables for construction and/or operation, losses in worker productivity, community resistance, and a poor company reputation.

Delays. Loucks (1978, p. 2) writes:

> Failure to take responsibility for the environmental costs associated with a development project could lead to a project being delayed or cancelled after an initial investment had been made. Since the financing of large-scale technologies requires intensive capital investments, any cancellations or project delays can result in considerable economic loss.

Delay is one of the most common and costly results of failure to adequately assess and deal with social impacts. A Massachusetts Institute of Technology paper prepared for the Energy Research and Development Administration quotes a number of representatives of large energy companies with projects in the rural West on this subject:

> In an inflationary era, delays in construction of a new facility increase costs substantially. Moreover, increases in potential costs are apt to be substantial as in the case of the Basin Electric Power Cooperative's Laramie River Station [West 1977, pp. 15-16].

Other company officials estimate that spending several hundred thousand dollars for growth management in the local community can prevent millions of dollars in expensive delays. Relationships with local residents can affect company decision making because locals have the capability of enacting regulations that retard or prohibit facility construction—or which make it easier. The MIT paper reports:

> When the Puget Sound Power and Light Company approached Skagit County with a proposal to construct a nuclear power plant there . . . the county could have prevented the facility's construction by doing nothing— i.e., by declining to reclassify 260 acres which had been zoned as "forestry/ recreation and residential" [West 1977, p. 20].

Background documents for the draft environmental impact statement for the Cyprus–Thompson Creek Project reveal that the values of the local community were clearly identified; further, the significance of those values for forecasting and dealing with the social impact of the project was recognized and acted on by the proponent. Consequently, the hearings process for the final EIS created no delay because there were no citizens' concerns that had not been already addressed.

The Loucks (1978, p. 57) study analyzes eight projects, at the point in the project development when the project was cancelled or delayed, to calculate percentage of lost capital/total capital costs and concludes: "The earlier in project development that environmental problems are identified the lower the percentage of lost capital/total capital costs."

Cancellation. It is rare for a project to be cancelled solely because of environmental issues that were neglected or inadequately managed, but it has happened (as at Kaiparowitz in southern Utah) and some observers believe it will happen more frequently as changing public attitudes and political developments become more influential in the 1980s. Cancellations have also occurred because delays have caused the projects to become economically too risky or unfeasible. Writing about the sluggish molybdenum market, *Business Week* (December 7, 1981) noted: "Within the next several months, four new mines are likely to be producing." And, in fact, proposed mines that were delayed, after initial investments had already been made (e.g. AMAX's in Gunnison County, Colorado, and in western Washington), did lose out to those that were about to become operational.

Uncertainties. Failing to adequately address the community's concerns may result in uncertainties in a project's timetable or actually bring on costly changes in design after commitments have been made. These problems can be avoided if good relationships have been developed and maintained. The MIT paper states:

> Robert Huff, a community developer also working for Atlantic Richfield, believes that cooperation with a variety of local communities has been highly beneficial for the company because of the communication, rapport, and respect that have resulted. Another major advantage that he identifies is that of being able to remain on schedule during construction [West 1977, p. 11].

Supporting Huff's concern, researcher-economist John Gilmore (1976, p. 535) says: "Besides fostering conflict, this sort of boom growth almost inevitably generates a situation that causes overruns in both time and the money required to get projects built and operating."

In Challis, Cyprus officials took early action to try to minimize inevitable uncertainties. The sociologists commented publicly on such action:

> Anticipation and delay are causing rumors and uncertainty. These "unknowns" are sometimes the hardest issues for action-oriented rural Wester-

ners to deal with. For that reason, the technical assistance of several Cyprus community consultants has been especially important in helping local city, school, and county officials and local businessmen find ways of "getting ready" for the expansion [*Challis Messenger*, May 8, 1980].

Productivity/Turnover. Scheduling uncertainties are also associated with the social problems of workers on the project. Turnover related to recruitment practices, the housing situation, and working conditions negatively affects productivity, according to a number of studies (Gilmore 1976; West 1977; Metz 1980). While the locals' interest in these matters parallels the company's, their reasons differ. The locals' overriding concern is with protecting the quality of their valued way of life, whereas (genuine humanistic concerns notwithstanding) company executives are understandably interested in protecting the social environment of the local community as a means of optimizing interaction between employee absenteeism, turnover, and productivity on the one hand and return on investment on the other. In the words of Robert Quenon of Carter Oil Company, "[We] want the best workers and that requires a desirable setting" (West 1977, p. 15).

In their study of energy development at Rock Springs, Gilmore and Duff (1975, p. 20) report: "The quality-of-life problems are more than mere inconveniences. They are directly damaging to industrial activity in Sweetwater County." Gilmore (1976, p. 536) attributed much of the difficulty of recruiting and retaining satisfactory employees to the quality-of-life problems in Rock Springs: "It is difficult to attract and retain a satisfactory work force, . . . for building and operating a power plant or gasification plant, . . . or for maintaining the county's roads and bridges. Industrial productivity and profits drop." And: "The best solution [to productivity problems] is that already advanced: to make Sweetwater County a more attractive place to which industrial labor can be attracted and retained" (Gilmore and Duff, 1975, p. 43).

Western Energy Company's Martin White told the MIT researchers: "Industrial history proves that undesirable working and living conditions result in less than optimal productivity. Conversely, history indicates that a good living environment will affect workers' attitudes favorably and, consequently, result in greater productivity" (West 1977, p. 6).

Community relations. In the early 1970s, some communities were willing to overlook the social costs of a large-scale project if their leaders were eager for economic growth. Mim Dixon (1975, p. 8), writing about the proposed Alaska pipeline, observed:

> The most logical group of people to be concerned about the adverse effects of the pipeline on the social environment would be those people who would be most directly affected, the residents of towns located in the pipeline corridor.

However, these were the people who thought they had the most to gain in terms of jobs, economic opportunities, and wealth. Located at the midpoint of the pipeline, Fairbanks sought to become the administrative, supply, and transportation center for the project. At the Department of Interior hearings on the draft EIS for the pipeline, a Fairbanks Chamber of Commerce representative strongly urged immediate construction "for the social good it will make possible." . . . The Mayor of Fairbanks testified at the Department of Interior hearing that pipeline opponents were "anti-God, they're anti-man, and they're anti-mind."

But in the 1980s, the intensification of resource development of the rural West is being met with increasing resistance from communities affected. This is exemplified by demands that the companies provide ever-increasing amounts of front-end money and that they make more specific their commitments to long-term obligations to the affected communities. As federal funding cutbacks continue and community resistance becomes more prominent, the company-funded impact mitigation programs that turn out to be cost-effective will be those that focus no less on the local community's social and cultural values than on its material needs.

A recent and dramatic example of the economic impact of community resistance to a project because of lifestyle issues is the "delayed" Mount Emmons molybdenum mine near the town of Crested Butte in Gunnison County, Colorado. Although AMAX publicly attributes the postponement to moly market conditions, spokesmen for other mining companies privately maintain that the politically astute resistance of residents of Crested Butte would have brought on a "no go" decision even if the nation's economic slump had not.[7]

In contrast, most Challis residents have supported the Cyprus project largely because of the attention the company paid to community relations during its first year in the community. *Next Year Country*, a documentary film about resource development in four Western states,[8] portrays the Cyprus-Challis relationship as the most accommodative of the four projects presented. National distribution of the film has given Cyprus exceptional public exposure as a good citizen in the community.

Company reputation. It is certainly in a company's interest to develop a reputation for being a good citizen. West's (1977) MIT report states:

> If publicized, sentiments about the manner in which a company carries out the task of developing an energy facility can either foster or undermine the image that corporation seeks to create. . . . [They can influence] congressional legislation, anti-trust deliberation, rate setting, policies of governmental regulatory agencies, and other factors vital to the future of any energy company [p. 20].

Even executives who feel only weakly motivated to work toward high environmental quality in the region of their planned facility are likely to give a high priority to sparing their corporation the notoriety that comes with despoiling a rural area. Various company representatives echoed the sentiment of Robert Valeu of Basin Electric Cooperative who recognized the urgency of "avoiding another Jim Bridger"—i.e., an especially problematic boomtown. A reputation for policies which are destructive to local communities is clearly disadvantageous for corporations which intend to maintain their presence in an area over the long term and which expect to be permitted to construct future facilities in other communities [pp. 14-15].

In the same report, R. Gale Daniels of Atlantic Richfield and other resource development executives express their belief that monetary successes in future developments will be dependent on the reputations their companies will have made for mitigating social impacts in previous projects. Consequently, some companies are moving ahead of government requirements for mitigation of social impacts in order to enhance their own self-interests. For example, in a private conversation with one of my research associates, an AMAX vice-president said: "Government sometimes says to the company, 'Don't worry about that political stuff; we've got that under control.' We [industry] sometimes have to push government to require us to do what we need to do to protect ourselves for the future."[9]

Recommendations

A resource development project can use a number of ways to avoid, or at least lessen, the kinds of problems described above. Seven such ways are summarized below.

Prevention. The following is one of the conclusions in Louck's (1978, p. 55) socioeconomic analysis of energy-related projects:

> The preliminary results of this research indicate that many of the excessive costs associated with large-scale energy developments are unnecessary costs and could have been avoided with an investment in adequate environmental management. Adequate environmental management is cost effective and its return on investment is high.

The cost effectiveness of preventing and minimizing social impact as opposed to mitigation (alleviation, softening) or any other reactive strategies is stressed again and again in studies of resource-related developments. Environmental problems identified early in project planning and development are far less costly to resolve. Key impact concerns which were unanticipated, usually because of inadequate and untimely assessment of the community, frequently result in economic loss to the developer. On the other hand, strategies which reflect these concerns from the beginning can prevent or minimize some significant impacts. The *Challis Messenger* of

September 3, 1981 reported our effort to recount the Cyprus–Thompson Creek Project's use of such strategy:

> The company's policy of hiring locals, using local contractors and suppliers, training locals for jobs, and even using the local paper . . . to disseminate information was a principal mitigation measure because it permitted sharing some of the economic benefits of the project with the people who were being asked to bear so many social costs.

Stable labor force. A stable labor force can become a reality if appropriate steps are taken in various areas. For example, respondents in the Gulf Canada (Cornerstone 1980a) study stressed the value of personal and social aspects of work. The development of work teams that have a vested interest in a project's success provides workers with greater continuity between their personal and work lives. A senior executive officer of a large mining company, speaking about his colleagues, said to me:

> We rely on vendor technology and that strips the mining engineer of the old rewards like global traveling and the excitement of discovery. Those who love what they do don't always get the right kind of feedback and recognition from the company.

My 1981 field notes indicate that most Cyprus employees found personal and social satisfaction on the job:

> In fact, both men and women described their work experience for Cyprus in these terms: "a team," "safety conscious," "supervisors and workers learning from each other," "respect," "exemplary safety and training programs," and "opportunities to advance."

Recommendations for increasing productivity include expanding training programs for unskilled people, tapping the labor pool provided by local women, and expanding services to the women of the community:[10]

> Wives are affected by all . . . [the quality-of-life problems]. Beyond that, two remedies are needed: (1) the newcomer wife should be actively welcomed to the community, and (2) the resident wife should be given a greater variety of ways to spend her time [Gilmore and Duff 1975, p. 43].

Other important considerations in maintaining a stable work force lie in developing programs that will address the newcomers' needs.

> The tools needed to accommodate and retain the new population include the institutions for timely and satisfactory provision of public goods and services. They also include expanded social service programs, . . . improved intracommunity communications, and adult education programs designed to maintain the community [Gilmore 1976, p. 539].

Growth management. Traditionally, industry has left the management of rapid-growth problems in the community to local and state governments and the private sector. More recently, some companies have recognized that it is in their own self-interest to provide ongoing technical assistance and grants, loans, tax prepayments, and other such help to beleaguered communities. A less obvious but more important factor in a company's cost-effective growth management policy was expressed by Gilmore in a private talk with me: "The big factor in making/not making a development situation work is the kind of relationship the mine or plant manager has with the locals and with his own workers. Almost any philosophy of development can work if this relationship is good—or fail if it is bad." It is unlikely that there is a better example of the validity of Gilmore's professional judgment than that demonstrated in the Cyprus Project at Challis, where the relationship of project manager M.M. McGee with the locals and with his own workers was a recurring theme in the success of the Cyprus–Thompson Creek Project.[11]

Helping to build the capacity of a community to cope with rapid growth is a way of decentralizing decision making and has the same payoffs, one being the ability to determine optimal site-specific use of social management funds. In the MIT report, C.E. Smith, Jr. of the Carter Mining Company emphasizes the value of timely growth management for the most effective use of a company's financial resources (West 1977, p. 17). For example, a company's generous assistance toward building a new school which comes after two years of project-related overcrowding that has strained students, teachers, and administrators to the breaking point is not as effective as providing enrollment projections, construction assistance, and temporary classrooms which prevent or minimize such serious disruptions in the school.

Effective use of funds. Even though a company has an efficient and well-staffed public relations unit, it is not usually cost-effective to try to substitute conventional public relations for growth management. What has worked for the company in one community will not necessarily be effective in another, and failure to understand what is most important to the local community can account for funding decisions which allocate an adequate budget for social impact management but assign those funds ineffectively. For example, it is probably not cost-effective to hire a dynamic and professionally sound urban planner to give technical assistance to a rural zoning board whose members were likely chosen because they opposed "telling a man what he can do with his own land."

There is no substitute for learning about the values of the community and taking that knowledge into account as early as possible in the project planning and as often as possible thereafter. Within weeks after the announcement that Cyprus would develop the Thompson Creek mine, its consultants used in-depth interviews with a cross-section of Custer County residents to assess their basic values and to construct a social description of the community. The value of this timely, comprehensive study was to inform Cyprus about the guiding principles that members of the community used to make decisions; as a result, Cyprus was able to avoid taking certain actions which would have clashed with residents' values and thus would have been negatively received by the small community of Challis.

Public involvement. Cost-effectiveness reports emphasize that public meetings are not synonymous with public involvement. The former provide some information dissemination services, but rarely are they designed to allow for significant public input. Consequent misunderstandings and misinformation about the community's real concerns, values, and needs will contribute to inappropriate plans and costly delays. Well-designed small workshops, meetings in settings which are congenial to the community's natural groups, and an ongoing open planning process that uses a locally selected advisory group will facilitate incorporating appropriate social concerns into the project, forestalling litigation and/or costly design changes. For example, Cyprus provided opportunities for both formal and informal public involvement in addition to holding regular public meetings. Consultants on community development met with small groups (e.g. senior citizens and high school students) to enlist their help in planning where and how the community should grow. A "kitchen cabinet," an advisory group of knowledgeable, representative, and influential locals, met regularly to keep the community and Cyprus accountable to each other. But the most effective public involvement was accomplished simply because Cyprus representatives and locals regarded each other as trusted partners as they tried to balance community lifestyle concerns with the company's economic ones.

Monitoring. Although social scientists have tried for many years to convince agencies and companies about the particular cost effectiveness which only ongoing monitoring can provide in communities where projects have brought rapid social change, the mandate and funding for such programs are rare and recent. Basin Electric Power Cooperative was obliged by law to develop a comprehensive social impact monitoring program for its Wheatland, Wyoming project, whereby a project council would receive monthly reports from the project, review and evaluate monitoring reports, and design and implement mitigation measures. However, probably because only token support was provided (Metz 1980, p. 7), monitoring at Wheatland has not been either an economic or social success, judging from widespread reports of social disorganization at that site.

Similiar reports come from the Cornerstone (1980a, b) studies, which found that very little monitoring of socioeconomic activities is occurring and that a conflict persists over whether monitoring is the responsibility of government or of industry. This situation is most unfortunate because evidence of the cost effectiveness of such monitoring, which points out opportunities to nip potentially expensive problems in the bud, should end industry's reluctance to accept that responsibility. Gulf Oil Corporation, recognizing that ongoing readings of social change are necessary to economic survival, has built an internal monitoring capability into its management structure (according to an article in *Managerial Planning*, September 1978). However, to the best of my knowledge, the Cyprus–Thompson Creek Project is the only one that voluntarily supported ongoing monitoring of the community's social concerns—and did so from the beginning.

Organizational structure. An AMAX vice-president, describing his company's gradual commitment to managing social impacts of their projects, told me: "For a long time it only got done because a few people in operations (sometimes staff, sometimes consultants) were strong enough to carry it out." Where and how responsibility for socioeconomic matters is assigned in a company's organizational structure indicates how aware its leaders are of economic benefits to be gained currently and in the future. Unless the assignment for social affairs is to either consultants or staff members who report directly to high levels in the company, it is not likely to have much effect because of the amount of clout required to act on the findings and recommendations of social analysts. Once the management structure is determined, successful implementation of these social analyses depends on three essentials: commitment of senior executive personnel, professional staffing or judicious use of consultants, and decentralization in decision making for specific projects.

> To be successful, [environmental management] must be the result of a corporate strategy that has a strong commitment from the highest level in the corporation . . . . Insuring that there is implementation of corporate commitment at all levels of decision-making requires that managers must have the responsibility for environmental concerns delegated to their operations [Loucks 1978, p. 67].

The relative speed and ease of Cyprus's successful entry into the community of Challis was directly related to the project manager's decision-making capability. My field notes record:

> One of the community's cherished values has been reliance on informal relationships and understandings. Members' distrust of (and bad experiences with) federal bureaucracies encouraged the development of a partnership

with the kind of private enterprise that they could identify with, i.e., one whose representatives could make decisions on the spot and bind agreements with a handshake.

Evidence from the literature on large-scale natural resource developments and other information acquired from social scientists and leaders of some of North America's largest oil, mining, and power plant companies show that the cost of adequate management of social problems related to industrial projects is minimal compared to the cost of managing them inadequately. Industry is learning expensive lessons about the necessity of introducing social impact management into the decision making, planning, and operations of their corporate structures. As rapid social change in the 1980s impinges upon public and private institutions, a social change management program for each project makes more and more good business sense. A Petro Canada official notes: "If a corporation ignores the environmental and social factors associated with its projects, it is at its own economic peril" (Cornerstone 1980a, p. 94).

In contrast to Bighole's contentious approach to doing its project at Sagebrush, what I have come to call an accommodative approach to doing natural resource development projects is highly cost effective, but it goes beyond narrow economic considerations to address a range of ethical and value issues in these projects. An accommodative approach shows promise of being much more likely than the traditional one to achieve an optimal balance between merely being profitable and being socially enlightened.

An Accommodative Approach to Resolving Ethical and Value Issues

This section has two purposes: (1) to draw attention to and examine ethical and value issues and conflicts inherent in rapid and massive development of energy and other natural resources in or near traditionally small, rural communities; and (2) to indicate how and why an accommodative approach to natural resource development minimizes and even may forestall these conflicts. The usual procedures employed in the industrialization process inevitably ride roughshod over the individual goals, cultural commitments, and social priorities of predevelopment residents. As a result, these methods not only exacerbate the ethical and value conflicts such development creates, but also preclude any real understanding and mutually acceptable interaction between the scientific, professional, and other worker communities involved on the one hand and the affected rural residents on the other with regard to the issues at stake. In contrast, implementation of a relatively accommodative approach provides for equitable local control while being responsive to the needs and rights of the industrial developer and of the consumers of its products. While the ethical and value issues are the same in either case, only the accommodative mode holds out real promise for minimizing and forestalling conflict.

Much of the following discussion is based on a study which colleagues and I did of scientists and engineers working for accommodative natural resource development projects in the rural West. (The aforementioned Cyprus Mining Company venture at Challis was one of these projects [Gold 1981].) The discussion focuses on (1) the kinds of ethical and value conflicts that these specialists and others get caught up in[12] and (2) a development method which appears to offer solutions to many of the sociocultural problems engendered by the traditional contentious approach to industrialization.

Background

The extensive experience which my longtime research colleagues, Alice Sterling and Kathy McGlynn,[13] and I have had in conducting community research in the rural West over the past decade has enabled us to become very familiar with how developers here normally pursue their economic and technological values and objectives. The typical approach is a contentious one which runs roughshod over the lifestyles, social systems, values, and other concerns of those who live in the many small towns which have been variously impacted by natural resource development activities in or near their vicinities (Gilmore and Duff 1975; Summers 1976; Carter 1977). Many locals naturally react sharply to the impact of such externally conceived, instigated, and controlled development, which they perceive as a threatening intrusion if not an invasion (Toole 1976; Parfit 1980). Specific contributors to social stress include characteristic lack of realistic discussion concerning pollution dangers, population increases, school demands, housing and water supply needs, and length of industrial operations (Gold et al. 1974b, 1975; Gold 1978, 1981). Tension, cynicism, continuing frustration, generation of rumors, feelings of alienation and vulnerability, hostility, and the like result when industrial plans are not made available in terms locals can understand and accept (Gold 1974a; Kohrs 1974; Cortese and Jones 1977; Murdock and Leistritz 1979).

Recognizing such problems, a few companies have recently attempted to employ an accommodative scheme. Ideally this approach involves locals in all the decision-making processes, which concern not only whether a proposed development should take place but, if so, in what manner, on what scope, at what rate, and with what controls (Hammond and Adelman 1976; Schneider and Gilmore 1976; McCarthy 1976; Swanson, Cohen, and Swanson 1979). In this way, the development proceeds only if differences in interests and values and in the handling of ethical issues can be reconciled enough to make acceptable sense to all concerned (McCarthy 1976; Selz-nick 1953). Such a procedure acknowledges that there are some doubts about the future viability and desirablity of unabatedly pursuing our technologically oriented lifestyle (Forbes 1968; Linder 1970; Boorstin 1975; Hirsch 1976; Johnson 1979; Borgmann 1980; Heilbroner 1980). In particular, many of the scientists and engineers associated with sudden and massive development projects have come to question their own ethical rules and social standards as they take note of the fact that (1) they are very instrumental in bringing largely undesired, sweeping, and irrevocable change to those who happen to live where change is taking place; and (2) their work is causing these local residents to pay enormous social costs so that those who live elsewhere may reap the benefits the development is designed to produce (Gold 1981). Such doubts (Barnet 1980), along with our research findings concerning accommodation, have called attention to a number of underlying as well as obvious ethical and value concerns (Glaser 1964; Schumacher 1973; Borgmann 1980).

The Issues

For present purposes, it is helpful to distinguish between the basic or underlying ethical and value issues and the obvious or immediate ones. There are three of the former. The first concerns the viability and validity of the current lifestyle (Easterlin 1973, 1974; Scitovsky 1976; Boorstin 1975; Johnson 1979). The second is the question of how the costs and benefits of the technological lifestyle are to be distributed (Rawls 1971; Rainwater 1974; Thurow 1980; Blocker and Smith 1980). The third is the issue of public discourse, including what kind of access citizens have to public policy debates and decisions and how able they are to talk in the public forum about their profoundest aspirations (Cantril and Roll 1971; Tribe, Schelling, and Voss 1976; Dworkin 1978; Hadley 1978; Nelkin 1979). These basic issues inform and guide the discussion of the obvious and immediate ones (detailed below). The interaction of the two kinds of problems is complex, primarily due to the fact that the basic issues are currently in a deeply unsettled state among both experts and laypersons (MacIntyre 1981). Hence the basic problems make themselves felt at the level of immediate issues in hidden, inconsistent, and misleading ways. At the same time, the encounter of large-scale industry with undeveloped rural areas provides a special focus for the interaction of immediate and fundamental concerns.

From the theoretical standpoint of ethics and values, conflict avoidance and mitigation which fail to consider the root issues and work in circuitous and indirect ways are unsatisfactory. It would, on the other hand, be equally unsatisfactory to force or press for a principled resolution when principles have not been openly discussed and received a substantial affirmation. As regards the development and approval of moral principles, students of values and ethics are inclined to demand a theoretical resolution before practical steps are taken. But such an ordering rarely occurs in fact and will not happen in the case of resource development. What does normally happen is the gradual, largely implicit, and practical reshaping of our moral vision, and in this process theoretical proposals and examinations constitute one important factor. Therefore a close study and monitoring of the forces, arguments, and procedures involved in resource development provide insights and materials for a better understanding of how issues of ethics and values inform public policy and of the constraints that practice imposes on the efficacy of theoretical work in the area of values and ethics (Borgmann 1980; Gold 1981, 1982a).

There is a more definite tie between theory and practice and between the underlying and immediate issues. Given the presently uncertain disposition of the basic issues, it seems that the accommodative approach to conflict avoidance and mitigation in resource development is more likely to allow for the kind of thoughtful debate that may lead to a satisfactory settling of the basic ethical issues. The accommodative approach is also more likely to protect the interest of the least powerful who are most vulnerable in the absence of strong and definitely agreed upon norms and values for resource development.[14] The following points, which summarize the major components of this approach, address the immediate issues and indicate how debate may be encouraged while protecting the interests of a vulnerable minority.

1. The company must develop both environmental and local community policies and be willing to negotiate their application with the community so that the process of balancing accountabilities (to the company, the community, the environment, and national needs) is visible and generally acceptable to all.

2. The company must be willing to have decisions influenced by consultants whose accountability is not solely to the company. E.g., a hydrologist who works for a reputable consulting organization or university and is therefore accountable to his profession and to the academic community is more apt to move the company toward accommodation than a hydrologist on the company payroll.

3. Top management must delegate enough authority to on-site organizational leaders, such as the project manager or superintendent, to enable them to make all but the most fundamental development-related (policy) decisions without clearing with the home office. These individuals are intimately acquainted with the local scene and thus in a much better position to make decisions that will be acceptable to the locals.

4. The company concerned must be "up front" regarding its plans. For

example, it must provide timely, extensive, and repeated news updates on its plans in order to help predevelopment residents accept the reality of a "go" decision; and it must offer continuous reassurance that opportunities of particular interest to locals will be available to them, that specific dates will be published regarding when job applications will be taken, that facts will be announced to dispell rumors, and the like. An open process of planning helps the people to see why, when the company has to change its plans, it may nevertheless be keeping its word about what it said it was going to do.

5. The open planning process must include visible participation on the local scene by top officials from the home office and a well-grounded program of local "capacity building," e.g., helping officials of the local (rural) community to learn about the modern (urban) planning principles and procedures needed for governing a rapid-growth town such as theirs.

6. As Scheffey (1968, p. 355) has noted, "a significant . . . research effort [must] be directed toward investigation of human and community values as they will ultimately determine resource development goals." Community members' social and cultural values must be understood and acknowledged by the company's scientists, engineers, consultants, and management personnel so that actions by the company, its construction contractors, and their personnel will not generate strife unwittingly. Ethnographic community studies done at the outset of proposed developments can provide much assistance in achieving such understanding of the way each rural community has evolved its distinctive pattern of values.

7. Provisions for public input must give local residents the capability of entering the planning process early and on equal status with the agency personnel, professionals, and company representatives, rather than placing them in the typical reactive stance. Knowledgeable locals who are reticent to speak out at public meetings are more inclined to voice their positions at the kinds of smaller, more informal gatherings which typify rural life. Provisions for such input would enable the compilation of a more realistic picture of the various facets of the community and of the issues of concern to residents.[15]

8. Outside consultants must gain firsthand acquaintance with the community which will be affected by the proposed development so that their decisions and recommendations will be grounded in the members' values and concerns and thus be more acceptable to them. Otherwise, consultants cannot understand the views and reactions of local residents and nip frustrations in the bud.

9. Scientists, engineers, and others working for the company must also make an effort to meet local residents. Each group must get to know the other too well for either to resort to treating the other categorically and impersonally; this knowledge will help forestall rumors, misconceptions, and paranoid thoughts and feelings about each other.

10. Company promises and commitments to the community must be honored. For example, if help for anticipated school expansion is promised, the company should come forth with this help at the time it is needed.

11. To be on more equal terms with resource development companies, local residents must strengthen their ordinary city/county government forces (e.g. the county commissioners, city council, planning and zoning boards), preferably even before environmental impact studies are started. This kind of capacity building is far preferable to strengthening the relatively ad hoc pressure groups which people have tended to turn to because they have lost faith and trust in local government.[16] This loss of faith is to a developer's advantage, since county commissioners might otherwise command the immediate attention of companies simply by flaunting their potential to use zoning authority to stop projects. Even assuming they wish to oppose a proposed project, they ordinarily are loath to use their full authority in this way because they sense they do not have their nominal constituents' blessings to take such drastic action. Oftentimes, too, county commissioners do not realize they have so much legal authority (through controlling land use in the county); moreover, they are usually doubtful of their moral mandate to exercise it.

12. For the community to be a full partner in the accommodation model, it must develop its own policies and procedures for identifying and protecting its chosen way of life. For example, local people need to have their own consultants to avoid feelings of being manipulated by outsiders not directly accountable to them. As such, community policy would do well to include provisions for hiring such personnel. Residents also need a broad-based community development organization with linkages to all governmental and other community groups.

13. The company must continually monitor local residents' perceptions and concerns and take these into account as the development proceeds. Otherwise, the misconceptions and rumors which accompany fears regarding change can quickly destroy a previously favorable company-community relationship, turning the developmental process into a contentious one.

14. Newcomers' desires and needs must be assessed and taken into account by both the company and the community in planning for development. For example, placement and availability of suitable housing are major issues that must be addressed.

15. Some provisions must be made for the impact of "bust" situations, such as the end of a construction period when a large, temporary work force is being withdrawn, or a partial or total shutdown of industrial operations occurs, either of which suddenly creates widespread unemployment in the community. "Bust" impacts cause at least as much social and economic stress as development. To minimize such impacts, the company might assist employees to find work and the community to diversify its economic base before implementing phase-out procedures.

The Basic Issue

The accommodative approach is undergirded by some kind of mutual understanding; but there are still conflicting interests. The largely tacit agreement that provides the framework of conflict in natural resource development is occasionally appealed to as a truism or common sense by the representatives of industry. This country and in fact this world are committed to a high and rising standard of living, and this commitment entails the exploitation of natural resources. To the extent that this principle remains unchallenged, the treatment of conflicts is just the transaction of the inevitable.[17] For the locals, it is the change from having a disproportionate share of the benefits of this principle to having a disproportionate share of its burdens. For the industrialists, it is the execution of a part of the master plan of the technological society. What gives industry its overpowering advantage over the locals is not just its money and legal staff but its consonance with this basic principle of contemporary society. When the inevitable comes to pass, the accommodation approach is clearly the most humane way to let it happen.

The accommodation approach can also be understood as a concession to the fact that the basic agreement on technological progress is no longer questioned. Obviously, the conflict between locals and industry is not just a clash between differing interests within the technological society, but as much, perhaps more, a conflict between a relatively pretechnological setting and the leading edge of technological progress. The deepest frustration of resource development lies in the fact that this conflict remains unresolved and unspoken in at least the official meetings, though it surfaces in the private remarks of locals. If that basic disagreement were to be put on the agenda, accommodation ought to be able to be achieved in the denial of a project as likely as in its implementation. This clearly is not the case. Industrialists are supremely confident of their cause and enormously tolerant of opposition as long as the progress of technology itself is not in question. If it is questioned, they become disquieted and refuse to see or understand the challenge. Hence, if rejection of a project is advocated through a challenge to the technological framework, industrialists try to force the challenge back into the framework by interpreting the locals' resistance as egotism within the framework. The locals are said to want the best of the two sides of the industrial world: good fishing and Porsches (or, for some, pickup trucks). The industrialists sometimes both soften and strengthen that charge by adding that they would act the same way if they were in the locals' shoes.

Predevelopment residents have a hard time sustaining the real force of their challenge to the technological framework for two reasons. First, so fundamental a charge is difficult to put into words, to clarify and justify in all its consequences, and to give voice to in public meetings. Second, the locals sense that a county, the usual political setting of such a conflict, is too small and weak a forum for the resolution of so basic an issue. A county may have the statutory means to prevent development, but it does not have the legal and financial strength to make its case prevail all the way up to the Supreme Court. Even if it did, a congressional reaction would be sure to follow. As we can see, even political entities of the magnitude of states have difficulty in asserting their rights in resource development.

How does the accommodation approach look in light of this basic issue? It seems unrealistic and misleading to include in its agenda the denial of a project as an equiprobable outcome (though it would be equally foolish to exclude it altogether). However, the accommodation approach best provides for the calm, the time, the information, and the expertise which are necessary if the basic issue of the sense of technological progress is to receive any thoughtful attention at all. Thus, every major resource development can provide something of a forum for and a contribution to a problem which has to be solved nationally if it is ever solved. It must be remembered that the accommodation approach puts restrictions primarily on needless and hasty development, not on the consideration and critique of development. On this score too, the accommodation approach is preferable to a conflictual one.

For these same reasons, the accommodation approach is also a preferable way to examine and act upon proposals to reorient and reorganize the very technological system to which our society has been committed. Schnaiberg's (1980, p. 137) comments on such changes are instructive:

> [Among] the potentially important changes in social responses to the modern technological system is the development of holistic alternatives. Intermediate technology of Schumacher [1973], or alternative technology, or the "soft path" of Lovins [1977], represent models of application of capital and labor that are different from the present industrial system. Importantly, such alternate systems of technology are not piecemeal attacks on the present system, but represent quite different organizational principles, with goals other than simply profit maximization and aggregate national economic growth. Neither are they, like the trenchant analyses of the 1960s, simply critiques of the present system, but proposals for what are seen as practical alternatives. This is, of course, a view from the proponents of such technological reorganization. Defenders of the present industrial system casually dismiss such counterproposals as the "Chinese laundry" system of labor-intensive production.

Within the framework of the present industrial system, an accommodative approach to doing energy and other natural resource development projects tends to minimize ethical and value conflicts historically part of such industrialization and still intrinsic to such traditional approaches to development as Bighole's. Ideally, implementation of a relatively accommodative approach provides for equitable local control while being responsive to the needs and rights of the industrial developer and of the consumers of its products. This approach fosters ongoing negotiations between the company and the community regarding all aspects of their relationship mutually regarded as important. Accordingly, the project proceeds only if differences in interests and values and in the handling of ethical issues can be reconciled enough to make acceptable sense to all concerned. Such working out of differences in standards of behavior and in conceptions of right and wrong adds much to the quality of life of the participants and thus to the social enlightenment of a cost-effective approach to resource development.

Some theoretical, methodological, and applied payoffs of the present findings and analyses are indicated in the concluding section, which ends with a reaffirmation of the moral and practical desirability of pursuing accommodative objectives in natural resource development projects.

Concluding Remarks

On Conceptualizing Gemeinschaft and Gesellschaft

The research findings reported here show that *Gemeinschaft* does not pale into insignificance and get taken over and is not simply superseded by *Gesellschaft* in rural industrialization/urbanization situations. What happens in these situations is that community outer structure may change considerably, some old and many new ties between outer-structural concepts and behavior may be in evidence, and the dominant character of the community may superficially appear to be less *Gemeinschaft* and more *Gesellschaft* than prior to industrialization, but the *Gemeinschaft* core is kept alive and well within the inner structure.

Remarkable as *Gemeinschaft*'s persistence may be, still more remarkable—owing largely to sociology's lack of attention to the dynamics of *Gemeinschaft*—is its waxing and waning in response to internal and external forces such as those reported in this story of Sagebrush. Conceptual payoffs of analysis of the ebb and flow of this basic and widespread form of human organization are fairly obvious in studies of the makeup, functioning, and change processes in communities, and the previous chapter gave many examples of such payoffs. Comparably productive should be studies of the ebb and flow of *Gemeinschaft* in other social organzations, such as industrial plants, hospitals, and the huge office complexes which abound nowadays. Although only barely indicated in this report, the potential for closely related conceptual payoffs should be equally great when more sociological

attention is given to waxing and waning of *Gesellschaft*. Practical or applied payoffs of these theoretical studies should be considerable, ranging
from better community planning for energy development projects to better
governmental policies for making the nation's cities more compatible with
the sociocultural goals and human strivings of the citizenry.

Sociology needs to recognize more clearly and certainly the interrela-
tionship between the *Gemeinschaft*-like inner structure and *Gesellschaft*-
like outer structure of the community. Such recognition would reveal that
outer-structural behavior is generic to community life and not peculiar to
the city. Outer-structural behavior may occur more usually and be developed to a finer art in the city, but I doubt that this is any more the case
than the assertion that inner-structural behavior occurs more usually and is
developed to a finer art in the small town. To be sure, inner-structural
behavior is the dominant interactional expectation and pattern of the rural
community, just as outer-structural behavior is the dominant interactional
expectation and pattern of the urban community. What needs to be understood is that both kinds of behavior occur in abundance in both kinds of
communities. In short, no community is totally *Gemeinschaft* or
Gesellschaft; all are interacting combinations of the two, as shown in the
present findings on ties, interactions, and interrelationships between inner
and outer structure.

Conventional sociological distinctions between urban and rural communities need to give due attention to the *Gemeinschaft* foundations of big
cities as well as of small towns and to the essential similarities in their
Gesellschaft veneers.[18] Relying heavily on demographic and related data to
define and draw hard lines between urban and rural communities appears,
in the light of present findings, to be misleading, for such conceptions fail
to take into account the facts of inner and outer structure in communities
of all sizes and descriptions, to the mix of *Gemeinschaft* and *Gesellschaft*
values in all, and to each community's way of trying to organize and
conduct itself to safeguard and realize its values. These sociocultural facts
of collective life must be taken into account in formal sociological analyses
which aim to typify communities as predominantly *Gemeinschaft* or
Gesellschaft.

Students of community change need to take advantage of the present
analysis of inner and outer structure when trying to identify and explain
how and why communities in given kinds of impact, growth, etc. situations
do/do not experience given kinds and degrees and rates of change. Such
analysis should also contribute to predicting, planning for, and coping with
community change.

The Sagebrush experience reveals that, after three years of construction
and a year of being operational, the Bighole project had the effect of doub-

ling the community's population, substantially increasing and modernizing its commercial sector, and noticeably bureaucratizing much of local
government—but the community's basic rural features and way of life
remained largely intact despite these indications of urbanization. Fischer
(1982, p. 235) observed some differences in behavior between public urban
and public rural places which suggest another dimension of urbanization
in towns like Sagebrush. Fischer noted that misunderstanding, distrust,
reluctance to help, and conflict "are more likely to occur in public urban
places than in the typically more homogeneous public rural places." The
key here is misunderstanding, which breeds distrust, which fuels misunderstanding, and so on. The rural person in his natural setting tends to be
trustful, helpful, and accepting. As the Sagebrush story indicates, this tendency is reduced when changes in the community force him to realize that
he is often misunderstanding and being misunderstood and that he had
better put up his outer-structural guard more certainly as the rule and not
the exception. In at least this important sense, urbanization did occur in
this industrialized rural Western community. As pointed out, however, it
would be incorrect to cite such findings of city-like behavior as evidence
that the small town is now basking in the cultural light of *Gesellschaft* and
can therefore be regarded as having been urbanized. No such inferential
leap regarding community transformation is made when social scientists
find in the big cities evidence of behavior commonly associated with their
conceptions of rural life. Just as much caution and restraint should be
exercised when tempted to say that Sagebrush has been urbanized by
Bighole's project as when tempted to conclude on the basis of Suttles's
(1968) findings about ethnic *Gemeinschaften* in Chicago that the big city is
being ruralized.

On Ways of Studying Community

   Much of what I have written about Sagebrush differs markedly with the
findings of standard sociological studies of industrially impacted rural
communities simply because the latter rely largely or entirely on a combination of secondary and questionnaire data and thus portray these communities in terms of attitudes rather than values, of socioeconomic factors
much more than sociocultural ones, of outer structure alone much more
than inner and outer structure, of what the investigator thinks the data
mean much more than what the residents say their utterances and actions
mean, and so on. Because so few sociological students of community use
ethnography as a principal research method, the reports of a vast majority
reveal little or nothing about how inner and outer structure work—alone
and/or in relation to each other, what holds the community together and
why, what the residents think makes life worth living in the community,

what members think are differences between the actual and the ideal in what is or may be happening in their community, and the like. The standard monograph on community is thus a gloss of these sociologically interesting and valuable topics because the standard research methods produce data which pertain more to indices than to the underlying actualities and place the investigator in the position of making many inferences about the social scene in question which he has no way of validating so long as he does not use ethnographic procedures.[19]

On Formulating and Carrying Out Strategies for Coal and Other Energy Development

As exemplified by the Bighole Energy Corporation's project at Sagebrush, a contentious approach to doing an energy development project has shown itself to be the work of an insensitive, poorly informed, and perhaps unwittingly tyrannical majority imposing its will regarding societal and industrial progress on those who happened to live where the desired coal was. The decision to establish a mine-mouth, coal-fired power plant at Sagebrush was made by the company's board of directors after evaluating the technical feasibility of such a plant and the demand for electricity in the urban areas it served many hundreds of miles from the selected plant site. Residents of Sagebrush were given no voice in the "go" decision which the board of directors made and were not even informed of the decision and its likely impact on their community until preparations for the project were well under way. In a word, the project was done *to* Sagebrush much more than *with* or *for* Sagebrush. From the very beginning and thereafter, Bighole's project was imposed on Sagebrush, allegedly in response to the need to develop the West's vast coal resources for the good of the region and thus of the nation. The project was, so far as Sagebrush was concerned, externally conceived and controlled and foisted in that manner on the community, whether or not the locals were willing and able to deal with resultant intervention in their lives.

Locals' response to the whole intervention process revealed the morally indefensible economic cost/benefit logic of the coal developers and thereby of the nation's entire system of centralized energy production and consumption which rationalized its existence in terms of this logic. The essential and overriding flaw in this line of reasoning was that it had no provision for taking into account sociocultural costs and benefits and, in effect, assigned them a zero value through leaving them out of cost/benefit ratios and other calculations of the amount of progress achieved through one development scenario or another. Such calculations are always in terms of dollars alone, for which reason matters of equity, justice, and just plain right and wrong are left out of account. Sagebrush ranchers' intensive experience with some of the standard bearers of this cost/benefit logic led them to discover some fundamental weaknesses in the structure and functioning of American society. Their plea for fair treatment was, in essence, a plea to the nation to set itself straight and stop pretending that progress consisted very largely, if not entirely, of technological, economic, and other *Gesellschaft* factors which, if properly attended to, would make everything else in life right. In other words, progress could not be achieved in any morally acceptable way unless technological and economic considerations were made servants rather than masters, i.e., unless *Gemeinschaft* issues were given priority in this pursuit.

In order to give due regard to *Gemeinschaft* priorities, a development project must use a planning scheme which is as sensitive to the political realities of the locals and the developer as it is to the sociocultural interests of the former and the economic interests of the latter. Commenting on such planning, Myrdal (1971, pp. 437, 439) calls attention to the social and political processes in which a development plan must be embedded if it is to make acceptable sense to those concerned:

> A plan is fundamentally a political program. It has to be produced in terms of the government's valuation. . . . The government itself is a part of the social system from which a plan cannot be separated. Moreover, a social system, including the attitudes of the government and the people, can change in the midst of a plan as a result of following the plan itself. The attitudes of the people and their institutions can represent obstacles to a plan. No government is entirely free to follow its own subjective valuations [p. 437].

> The optimal plan, then should . . . be regarded as a steadily forward-moving pattern of policies that has to be modified continually in the light of newly emerging events, changing causal connections, and changing valuations among the rulers as well as the ruled. But planning, in the final instance, can never be a substitute for policy-making. On the contrary, its value premises must come from and by the political process. These value premises cannot be simple and general; they must be as specific and complex as the valuations that determine, and become determined by, the political process. It would be impossible, for example, to work out a plan for animal husbandry in India that did not take into account the common aversion to slaughtering cows. An agricultural policy dealing with land ownership and tenancy must be framed so that the government will find them both feasible and desirable in view of the actual power situation in a country.

> All planning thus implies political choices [p. 439].

It is evident from the foregoing that Bighole's contentious approach is a far cry from "the optimal plan" for development.

In contrast to Bighole's contentious approach to doing a coal development project is an approach which *does* adequately take into account sociocultural costs and benefits along with technical and economic ones and *does* provide for giving locals a meaningful and equitable voice in determining whether the project is "go" or "no go " and, if the former, how it is to be designed and implemented so as to give appropriately negotiated weight to safeguarding and enhancing the locals' values along with those of the energy industry and its consumers. This desirable approach to energy and other natural resource development is highly accommodative, as it is designed to use negotiation processes to minimize the social and economic costs of the contentiousness inherent in the traditional approach to resource development exemplified by Bighole. Through using an accommodative model of energy development to circumvent social injustices and through using fundamental democratic processes of assessment and negotiation to ensure that differences in social and cultural values are reconciled fairly, humanely, and justly, the Bigholes of the energy industry should almost certainly be able to avoid some and minimize other human problems of the sort we observed at Sagebrush. An accommodative approach is desirable not only because it fosters a climate for doing right by all concerned in and with an energy development project. It is also desirable in that it contributes to creating work and living situations which tend to atract and retain as project employees people who will fit in (as socially sensitive human, not as automatons) and become productive members of the company and the community. In short, the "right" way, the way which avoids and minimizes social impact, should appeal to energy development companies for the additional reason that it is likely to be more cost-effective, during and after construction of a project, than the much more contentious approach used by traditional companies like Bighole (Cottrell 1970).

Summary

Being a traditional resource development company, Bighole was so concerned about economic and technical aspects of its project that it paid little or no attention to the effects of the project on the lives of those who happened to reside in the vicinity of the site selected for the coal mine and power plant. Sagebrush gradually learned that Bighole's game plan called for doing the project in a strictly economically cost-effective way, and this end pretty well justified whatever means seemed expedient for trying to complete the project under budget and on time.

Bighole's use of this narrow concept of cost effectiveness created such a contentious relationship between the company and the community that it backfired, for it led locals to take actions which resulted in costly delays in completing the project. Throughout all this penny-wise interaction with the locals, it simply never occurred to Bighole's management that giving more weight to the community's social and cultural concerns could have saved the project a lot of time, money, and hassle.

Really cost-effective natural resource development is exemplified by Cyprus Mining Company's molybdenum mining project near Challis, Idaho, because the project has been faithful to the spirit as well as the letter of NEPA and has made a significant effort to accommodate its essentially economic goals to the social and cultural values of the locals. The accommodation approach to natural resource development used by Cyprus is a good example of a project which is environmentally sound and socially enlightened, a combination which not only makes for good corporate citizenship but is so effective in saving time, money, and hassle in getting the project into production that it is truly cost-effective in the broadest sense.

Notes

1. Or at least that part of the nation which would receive Bighole's electricity, either from the regional power grid to which the new power plant would be connected or from the coal which the new mine would ship to power plants outside this power grid.
2. As Ophuls (1977, p. 176) has noted with reference to nuclear energy development, "honesty and 'progress' may not be compatible."
3. Note, too, the explanation which Friesma and Culhane (1976, pp. 340-41) offer regarding the actualities of company and public agency behavior in contrast to some of the more hopeful expectations regarding output of agencies responsible for doing NEPA-related research, policy formulation, and decision making: "The expectation that NEPA will cause federal agencies to produce scientific, holistic, optimizing, evaluating, mitigating, and coordinating policy seems to be the latest manifestation of the rational decision-making perspective on bureaucratic behavior. . . . [But] public administration behavior is not scientific management; it is politics" (quoted in Schnaiberg 1980, p. 321).
4. No attempt will be made in this discussion to calculate the cost effectiveness of social impact prevention and mitigation from the viewpoint of the community where the development occurs, nor from the perspective of the consumers of the project's products. The community's views on this topic are discussed in much of the remainder of this book.
5. Early in Cyprus's project at Thompson Creek, the company was sold to Standard Oil of Indiana and became part of the Amoco Minerals division of that large firm. While many of the original policies and procedures that were established when Cyprus was a small, independent, and unusually progressive mining company remained pretty much intact when taken over by this large oil company, some were not, especially those which permitted managers on the ground to exercise considerable influence on top management policies for the project. A notable example concerns housing for those slated to be part of the mine's permanent work force. Company representatives on the scene recommended that the houses being constructed for permanent employees be made available on very attractive terms, which would include a guarantee by the company to buy back houses at full value if the project were aborted or cur-

tailed. Top management of Amoco Minerals resisted offering this guarantee and accepting some other recommendations for the housing program that managers on the ground had made. As a result, the company failed to attract nearly enough buyers for the houses it had built for permanent employees. When top management finally got around to realizing that these employees did not regard the housing policies as sufficiently in their interest, it changed them to what local officials had recommended in the first place. But by then it was too late, for the great majority of permanent employees had already committed themselves to other living arrangements. Consequently, a painfully noticeable number of the houses built in 1981 for the mine's employees still (mid-1984) stand empty as a continuing, highly visible reminder of this failure on the part of top management to understand and support policy recommendations of middle management officials on the ground.

6. According to the Loucks report, this project suffered a $7.1 million overrun due to environmental factors which could have been competently managed at a cost of $1.15 million. See Loucks (1978, pp. 39-44) for a detailed account of the method for calculating overrun costs.

7. As this book goes to press, I have been hearing from mining industry sources that AMAX has written off its abortive, 100-million-dollar effort to get the Mount Emmons Project under way and is turning over to another firm the task of completing development of a molybdenum mine at Mount Emmons.

8. This film had its first showing on public television on January 30, 1982.

9. Sterling and I interviewed AMAX officers for a National Science Foundation study (Gold 1981). As indicated in note 4, chapter 2, this and other such quotes are from our fieldwork files.

10. More information is needed on the cost effectiveness of programs to expand employment opportunities for women and to help integrate newcomer wives into the community. The most helpful source of such information currently available is Moen et al. (1981).

11. McGee was transferred to another project near the end of 1983. This transfer occurred about a year after my colleagues and I had completed our research assignment for Cyprus and about three years after Cyprus had been acquired by Standard Oil of Indiana.

12. Ethical considerations here pertain to the professionally acceptable codes and standards of behavior or practice, including judgments of what is morally right and wrong. Adherence to such moral principles means subscribing to a particular set of values.

13. I gratefully acknowledge the assistance of Sterling and McGlynn and of University of Montana philosopher Albert Borgmann in preparing this section on resolving ethical and value issues in natural resource development projects. Professor Borgmann's sterling prose is very evident in this section which is based on a paper that he and I wrote (Gold and Borgmann 1982).

14. A comparison of accommodative and contentious approaches to resolving ethical and value issues would be necessary to test this hypothesis. The present discussion begins this comparison, mindful of the observation that "the problem for [recent and emergent Western society] is how to adjudicate the claims of group versus group, where the problem is clearly right versus right, rather than right or wrong; of weighing the claims of group memberships against individual rights, of balancing liberty and equality, equity and efficiency" (Bell 1976, p. 26).

15. For example, one company required building contractors to be bonded. This requirement engendered frustration and resentment because, according to a Sagebrush businessman, "a good local reputation is all that is necessary in our town."

16. Ad hoc pressure groups usually have charismatic leaders who get so far ahead of their constituencies that they become ineffective and render their groups easy pickings for traditional companies. Established local governments are much less likely to have charismatic leaders and so tend not to have this problem. The grass roots origins of protective associations, such as the one at Sagebrush, also tend to lessen the likelihood of a special interest stigma.

17. The small community which organizes life in the *Gemeinschaft* manner is so inclined to try to avoid or minimize conflict that it is simply not prepared to handle conflicts of the sort suffered by Sagebrush. As Swanson, Cohen, and Swanson (1979, p. 64) point out, citing Donahue (1974, p. 126): "Donahue believes the acceptable threshold of conflict in smaller towns is lower than in big cities because the small towns 'tend to repress conflict and to forestall action when conflict occurs.'"

18. Fischer (1982, p. 262) arrives at a similar conclusion: "What I have labeled the diversity of communities perspective (within which I include subcultural theory) leads to arguments that urbanism helps generate varieties of social worlds within which people build communal and supportive networks. These diverse worlds may give rise to seeming deviance, and they may clash with one another, but they are internally integrated. If we accept, at least for discussion, that this conclusion is valid, what might it imply for the sociology of community? It suggests that the discipline should leave behind the simple question whether urban life is disintegrative to pursue how rural and urban life are differently integrated." Systematic analyses of inner and outer structure in the manner begun in the Sagebrush story should help in this pursuit.

19. Stretton (1976, esp. pp. 138-46) has an excellent section on research methods which points out how sterile and misleading so-called objective social science research often turns out to be, because it pretends to be value-free rather than facing up to dealing with the inescapable influence of values on research.

References

Barnet, Richard J. 1980. *The Lean Years: Politics in the Age of Scarcity.* New York: Simon & Schuster.

Bell, Daniel. 1967. "Notes on the Post-Industrial Society." *Public Interest* (Spring): 102-18.

_____. 1976. *The Cultural Contradictions of Capitalism.* New York: Basic Books.

Blocker, H. Gene, and Smith, Elizabeth H. (eds.). 1980. *John Rawls' Theory of Social Justice.* Athens: Ohio University Press.

Boorstin, Daniel Joseph. 1975. *Democracy and Its Discontents.* New York: Vantage.

Borgmann, Albert. 1980. "Should Montana Share Its Coal? Technology and Public Policy." *Research in Philosophy and Technology* 3:287-311.

Cantril, Albert Hadley, and Roll, Charles W., Jr. 1971. *Hopes and Fears of the American People.* New York: Universe.

Carter, Luther J. 1977. "Coal: Invoking 'the Rule of Reason' in an Energy-Environment Conflict." *Science* 198:276-80.

Casper, Barry M., and Wellstone, Paul David. 1981. *Powerline: The First Battle of America's Energy War.* Amherst: University of Massachusetts Press.

City of Detroit, Community and Economic Development Department. 1980. "Final Environmental Impact Statement: Central Industrial Park" (December).

Cornerstone Planning Group. 1980a. "Development of Socio-economic Principles and Practices: The Resource Sector's Socio-economic Practices and Trends." Study Three for Gulf-Canada Resources.

_____. 1980b. "The Government's Socio-economic Regulatory Requirements, Practices, and Trends." Study Two for Gulf Canada Resources.

Cortese, Charles F., and Jones, Bernie. 1977. "The Sociological Analysis of Boom Towns." *Western Sociological Review* 8:76-90.

Cottrell, Fred. 1970. *Energy and Society: The Relation between Energy, Social Change, and Economic Development.* Westport, Conn.: Greenwood.

Davis, David Howard. 1982. *Energy Politics,* 3rd ed. New York: St. Martin's.

Dixon, Mim. 1975. *What Happened to Fairbanks? The Effects of the Trans-Alaska Oil Pipeline on the Community of Fairbanks, Alaska.* Boulder, Colo.: Westview.

Donahue, George. 1974. "Feasible Options for Social Action." In *Communities Left Behind,* ed. Larry E. Whitney. Ames: Iowa State University Press.

Douglas, Jack. 1976. *Investigative Social Research: Individual and Team Field Research.* Beverly Hills, Calif.: Sage.

Dworkin, Ronald. 1978. "Liberalism." In *Public and Private Morality,* ed. S. Hampshire. New York: Cambridge University Press.

Easterlin, Richard Ainley. 1974. "Does Economic Growth Improve the Human Lot?" In *Nations and Households in Economic Growth,* ed. P.A. David and M.W. Reder. New York: Academic Press.

_____. 1973. "Does Money Buy Happiness?" *The Public Interest* 30:3-10.

Eggan, Frederick Russell, et al. 1955. *Social Anthropology of North American Tribes.* Chicago: University of Chicago Press.

Erikson, Kai T. 1976. *Everything in Its Path: Destruction of Community in the Buffalo Creek Flood.* New York: Simon & Schuster.

Ewald, William R., Jr. (ed.). 1968. *Environment and Policy: The Next Fifty Years.* Bloomington, Ind.: Indiana University Press.

Fischer, Claude S. 1982. *To Dwell among Friends: Personal Networks in Town and City.* Chicago: University of Chicago Press.

_____. 1976. *The Urban Experience.* New York: Harcourt Brace Jovanovich.

Fitch, Lyle C. 1968. "National Development and National Policy." In *Environment and Policy,* ed. William R. Ewald, Jr. Bloomington, Ind.: Indiana University Press.

Forbes, R.J. 1968. *The Conquest of Nature: Technology and Its Consequences.* New York: Praeger.

Friesma, H. Paul, and Culhane, P.J. 1976. "Social Impacts, Politics, and the Environmental Impact Statement Process." *Natural Resources Journal* 16:339-56.

Galbraith, John Kenneth. 1971. *The New Industrial State.* Boston: Houghton Mifflin.

Gans, Herbert. 1962. *The Urban Villagers.* New York: Free Press.

Gilmore, John. 1976. "Boom Towns May Hinder Energy Resource Development." *Science* 191:535-40.

Gilmore, John, and Duff, Mary. 1975. "A Growth Management Case Study: Sweetwater County, Wyoming" (App. A). Denver: University of Denver (mimeographed).

Glaser, Barney G. 1964. *Organizational Scientists: Their Professional Careers.* Indianapolis: Bobbs-Merrill.

Gold, Raymond L. 1982a. "Accommodation Preempts Confrontation." *Public Relations Quarterly* (Fall): 23-28.

_____. 1982b. "Commentary on 'Local Social Disruption and Western Energy Development.'" *Pacific Sociological Review* 25:349-56.

_____. 1982c. "Community Life-Style and Values Must Be Guarded by Developers, Study Says." *Engineering and Mining Journal* 183:55.

_____. 1981. "An Accommodation Approach to Resolving Ethical and Value Issues in Natural Resource Development." Final Report to National Science Foundation, 0SS78-24551 (November 30).

_____. 1978. "Toward Social Policy on Regionalizing Energy Production and Consumption." In *Energy in America: Social and Behavioral Dimensions,* ed. S. Warkov. New York: Praeger.

_____. 1977. "Review of Investigative Social Research: Individual and Team Field Research by Jack Douglas." *Contemporary Sociology* 6:654-55.

_____. 1974a. "How Southeastern Montanans View the Coal Development Issue." *Western Wildlands* 1:16-20.

_____. 1974b. "Social Impacts of Strip Mining and Other Industrialization of Coal

Resources." In *Social Impact Assessment,* ed. C.P. Wolf. Milwaukee: Environmental Design Research Association.

Gold, Raymond L., and Borgmann, Albert. 1982. "Resolving Ethical and Value Issues in Natural Resource Development" (unpublished).

Gold, Raymond L., et al. 1978. "A Social Impact Assessment Primer." Missoula, Mont.: University of Montana (mimeographed).

———. 1976. "Final Report: A Social Impact Assessment of the Vicinity of the Beartooth Face/Stillwater Planning Unit." Missoula, Mont.: University of Montana (mimeographed).

———. 1975a. "Study of Social Structure and Service Impact of Proposed Expansion of Decker Coal Company Strip Mine Operations." Missoula, Mont.: University of Montana (mimeographed).

———. 1975b. "Final Report: A Study of Social Impact of Coal Development in the Decker-Birney-Ashland Area." Missoula, Mont.: University of Montana (mimeographed).

———. 1974a. "A Comparative Case Study of the Impact of Coal Development on the Way of Life of People in the Coal Areas of Eastern Montana and Northeastern Wyoming." Missoula, Mont.: University of Montana (mimeographed).

———. 1974b. "A Social Impact Study of Colstrip Generating Plants #3 and #4." Missoula, Mont.: University of Montana (mimeographed).

Hadley, Arthur Twining. 1978. *The Empty Polling Booth.* Englewood Cliffs, N.J.: Prentice-Hall.

Hammond, Kenneth, and Adelman, Leonard. 1976. "Science, Values, and Human Judgment." *Science* 194:389-96.

Heberle, Rudolf. 1966. "The Sociological System of Ferdinand Tönnies: 'Community and Society.'" In *An Introduction to the History of Sociology,* abr. ed., ed. Harry Elmer Barnes. Chicago: University of Chicago Press.

Heilbroner, Robert L. 1980. *An Inquiry into the Human Prospect,* 2nd ed. New York: W.W. Norton.

Heller, Walter. 1966. *New Dimensions of Political Economy.* Cambridge: Harvard University Press.

Hirsch, Fred. 1976. *Social Limits to Growth.* Cambridge: Harvard University Press.

Homans, George C. 1950. *The Human Group.* New York: Harcourt Brace.

Hughes, Everett Cherrington. 1943. *French Canada in Transition.* Chicago: University of Chicago Press.

Hunter, Albert. 1974. *Symbolic Communities: The Persistence and Change of Chicago's Local Communities.* Chicago: University of Chicago Press.

Johnson, Sue, and Weil, Esther. 1977. "Social Aspects of Power Plant Siting." Lexington, Ky.: Ohio River Basin Study, University of Kentucky (mimeographed).

Johnson, Warren A. 1979. *Muddling toward Frugality.* Boulder, Colo.: Shamala.

Kneese, Allen V. 1973. "The Faustian Bargain: Benefit-Cost Analysis and Unscheduled Events in the Nuclear Fuel Cycle." *Resources* 44:1-5.

Kohrs, Eldean V. 1974. "Social Consequences of Boom Growth in Wyoming." Paper read at Rocky Mountain Association for the Advancement of Science meeting in Laramie, Wyoming.

Lauer, Robert H. 1982. *Perspectives on Social Change,* 3rd ed. Boston: Allyn & Bacon.

Liebow, Elliot. 1967. *Tally's Corner.* Boston: Little, Brown.

Linder, Staffan. 1970. *The Harried Leisure Class.* New York: Columbia University Press.

Lofland, Lyn. 1973. *A World of Strangers.* New York: Basic Books.

Loucks, Diane. 1978. "The Impact of Environmental Assessment on Energy Project Development." M.A. thesis. Toronto: York University.

Lovins, Amory B. 1977. *Soft Energy Paths: Toward a Durable Peace.* New York: Harper & Row.

MacIntyre, Alasdair C. 1981. *After Virtue: A Study in Moral Theory.* Notre Dame, Ind.: Notre Dame University Press.

Malinowski, Bronislaw. 1941. *Sexual Life of Savages in Northwestern Melanesia.* New York: Halcyon.

McCarthy, Jane E. 1976. "Resolving Environmental Conflicts." *Environmental Science and Technology* 10:40-43.

Metz, William C. 1980. "The Mitigation of Socioeconomic Impacts by Electric Utilities." *Public Utilities Fortnightly* (September 11): 3-11.

Moen, Elizabeth, et al. 1981. *Women and the Social Costs of Energy Development.* Boulder, Colo.: Westview.

Murdock, Steve H., and Leistritz, F. Larry. 1979. *Energy Development in the Western United States: Impact on Rural Areas.* New York: Praeger.

Myrdal, Gunnar. 1971. *Asian Drama: An Inquiry into the Poverty of Nations,* abr. Seth S. King. New York: Pantheon.

Nelkin, Dorothy (ed.). 1979. *Controversy: Politics of Technical Decisions.* Beverly Hills, Calif.: Sage.

Nisbet, Robert A. 1966. *The Sociological Tradition.* New York: Basic Books.

Ophuls, William. 1977. *Ecology and the Politics of Scarcity: Prologue to a Political Theory of the Steady State.* San Francisco: W.H. Freeman.

Palen, J. John. 1979. "The Urban Nexus: Toward the Year 2000." In *Societal Growth,* ed. A.H. Hawley. New York: Free Press.

Parfit, Michael. 1980. *Last Stand at Rosebud Creek.* New York: E.P. Dutton.

Power, Thomas M. 1980. *The Economic Value of the Quality of Life.* Boulder, Colo.: Westview.

Rainwater, Lee. 1974. *What Money Buys: Inequality and the Social Meanings of Income.* New York: Basic Books.

Rawls, John. 1971. *A Theory of Justice.* Cambridge: Harvard University Press.

Scheffey, A.J.W. 1968. "Comments on Fischer." In *Environment and Policy,* ed. William R. Ewald, Jr. Bloomington, Ind.: Indiana University Press.

Schnaiberg, Allan. 1980. *The Environment: From Surplus to Scarcity.* New York: Oxford University Press.

Schneider, Richard, and Gilmore, John. 1976. "Report on the Denver Workshop on State-Local-Federal Relationships in Social Impact Assessment." Denver: University of Denver (mimeographed).

Schumacher, E.F. 1973. *Small Is Beautiful: Economics as if People Mattered.* London: Blond & Briggs.

Scitovsky, Tibor. 1976. *The Joyless Economy.* London: Oxford University Press.

Selznick, Philip. 1953. *TVA and the Grass Roots: A Study in the Sociology of Formal Organizations.* Berkeley: University of California Press.

Shibutani, Tamotsu. 1978. *The Derelicts of Company K: A Sociological Study of Demoralization.* Los Angeles: University of California Press.

Simmel, Georg. 1950. *The Sociology of Georg Simmel,* ed. Kurt H. Wolff. Glencoe, Ill.: Free Press.

Stretton, Hugh. 1976. *Capitalism, Socialism, and the Environment.* Cambridge: Cambridge University Press.

Summers, Gene F., et al. 1976. *Industrial Invasion of Nonmetropolitan America: A Quarter Century of Experience.* New York: Praeger.

Suttles, Gerald D. 1968. *The Social Order of the Slum: Ethnicity and Territory in the Inner City.* Chicago: University of Chicago Press.

Swanson, Bert E.; Cohen, Richard A.; and Swanson, Edith P. 1979. *Small Towns and Small Towners: A Framework for Survival and Growth.* Beverly Hills, Calif.: Sage.

Thurow, Lester C. 1980. *The Zero-Sum Society: Distribution and the Possibilities for Economic Change.* New York: Basic Books.

Tönnies, Ferdinand. 1887. *Gemeinschaft und Gesellschaft.* Leipzig: Fue's Verlag.

Toole, K. Ross. 1976. *The Rape of the Great Plains: Northwest America, Cattle, and Coal.* Boston: Little, Brown.

Tribe, Laurence H.; Schelling, Corinne S.; and Voss, John (eds.). 1976. *When Values Conflict: Essays on Environmental Analysis, Discourse, and Decision.* Cambridge: Ballinger.

West, Stanley A. 1977. "Energy Impacts: Opportunities for Company-Community Cooperation in Mitigating Energy Facility Impacts." Cambridge: MIT Press (mimeographed).

Whitehead, Alfred North. 1933. *Adventures of Ideas.* New York: Mentor.

Wildavsky, Aaron. 1967. "Aesthetic Power or the Triumph of the Sensitive Minority over the Vulgar Mass: A Political Analysis of the New Economics." *Daedalus* (Fall): 1115-28.

Index

Accommodating natural resource development, 150-58, 161-63. *See also* Development

After construction, 71-91. *See also* Newcomers; Ranchers; Sagebrush; Sagebrush community

AMAX, 142, 144, 145, 149

Amoco Minerals, 164n5

Apex Consultants, 45-49

Before development, *See* Sagebrush; Sagebrush community

Bell, Daniel, 114, 124-25

Bighole Energy Corporation, 25, 35, 53-54, 75, 133-38, 161

Borgmann, Albert, 165n13

Bureau of Land Management (BLM), 19, 45-50, 51n11, 55

Businessmen. *See* Sagebrush businessmen

Challis, Idaho, 139-40, 142, 144, 147, 148, 151, 164

Challis Messenger, 143, 145

Coal development: politics of, 133-34; strategies for, 161-63

Coal leases, 51n11

Community: change analysis, 149-50; ideal and actual, 33-34; membership invulnerability, 123-24; service failures, 42-43; study procedures, 160-61. *See also* Sagebrush community

Community development, cost-effectiveness in, 138-50

Construction period, 62-67

Contentious natural resource development, explanation of, 151-52, 156-58, 161-63. *See also* Development

Cornerstone Planning Group, 140, 146, 148, 150

Costs of development (to locals): economic, 60-61; recreational, 61-62; social, 61-63. *See also* Development

Costs, socially unenlightened development, 141-45. *See also* Development

County commissioners' role, initial impacts of project on, 41

Cyprus–Thompson Creek Project, 139-44, 146-49, 151, 164n5

Davis, David Howard, 133-34

Detroit, 3, 5, 11, 93

Development: accommodation in, 150-58, 161-63; contentiousness in, 151-52, 156-58, 161-63; costs and/or benefits of, 60-63, 114-15, 141-45; defining its situation, 34; visual and auditory impacts of, 64

Dixon, Mim, 6, 143-44

Duff, Mary, 143

Energy companies, typical project-related behavior of, 136-38

Environmental Impact Statement (EIS) process, 44-50, 108, 135-36; Apex's role in, 45-50; public involvement program in, 45-50; social impact assessment aspect of, 46-49

Erikson, Kai T., 101-2, 105

Ethnography: defined, 5-6; its use in community study, 160-61

Fischer, Claude S., 160

Fitch, Lyle C., 136

French Canada in Transition, 3

173

Galbraith, John Kenneth, 134

Gemeinschaft: defined, 2; fitting new people in, 95; humanizing role of, 93-94; in disasters, 93; membership aspects of, 6, 35, 99; persistence of, 124-28; pretense in, 106-7; rites of (re)affirmation in, 99-101; sociocultural attributes of, 95-97; vulnerability of, 6-7; waxing and waning of, 33-34, 99-104, 129n7

Gemeinschaft and *Gesellschaft:* balance between, 94-95; conceptualization of, 158-60; evolutionarily conceived, 2-3; evolutionist concept reexamined, 3-5; ideal-typical relationship reexamined, 4-5, 12n13; inner- and outer-structural aspects of, 8-9, 12n10; interdependencies of, 98

Gesellschaft: defined, 2; membership aspects of, 94; pretense in, 107; sociocultural attributes of, 97-98

Gilmore, John, 142, 143, 146

Heberle, Rudolf, 4-5

Helping networks. *See* Sagebrush community

Housing. *See* Sagebrush

Hughes, Everett Cherrington, 3, 93

Industrialization, 11n1

Inner structure: defined, 7-8; impact vulnerabilities of, 121-22; predominance of, 113-14; examples and analyses of impacts on, 115-18; protections of, 104-5

Inner- and outer-structural behavior: examples of contrasts between, 108-12

Inner and outer structure: differential effects of impacts on, 115-20; maintaining connections and relationships between, 43; pretense in, 106-8; usual sociological portrayals of, 104-6; relationship between, 9; relative vulnerabilities of, 120-22; value-related aspects of, 112-13

Johnson, Sue, 138

Junction City, 15, 25, 26

Law enforcement, 22, 76-77. *See also* Sagebrush community

"Lease Hounds": inner-structure penetration of, 54, 134

Lifestyle, versus money, 34

Local government, informal style of, 25. *See also* Sagebrush

Loucks, Diane, 141, 142, 145, 149

Lovins, Amory B., 157

McGee, M.M., 147, 165n11

McGlynn, Kathy, 151, 165n13

Membership. *See* Sagebrush community

Merchants. *See* Sagebrush businessmen

Mineral rights to Western land, ownership of, 55

Modernization, 11n1

Moen, Elizabeth, 165n10

Mountain State Resource Council, 38, 47, 48, 135

Mutual trust, pragmatic and moral aspects of, 33

Myrdal, Gunnar, 125-26, 162

National Environmental Policy Act (NEPA) of 1969, 48, 137, 139, 164

Natural resource development, political aspects of, 162

Newcomers. *See* Sagebrush

Next Year Country, 144

Nisbet, Robert A., 3

Outer structure: defined, 7; impact vulnerabilities of, 120-21; impacts on, 118-19; initial project impacts on, 41-43; stripping away veneers of, 12n10

"People pollution": anxieties about, 27, 36; fear realized, 56-57

Population. *See* Sagebrush; Sagebrush community

Power, Thomas M., 114

Predevelopment residents, defined, 69n8

Pretense: *Gemeinschaft* and *Gesellschaft* situations of, 106-8; uses and misuses of, 106-8

"Prodevelopment" and "antidevelopment" ranchers: differences between, 68n3

Public land-use planning, local antipathy toward, 60

Quality of life, relationship of economic development to, 114

Ranchers: accommodative inclinations of,

59; after construction, 85-89; and land developers, 34-35; anticipatory impacts on, 40; business values of, 35; change in status of, 39, 58-59; divergency of development supporters among, 55; estrangement of development supporters among, 58; family pride of, 36-37; growth in interdependency awareness of, 57; ideal and actual community of, 56; impact vulnerability of, 56-59; "Indianization" of, 39; lifestyle interest protection of, 38-39; relationship to the land, 37, 51n9; views at the outset of development, 53-59; vulnerabilities of, 33-40. *See also* Sagebrush community; Vulnerability

Rangeland County: annual fair and rodeo festival in, 24-25; population of, 15

Rangeland Protective Association, 38, 39, 43, 47, 59, 73, 80, 86, 90, 97, 135

Recommendations of this study, 145-50

Recreation, 23-25, 61-62, 122-23

Resource Assessment, Inc. (RAI), 140

Sagebrush: housing situation in, 60, 71-73; impacts on population of, 67, 72-73; longtimers' after-construction situation in, 73-83; newcomers in, 56-68 *passim*, 73-91 *passim;* population of, 27n1, 73; positive aspects of development at, 65; voluntary associations in, 17-18, 74-75. *See also* Sagebrush community

Sagebrush businessmen, effects of development on, 65, 77-82

Sagebrush community: a composite, 10; first reactions to Bighole's project in, 25-27; helping networks in, 20-23, 60-61, 74, 83-84; historical background of, 15-16; inner- and outer-structural ties reestablished in, 82-83; keeping ranching "country" in, 87-88; law enforcement and crime in, 22, 76-77; lifestyle and values of, 20-25; membership and individuality in, 22-23, 123; merchant and rancher differences in, 85-86; physical description and history of, 15-18; population of, 15, 69n15, 73; predevelopment

people of, 18-20; Rangeland Protective Association activities in, 88; religious aspects of, 18; rural neighborhoods in, 19-20, 27; "selling out" in, 88; the elderly in, 18-19, 60, 61, 74. *See also* Rangeland Protective Association; Sagebrush

Sagebrush schools: impact of development on, 63-64, 73-74

Scheffey, A.J.W., 154

Schnaiberg, Allan, 48, 139, 157

Schools. *See* Sagebrush schools

Schumacher, E.F., 157

Social circles: loosening of, 73, 83, 88, 103; tightening of, 3-4, 34, 43-44, 66, 95, 101-2

Social impact assessment. *See* Environmental Impact Statement (EIS) process

Social Research and Applications (SRA), 140

Socialization process, humanizing aspects of, 93-94

Sociological sampling, 6

Sterling, Alice, 151, 165n8, n13

Suttles, Gerald D., 28, 160

Tönnies, Ferdinand, 1, 3, 4, 5

Trespass, concept and behavior of, 31-35

Uncertainty regarding a proposed project and its consequences, 34-36, 58

Urbanization, 11n1

Values, differences between industrialists and ranchers, 58-59, 65

Visual and auditory impacts of development, 64. *See also* Development

Voluntary associations, 17-18, 74-75. *See also* Sagebrush

Vulnerability: discussion of, 115; of *Gemeinschaft,* 6; of *Gemeinschaft's* inner structure, 121-22; of *Gemeinschaft's* outer structure, 120-21; of ranchers, 33-40, 56-59; of townspeople, 41-44

West, Stanley A., 141, 142, 143, 144-45, 147

"You can't stop progress," 43